June 1999

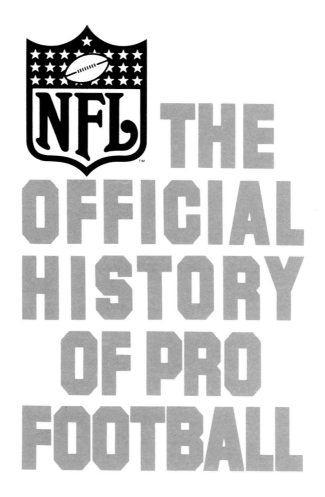

THE OFFICIAL HISTORY OF PRO FOOTBALL

Dear Ed,

To my favorite student!

Wishing you the very best life has to offer!

God Bless You

Don't lose faith.

Sincerely,
Kate

★ ★

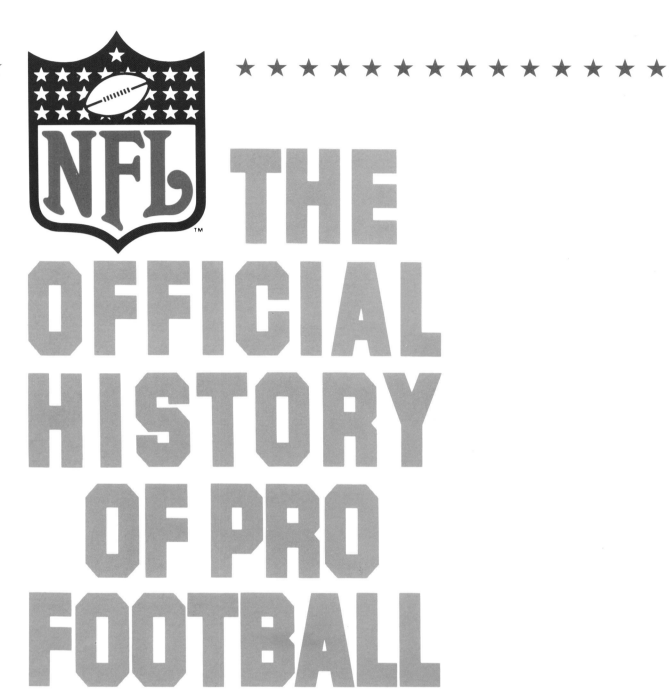

NFL THE OFFICIAL HISTORY OF PRO FOOTBALL

BEAU RIFFENBURGH
and JACK CLARY

★ ★

CRESCENT BOOKS
NEW YORK

This 1990 edition published by Crescent Books,
Distributed by Outlet Book Company, Inc.
A Random House Company, 225 Park Avenue South,
New York, New York 10003

Copyright © NFLP Inc. 1990

ISBN 0-517-02891-3
8 7 6 5 4 3 2 1

Printed and bound in Hong Kong

PHOTOGRAPHIC ACKNOWLEDGEMENTS

*All of the photographs in the book were obtained from the libraries of NFL Properties Inc, and the Pro
Football Hall of Fame:*

ABC-TV, NFL Photos 98; All Sport, NFL Photos 118 (left); Bob & Sylvia Allen, 157 (top); Arthur Anderson, NFL Photos 188 (top); Charles Aqua Viva, 127 (bottom); Eric Lars Bakke, 116 (left); George Bartell, Artist, 54 (bottom); Bauer, 39 bottom; John E. Biever, 88 (bottom), 109 (top), 112 (left), 158; Vernon Biever, 87, 89, 126 (bottom), 141 (bottom), 148; David Boss, 81 (left), 108 (bottom), 133 (bottom), 175, Peter Brouillet, 118 (right); Merv Corning, Artist, 66, 125 (top), 127 (right), 131 (top), 133 (top), 137 (top), 139 (bottom), 144 (top), 146 (top), 149 (top), 152, 154, 156, 159, 160 (left), 162, 166 (top), 168, 170 (right), 173 (right), 174 (top), 177 (top), 180 (top), 183, 186; Dave Cross, 189 (bottom); Bill Cummings, 179 (bottom); Brian Drake, 115 (center right); Malcolm W. Emmons, 36, 86 (top), 98 (bottom), 128 (right), 132 (top), 135 (bottom); Nate Fine, 99, 145, 169 (top); James F. Flores, 100 (main), 125 (bottom); George Gellatly, 78; George Gojkovich, 106 (left), 111; Pete J. Groh, 179 (top); H. Lee Hansen, 67, 71, 72; Paul Iverson, 112 (top); Paul Jasienski, 116 (top), 181; Fred Kaplan, 75 (top), 94 (top), 105 (inset); Amos Love, 160 (center); Richard Mackson, 114 (top), 177 (bottom), 184 (top); Robert Mayer, 116 (right); John McDonough, 174 (bottom); Al Messerschmidt, 101 (top), 107 (center), 164, 167 (bottom), 169 (bottom), 170 (left), 172 (x2); Peter Read Miller, 105 (bottom), 106 (right), 151, 157 (bottom), 165, 176, 185; Ronald Mosiati, 126 (top); NFL Photos 8, 9, 10, 11, 12, 14, 15, 16, 17, 19, 20, 21, 22, 25, 26, 27, 28, 29, 30, 31, 32, 33, 34, 35, 37, 38, 39 top, 40, 41, 42, 43, 44, 45, 46, 47, 48, 49, 50, 51, 52, 54 (center x2), 55 top, 56, 57 top, 57 bottom, 58, 59 top, 59 left, 59 right, 60, 61, 62 bottom, 64 top, 64 bottom, 68, 70 (x2), 73 (top), 74 (bottom), 74, 75, 77 (bottom and right), 83, 85, 88 (top), 90, 94 (bottom), 96, 97, 100, 102, 105 (center), 107 (bottom), 110 (center), 113 (bottom), 119 (bottom), 121, 124, 128 (left), 129, 142, 153; Darryl Norenberg, 91, 107 (bottom), 103 (left), 119 (top); Peter Palombi, Artist, 55 (bottom); Hy Peskin, Sports Illustrated, NFL Photos 84; Dick Raphael, 103 (right), 130, 132 (bottom), 136, 137 (bottom), 138 (center), 140, 143, 146 (bottom); Russ Reed, 93 (top), 131 (bottom), 134; Fred Reinert, Cleveland Plain Dealer, NFL Photos 62 (top); Frank Rippon, 79, 82, 83, 86; George Robarge, 108 (top); Bob Rosato, 180 (bottom), 184 (bottom), 188 (bottom); George Rose, 155 (center), 173 (top), 189 (top); Daniel Rubin, 81 (right); Manny Rubio, 113 (top), 123, 163, 167 (top); Russ Russell, 139 (top), 141 (top); Chris Schwenk, 114 (bottom); Carl Skalak, 147; Bill Smith, 112 (center); Robert L. Smith, 93 (bottom); Chuck Solomon, 115 (left); Jim Spencer, 101 (bottom); Paul Spinelli, 120, 178; Vic Stein, 67 (top), 73 (bottom), 76, 77 (upper left); Damian Strohmeyer, 115 (bottom right); Tony Tomsic, 69, 80, 86 (bottom), 104 (top), 110 (bottom), 135 (top), 138, (top), 144 (bottom), 150, 155 (top & bottom), 166 (bottom), 182; Gregg Trott, 117 (bottom), 187; Herb Weitman, 104 (bottom); Lou Witt, 92, 95, 111 (left), 149 (bottom); Michael Zagaris, 105 (top), 117 (top), 121 (bottom), 122, 171.

CONTENTS

INTRODUCTION

The National Football League embarks on its eighth decade of existence with pride in the accomplishments of the many contributors who have lifted professional football to the pinnacle of fan recognition, and with the promise of a most invigorating future of extraordinary athletic achievements and expansion that will make our game a truly international enterprise. This lavishly illustrated book will give readers of all ages and knowledge of the game an entertaining insight into the history and also the characters who have made pro football the spectacle it is today.

The history of the NFL in the United States permits us to reflect on the struggle, development, and maturity of the past 70 years. Now, in the 1990s, we can aspire – and, I am confident, accomplish – goals that were merely dreams a few years ago. Modern communications introduced live NFL games to countries across the Atlantic and Pacific in the 1980s. Today, we play international games before sellout crowds in those places.

NFL football is the number-one spectator sport in the U.S. We are ready to move forward and expand our form of sports entertainment around the globe.

Paul Tagliabue

PAUL TAGLIABUE *Commissioner*

ROOTS OF PRO FOOTBALL

Football moves from the Ivy League of Princeton, Harvard and Yale to the industrial heartlands of Akron, Canton and Massillon, Ohio, and Allegheny, Latrobe and Pittsburgh, Pennsylvania.

The Ohio League
The Roots of Pro Football

It is perversely appropriate that American football, a game that the National Football League is in the process of exporting to the rest of the world, had its roots in two games among the most popular throughout the world, although neither is particularly successful in the United States – association football (or soccer) and rugby.

Varieties of soccer – games involving kicking a ball – can be traced back at least 2,000 years. However, it was not until 1823 that the first important step in the evolution of American football occurred in England. That year, William Webb Ellis of the Rugby School picked up the ball and ran with it during a soccer game. The rules forbade advancing the ball any way except kicking it, and the other players were outraged. Nevertheless, Ellis's innovation became the basis of rugby, a new game that would influence American football because the runner could carry the ball as well as kick it.

Throughout the middle decades of the nineteenth century, soccer and rugby both became popular in the United States. On November 6, 1869, Rutgers and Princeton played what is officially considered the first American college football game, although it used rules more like those of association football than modern American football. Each team had 25 players, the ball was advanced by kicking it or butting it with the head, and the goal posts were 25 yards apart. Rutgers triumphed, six goals to four.

During the next seven years, rugby gained favor over association football with the major eastern schools. However, different schools played with slightly different rules until 1876, when, at the Massasoit Convention, the first rules were written for the game then known as rugby football were written. At the same time, an informal intercollegiate organization was formed to establish and regularly review the rules of the new game.

In the next decade, under the guidance of Walter Camp of Yale University, the man known today as "the father of American football," the game adopted a number of the rules that distinguished it from soccer or rugby. In 1880, Camp convinced his associates that the number of players on a team should be dropped from 15 to 11 and that the scrum to put the ball in play should be replaced by the center's snap to the quarterback. Two years later, Camp created the system of downs, in which a team needed to gain five yards in three plays or lose the ball. This inspired the first pre-arranged play strategy, spoken signals, and chalk lines parallel to the goal line. Point values were set in 1883, further differentiating the game from soccer. In 1885, the first referees were hired and allowed to assess penalties.

In 1888, Camp proposed – and the convention passed – a rule permitting legal tackling not just above the waist, but down to the knees. The rule opened the era of the mass formation, in which offenses contracted and bunched themselves around the runner. Dangerous formations, such as the Wedge, the Shoving Wedge, and the Flying Wedge, appeared, and the play on the field became brutal and dangerous.

By 1890, college football had risen to national popularity. Concurrent with its growth was the rise of athletic clubs throughout the United States. Such clubs emerged after the Civil War, with the first – the New York Athletic Club – founded in 1868. These athletic clubs had several important social functions. Through competitive athletics, American men, while still retaining their gentility, could break from the stifling Victorian mold of the day. The new form of football, which was aggressive and occasionally violent, served this need especially well.

The Birth of Pro Football

Popular functions of the athletic clubs were more social than athletic. The members were able to enjoy both the excitement of sporting events and the chance to engage in friendly – or serious – wagers on those games. The older or more sedentary members were able to enjoy the personal benefits of associating with athletes. Membership in a successful athletic club also could be the beginning of an individual's climb toward joining society's elite, who banded together in the more exclusive university or metropolitan men's clubs. But

Opposite: *William Walter (Pudge) Heffelfinger was paid $500.00 to play for the Allegheny Athletic Association in 1892, making him the first professional football player on record.*

Walter Camp

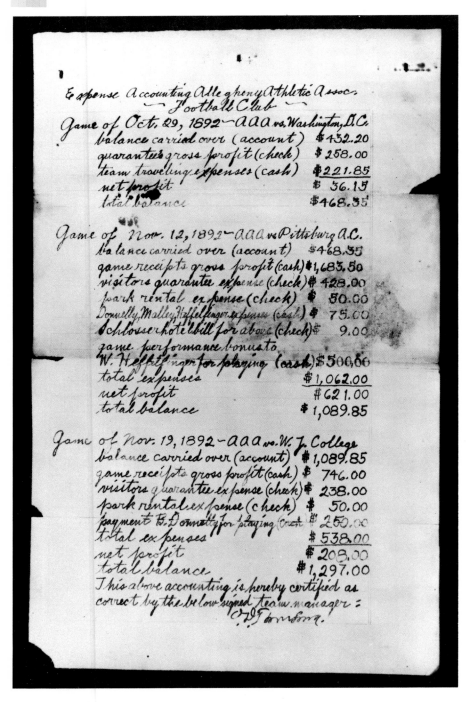

Expense Accounting Allegheny Athletic Assoc.
— Football Club —
Game of Oct. 29, 1892 – AAA vs. Washington, D.C.
balance carried over (account) $432.20
guarantees gross profit (check) $258.00
team traveling expenses (cash) $221.85
net profit $36.15
total balance $468.35

Game of Nov. 12, 1892 – AAA vs. Pittsburg A.C.
balance carried over (account) $468.35
game receipts gross profit (cash) $1,683.50
visitors guarantee expense (check) $428.00
park rental expense (check) $50.00
Donnelly, Malley, Heffelfinger expense (cash) $75.00
Schlosser hotel bill for above (check) $9.00
game performance bonus to
W. Heffelfinger for playing (cash) $500.00
total expenses $1,062.00
net profit $621.00
total balance $1,089.85

Game of Nov. 19, 1892 – AAA vs. W.J. College
balance carried over (account) $1,089.85
game receipts gross profit (cash) $746.00
visitors guarantee expense (check) $238.00
park rental expense (check) $50.00
payment B. Donnelly for playing (cash) $250.00
total expenses $538.00
net profit $208.00
total balance $1,297.00
This above accounting is hereby certified as
correct by the below signed team manager:
O.D. Thompson.

Allegheny Athletic Association's expense account for three games in 1892.

movement up the social ladder from the athletic clubs depended upon the success of the clubs' athletic fortunes. Thus, the sports ceased to be played simply for the love of the game, and winning became the all-important goal. How to win while maintaining a socially desirable clientele – and barring entry to those of moderate social status – became a major issue for the athletic clubs, especially because many of the best athletes possessed neither money nor the status desired by the memberships.

The solution for many athletic clubs, adopted in the 1890s, involved admission of men who did not become full-fledged members but who competed for the clubs in exchange for use of facilities and receipt of expenses for their efforts. Special-qualification membership was the clubs' first step toward professionalism, but because the general public felt negatively toward professionals in athletics, the clubs maintained fronts of strict amateurism. This entailed somewhat questionable dealings. For example, an athlete would be awarded a watch that he subsequently sold to a pawn shop for $20. The club then repurchased the watch from the pawn shop and later gave it away to the same athlete.

Other early steps toward professionalism were taken in western Pennsylvania in 1890. The previous

year, the Allegheny Athletic Association (AAA) had been formed in the city of Allegheny, Pennsylvania, an area that today is part of north Pittsburgh. In most sports, the AAA was little competition for the older East End Gymnasium Club (EEGC), which in 1892 became the Pittsburgh Athletic Club (PAC). In 1890, however, the AAA found an area in which it could compete – football. Several members of the AAA, notably John Moorehead and O.D. Thompson (both of whom had been at Yale with Camp), previously had played football, so the forming of a team was a natural development. Moreover, the team immediately gave the AAA a strong following because the East Enders did not play football. The AAA finished its six-game season with an impressive 3-2-1 record against some strong teams. The EEGC organized a team late in the year and scheduled two games, but played only one. The star of the East Enders was William Kirschner, a physical education instructor at the EEGC.

A bitter rivalry developed between the two clubs in 1891. The AAA dropped to a 2-2-1 record, which forced the resignation of Thompson, who had served both as manager and captain of the team. The East Enders, behind Kirschner, rolled to a 7-0 record. But it was at the cost of being labeled "semi-pro." It was noted in the Pittsburgh papers that Kirschner's salary nearly doubled during the football season, while his classes were cut in two. The papers sometimes made two-edged remarks about Kirschner's dubious status, although no one accused him outright.

Local newspapers regularly called for a meeting of the two teams throughout the 1891 season, but Thompson, perhaps fearing a one-sided loss because his team didn't have the time to practice together that the EEGC team had, carefully avoided a contest.

In 1892, however, the AAA and PAC scheduled a game for October 21. The AAA opened its season with a victory, and the PAC with three consecutive wins. As expected, the teams were undefeated when they met. On game day, more than 3,000 spectators overflowed PAC Park, and other people crowded windows and roofs of surrounding buildings. The game ended in a 6-6 tie. As a result, the two clubs divided $1,200 in gate receipts. Each also added about 100 new members in the following two months.

New hostilities flared quickly, however. The PAC accused the AAA of purposely trying to injure Kirschner, who had been knocked out of the game with an ankle injury. The Three A's, as they were called locally, dismissed the accusation with the retort that Kirschner was a professional and should not have been playing anyway. E.V. Paul of the AAA announced he was willing to bet anyone that the PAC had used a pro, and he said he didn't mean Kirschner.

Paul's comment proved accurate. The PAC had played the game with a new center, a man who had been introduced by PAC captain Charley Aull as an old friend named "Stayer," whom he happened to meet on the street and who agreed to replace the injured regular center. A week after the game, it was disclosed that "Stayer" actually was A.C. Read, the captain of the Penn State football team.

Although no one could prove that Read actually had been paid, and Aull had not tried to present him as a PAC member, the Penn State center definitely was imported talent. His use by the PAC had escalated the situation. In the prevailing climate, neither club would hesitate to take the final step to professionalism.

A rematch was scheduled for November 12, three weeks after the first game. Almost immediately, charges began to surface that one team or the other was trying to hire ringers (or players imported solely for the game), with frequent mention of the names of William (Pudge) Heffelfinger and Knowlton (Snake) Ames, two former All-Americas who currently were playing with the traveling Chicago Athletic Association team.

George Barbour, the PAC manager, denied all charges, but, on November 7, he traveled to Chicago with a large sum of money to pay Heffelfinger and Ames to join the PAC. Unfortunately for Barbour, both had quit the Chicago AA team over the benching of a teammate, and currently were in Pittsburgh. The timing could not have been worse for Barbour, or better for AAA manager Billy Kountz.

When game time rolled around at Exposition Park in Allegheny, Heffelfinger and his former Chicago AA teammates Ed Malley and Ben (Sport) Donnelly indeed were at the game. But they were lined up with the AAA. Ames had decided to forego the game rather than risk his amateur status.

Upon seeing Heffelfinger and company, the PAC immediately protested the AAA ringers and walked off the field. All bets were off, the PAC insisted. But it offered to play a scrub game. While the crowd of 3,000 grew restive and the regulars argued, the substitutes began to play. The Pittsburgh Press recorded the scene: "Confusion reigned dire all this time and it seemed as though the best advertised and most promising event of the football season was about to wind up in a farce. The Allegheny men claimed that they had only followed the East Enders' example in

that they had got these three men. It was cited that on Columbus Day the East Enders had played a State college man at center under an assumed name and the A's made a virtue of the fact that they had not complained at the time."

Ultimately, after more than a half-hour of argument, the real game was played. Because of the long delay and the approaching darkness of night, the halves were shortened to 30 minutes each, rather than the 45 then common. Predictably, the AAA won with the help of the three Chicago players. Midway through the first half, Heffelfinger jarred loose a fumble, picked up the ball, and stormed 35 yards to a touchdown. The conversion attempt was missed, and the final score was 4-0.

After the game, Heffelfinger was paid $500, plus $25 for expenses, and Malley and Donnelly each received $25 for travel. The first acknowledged pro football player had made his appearance, although it is highly likely that Heffelfinger (and others) had been paid all along by the Chicago AA. Two facts support this premise: Heffelfinger had quit his job in Omaha, Nebraska, to play football, and that Northwestern University (from the Chicago suburb of Evanston) had refused to play the Chicago AA because it wasn't considered amateur.

The controversy over professionalism raged in the Pittsburgh papers for weeks, but it wasn't enough to stop the AAA from paying Donnelly $250 to play against Washington and Jefferson College seven days later. The AAA and PAC each threatened

1894 Greensburg (Pennsylvania) Pros.

FRANK HARGRAVE   TOM DONOHOE   CHARLES JAMISON   JOSEPH WENTLIN

BILL THEURER   LAWSON FISCUS

RICHARD COULTER   CHARLES COPELAND   MORRISON BARCLAY

LLOYD HUFF   W. C. L. BAYNE

TOM JAMISON   LEO FURTWANGLER

ED MECHLING   JOHN CRIBBS

to turn in the other to the Amateur Athletic Union, the organization that policed amateur sports, but because each had professional skeletons in their closets, they both backed off and decided to wait until the next year, when they again could settle the issue on the field.

In 1893, the AAA and the PAC split two games, with the PAC winning 6-0 at Exposition Park, and the Alleghenys evening the score, 8-4 at PAC Park. The year was far more significant for several other reasons, however. On October 4, the PAC, represented by George Barbour, signed a player to a formal pro football contract that read, "I agree to participate in all regularly scheduled football games of the Pittsburgh Athletic Club for the full season of 1893. As an active player I agree to accept a salary of $50 per contest and also acknowledge that I will play for no other club during PAC games." Although the contract is torn across the signature, it is believed that the player was Grant Dibert, a halfback who had been with the East Enders since 1890. Several other PAC players undoubtedly were paid, but the AAA certainly had three pros on its roster all season—Ollie Rafferty, Jim Van Cleve, and Peter Wright. After losing their opening game, the Alleghenys also went outside their club to hire the first full-time coach, Sport Donnelly.

Pro football spread outside the immediate Pittsburgh area in 1894. The Greensburg Athletic Association offered former Princeton and AAA star Lawson Fiscus, then teaching in the town of South Fork, Pennsylvania, $20 a game to play for its team. Fiscus accepted, and Greensburg became the third football team to turn pro in as many years.

In September, 1895, the AAA found itself under investigation by the Amateur Athletic Union. If the AAU discovered that the AAA had been paying players, it would declare the club professional. No other team would dare play them, and the club's membership would dramatically fall. Hoping to avoid punishment, the AAA simply decided not to play in 1895.

The void in Pittsburgh football was filled by a new team, the Duquesne Country and Athletic Club (DC&AC, or Duquesnes), which challenged the PAC to a series of games. William C. Temple, a steel magnate who managed the Duquesnes, promised that only amateurs would play for his team, but, after a slow start, the Duquesnes began paying players.

Meanwhile, 40 miles away, Dave Berry, manager of the Latrobe YMCA team, desperately was searching for a quarterback for his opening game with the Jeannette Athletic Club. He offered 18-year-old John Brallier, who had quarterbacked Indiana Normal the year before, $10 and expenses to play for him. Brallier accepted, and played his first professional game on August 31.

Although players had been paid for three years, none ever openly admitted it. Brallier, on the other hand, was proud of what he considered an original act, and never told anything but the truth about his payday. For most of his life a dentist of indisputable integrity, Brallier's openness got him recognized as the first pro football player.

It was not until the 1960s that a mysterious pro football researcher gave Dan Rooney of the Pittsburgh Steelers a paper indicating that Heffelfinger actually had been paid three years before Brallier. When Rooney read the paper, he realized that he had a piece of research of incalculable importance. Unfortunately, by that time the man had left. As Rooney can best recall, the visitor's name was Nelson Ross. Rooney tried to track down Ross, but the man never was found. Proof of Ross's claims eventually surfaced in two places. Dick McCann of the Pro Football Hall of Fame discovered a page torn from an 1892 account ledger prepared by O.D. Thompson, the manager of the AAA. The ledger included the line, "Game performance bonus to W. Heffelfinger for playing (cash) $500." Then, J. Thomas Jable of William Paterson College published an article in which he reviewed and confirmed Ross's main points. Jable also added clarifying and insightful material from his own research.

1895 Latrobe (Pennsylvania) YMCA team.

Since the truth came to light about the earlier pros, Brallier has been considered the first admitted pro, in actuality a more honorable designation.

The 1896 season included five professional teams, but it is best remembered for the two-game season of the AAA. During the winter of 1895, the AAU finally disciplined the Alleghenys. The club was found guilty of paying cash to players and was permanently barred from any kind of competition with other AAU members. The punishment was a mortal blow to the club, and, by the time the 1896 season arrived, about the only members the AAA had left were the football players. At a meeting on October 27, they decided not only to field a football team in defiance of the AAU but to make it their best ever. To lead the club, they turned again to Sport Donnelly.

Donnelly immediately contacted some of the best pros in the country – Heffelfinger, Tom (Doggie) Trenchard, George Brooke, and Landgon (Biffy) Lea. He offered each man $100 a game, plus expenses. Donnelly scheduled only two games, but they were back-to-back on November 10 and 11 against the Duquesnes and the PAC. His 12-man team not only was thin, it had only one day of practice together before playing the games. Nevertheless, the AAA won both games, 12-0 over the Duquesnes and 18-0 over the PAC.

Despite the Alleghenys' victories, the $2,400 the club had to pay the players was not offset by the paid attendance. The club was completely broke and, for all intents and purposes, ceased to exist. It left an incredible legacy, however. It had the first known pro in 1892, the first regularly salaried players and the first full-time coach in 1893, and the first completely professional team in 1896.

The AAA had come and gone, but it was just the first of a growing number of pro teams. The sport spread across the country. The Copper Kings of Butte, Montana, were put together by a rich copper mine owner. The Copper Kings were one of the country's best clubs until the AAU declared them professional, and other teams, usually professional, refused to play them. Other teams were located in Seattle, San Francisco, Los Angeles, Detroit, and Youngstown, Ohio.

Most of the research on the period from 1897 to 1901, however, includes little except that done about the Pennsylvania teams. They generally are considered to have been the best during the period; the top Pennsylvania team of any year undoubtedly would have been correct in calling itself the national professional champion.

Of course, teams still were frightened to openly admit they were professional. An AAU sanction would have killed most teams – like the Copper Kings – because opponents, whether other pros, amateur associations, or colleges, would have stopped playing them. So teams played for local or regional championships, with the only generally recognized national champion being the best college team.

In 1897, Latrobe, then known as the Latrobe Athletic Association, went entirely professional, signing players from as far away as the East coast and Iowa. Walter Okeson, an All-America end at Lehigh who would go on to fame as the head of the NCAA Rules Committee, was signed as coach. The Latrobe team went 10-2-1, losing only to the Duquesnes until a season-ending 6-0 defeat by arch-rival Greensburg. The Greenies finished with the best record among athletic clubs in the state, but

If it had not been for preservation of the Allegheny Athletic Association's expense account, John Brallier, not Pudge Heffelfinger, would be the first known professional football player.

were not as highly regarded as Washington and Jefferson College, which had the same record.

The Spanish-American War (April-August, 1898), was not a long or particularly bloody war by modern standards, but it did help change the face of pro football in Pittsburgh. The Duquesne Country and Athletic Club had fielded the best team in Pittsburgh since 1895 (with the exception of the AAA's two-game wonders of 1896). In 1898, the Duquesnes decided to build an even better team, while dispelling rumors of either Greensburg or Latrobe being as good. After the 1897 season, the club had signed a number of good players to contracts for the next year. When many of the players went into the army in the spring, the DC&AC signed up replacements, many of them even better than the originals. At the end of the war, the Duquesnes found themselves with an overabundance of talent.

When it became apparent that the DC&AC could not financially survive while paying its players, William C. Temple, its chairman, took over the payments to the athletes, thus becoming the first pro football team owner in history. The fiction that everyone was playing for an amateur athletic club was held to in public, even when newspapers openly wrote of players being under contract. As a result, it is not entirely clear when Temple became owner – as early as 1898 or as late as 1901 – but there is little doubt that he was the first.

The Duquesnes had become the best pro team in Pennsylvania and, almost certainly, in the country – the first pro team that could claim to be as strong as the best college teams of the day. On Thanksgiving Day, the Duquesnes defeated powerful Washington and Jefferson 11-0 (under new scoring rules, a touchdown had increased from four to five points, while a conversion had dropped from two points to one). They accomplished the same feat the next year,

Right: Amos Alonzo Stagg is considered one of the most innovative coaches in American football history.

Below: Shelby Athletic Association.

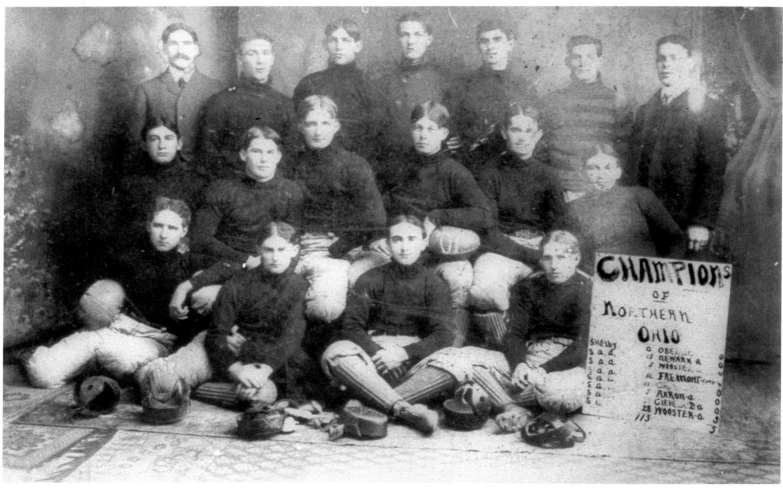

going 10-0, and defeating Penn State and Bucknell in the process.

In 1900, many of the best players from the DC&AC joined the new Homestead Library and Athletic Club (HLAC), an organization that had existed since 1894 in the Pittsburgh suburb of Homestead, where the Homestead Steel Works, with the world's largest blast furnaces, was located.

In 1901, the HLAC fielded the best athletic club team ever organized. In going 11-0, the Steelers, as they were known, outscored their opponents 313-12. Unfortunately, because of bad weather, a lack of strong local rivals, and the team's own power, the HLAC drew small crowds and lost $8,000. Losses off the field stopped the HLAC like no other football team could; immediately after the season, the Steelers began to break up.

Losing money was not an unusual occurrence at the time in western Pennsylvania. Greensburg, Latrobe, and the Lalus AC, which had succeeded the PAC as the second Pittsburgh athletic club power, all had financial problems. Yet across the state in Philadelphia, football was about to catch on, and it could thank professional baseball for helping out.

In 1902, the established National League and the new American League were in the midst of a war that saw each stealing the other's players. Nowhere did emotions run higher than in Philadelphia, where Connie Mack's Athletics, the American League champions in 1902, had signed several of the Phillies despite their having valid contracts, only to have the Phillies get the players back by going to court. When Phillies owner John I. Rogers organized a football team, Athletics owner Ben Shibe asked Mack to join with former Penn tackle Blondy Wallace and put together a stronger team. But the best players in the state were in the west, so Rogers and Shibe called in Dave Berry, former manager of Latrobe. Berry

gathered much of the HLAC team and, in short order, joined Rogers and Shibe in what they called the National Football League. Granted, the new three-team league was not actually national, but it was the first pro football league of any type. Even more important, by openly admitting they were pros, the three teams encouraged others to do the same.

The historical highlight of the NFL season was the Athletics' 39-0 victory over the Kanaweola AC at Elmira, New York – the first night game in pro football history. In league play, the three teams finished with 2-2 records, each splitting with the other two. All three claimed the championship, but Berry, who had been named league president, proclaimed his Pittsburgh Stars champions because they had the best point ratio. Berry's team had quickly alienated the fans of Pittsburgh by practicing in Greensburg, but it did generate some interest by signing Christy Mathewson, the Baseball Hall of Fame pitcher with the New York Giants, as its fullback. The Athletics countered with Rube Waddell, Mack's talented but flighty pitcher.

In December, 1902, Tom O'Rourke, manager of Madison Square Garden, decided to match the five best teams in the country in what he called the "World Series." Although the three NFL teams and the Watertown (New York) Red and Blacks were the class of the nation, none of them wanted to play. So O'Rourke ended up with the Orange (New Jersey) AC and four New York teams – the Syracuse AC, the Warlow AC, the Knickerbockers, and a team made of players from both the Phillies and the Athletics, but simply named "New York." Syracuse won three straight games to capture O'Rourke's national championship.

O'Rourke, encouraged by his earnings and by the fact that the two major baseball leagues adopted his idea and played a World Series in 1903, again put on a

The 1902 Philadelphia Athletics were coached by Connie Mack (middle row, fourth from the left), who also managed the baseball team bearing the same name. The team finished 11-2-1.

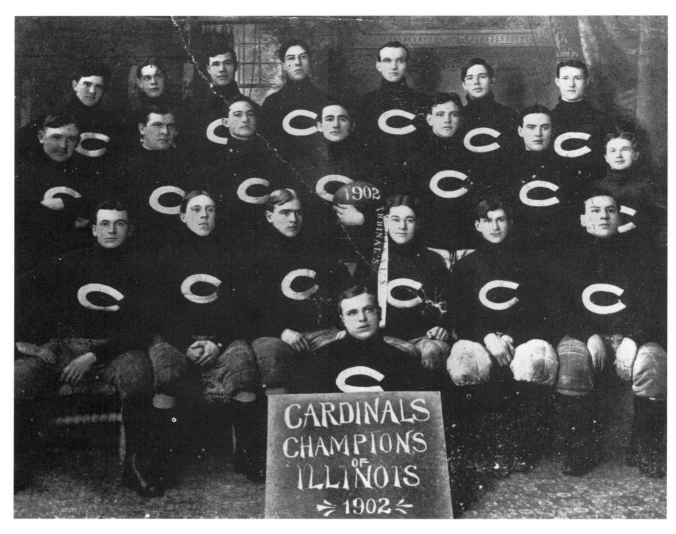

football World Series in 1903. This time the contestants were the Orange AC; the Oreos AC of Asbury Park, New Jersey; a club from Franklin, Pennsylvania; and the Watertown Red and Blacks, who, for the third year in a row, claimed to be the pro national champions. The Franklin team, however, proved otherwise, shutting out Watertown in the finals.

Despite the success of the Franklin team, 1903 marked the beginning of a decline of pro football in Pennsylvania. First, the Pittsburgh Stars folded. Then, the PAC was hurt when four of its players were hired by the Massillon Tigers, the first Ohio team openly to turn pro. Massillon's example was followed by many teams in Ohio. As the best players began to move to the Buckeye State – to Massillon, Canton, Akron, Shelby, Dover, and Columbus – the clubs and teams in Pennsylvania and New York declined, and many became extinct.

By 1905 pro football had for all purposes ended in its birthplace and most other areas of the eastern U.S., but it was just beginning in Ohio – the cradle of the sport.

Pro Football Comes to Ohio

Few football fans today have heard of Ohio's Stark County, and those who drive through it on their way elsewhere may wonder just what the area near the center of the nation's Amish population has to do with the sport. A newcomer to the pro football scene might be surprised to learn that New York or Los Angeles or even Green Bay does not host the Pro Football Hall of Fame. Instead, it's located in Stark County's largest city, Canton, which was selected as the Hall of Fame site because the NFL's organizational meetings were held there in 1920. But Canton also could have been

selected for older, perhaps better, reasons. For that matter, so could have Massillon, Stark County's second-largest city. Those two cities, and their natural rivalry, opened the door to pro football growth in Ohio.

As in Pennsylvania, pro football in Ohio had its roots in teams sponsored by athletic clubs. The first known club football team in the state was the Dayton AC in 1889. It was joined by teams from the Cleveland AA in 1891, the Akron AA in 1894, and the Canton AC and Youngstown AC in 1895. Ohio had strong amateur competition from the start, and state champions were proclaimed from 1895 to 1902.

In 1903, a decision was made that revolutionized the game of football. Through much of the 1890s, Massillon had fielded amateur teams made up of local players. They rarely could compete with Canton. The string of losses was not only embarrassing, but costly – the men of Massillon always lost large amounts wagered on the games.

By 1903, the football enthusiasts of Massillon had had enough. They met at the Hotel Sailor on September 3 to find a solution. A new team was organized, with Jack Goodrich as manager and Ed Stewart as coach. When the city's sporting goods store only could supply jerseys with striped sleeves, the town adopted the nickname Tigers.

Although many towns throughout Ohio organized teams the same way Massillon did, the Tigers were not just any team. For one thing, they made sure to spend time practicing together, which other town teams did not do. For another, they appeared to have some real talent on the squad. Guard Frank Botoner, a 32-year-old policeman; Goodrich, who was a halfback as well as the manager; Stewart, the coach quarterback, and editor of the Massillon Evening

Independent; and Mully Miller, a 170-pound fullback and the group's real star, immediately gave the Tigers a strong team.

After losing its opener 6-0 to Wooster College, Massillon rapidly became one of the best teams in the state, winning its next four games. Then the Tigers easily disposed of Canton 16-0, before beating a team from Cleveland. At that point, Massillon challenged Akron to a game for the state title.

The championship the Tigers were pursuing was not official. In a practice dating back to the 1890s, the championship of the state was awarded by popular acclaim at the end of the season. All games played were considered, but some games were more important than others. Victories over big-city title contenders were much more important than wins against small-town teams, although a loss against one of the lesser teams could eliminate a contender from the title picture. In 1903, the East End team of Akron had been recognized as the state champion for several years.

The East Ends initially dismissed Massillon's attempt to schedule a game, but the Tigers continued to pursue their claim. Finally, a game between the Tigers and the East Ends was set up for December 5, with an agreement that the winner would receive 75 percent of the gate and the loser 25 percent. Almost immediately, stories appeared claiming that Massillon wanted to win at any cost. On December 2, the Akron Beacon Journal announced that the Tigers had hired four members of the old Pittsburgh Athletic Club. The four were Bob Shiring, who had been the center for the Pittsburgh Stars in 1902, meaning he was the best center in western Pennsylvania (and probably the country); the McChesney brothers – Harry, a back who was one of the best

punters available, and Doc, a lineman who could play tackle or end equally well; and a man whose last name was either Peiper or Peiffer, depending on the source, and whose first name still is unknown but who possessed a sterling reputation as a tackle.

Massillon's tactics infuriated the Akron paper, but not as much as what happened on the field. In the first half, Doc McChesney recovered a fumble for a touchdown. In the second half, Massillon scored on a tackle-around play. The Tigers proceeded to win the Ohio Independent Championship 12–0.

The controversy about Massillon's use of pros raged in northern Ohio for weeks, but the Massillon team was not bothered in the slightest, nor were the managers of other Ohio teams. By the beginning of the 1904 season, at least five teams besides Massillon – Canton, Dover, Shelby, Lorain, and Salem – had begun paying players openly.

Actually, recent research by Joe Horrigan of the Pro Football Hall of Fame indicates that the Shelby team had been paying players since 1902. Despite Shelby's precedence in hiring pros, however, Massillon must be accorded the place of honor on the road to pro football in Ohio because it was the Tigers who opened the floodgates for a previously unpopular process, and who initiated the importation of out-of-state talent.

Shelby also receives credit in one other historical note. On September 16, 1904, Charles W. Follis signed a contract to play for the Shelby AC. Although Shelby had been paying some of its players since 1902, Follis had played for the team in exchange for working at the Howard Seltzer and Sons Hardware Store. His actual signing of a full-season contract in 1904 not only indicated how valuable he was considered, but made him the first verified black

Amos Alonzo Stagg's 1903 University of Chicago team demonstrate the T-formation.

professional football player. Follis's outstanding play as a halfback was a major reason Shelby went 8-1-1 in 1904, losing only to Massillon.

Meanwhile, the collection of Ohio teams informally known as the Ohio League began to be recognized as official. Starting with Massillon's first pro championship in 1903, the league used the same rules for determining a pro champion (or independent champion as it still was known in the early years) that the amateur teams in Ohio had used in the 1890s. The members of the league played most of the other teams once or twice a year, allowing for a champion to be decided by consensus. Although there sometimes were differing opinions about which team should be champion, the system generally worked well. The top teams in this unofficial league became so strong that each year the best of them was able to call itself, deservedly, the "U.S. Professional Champion."

The 1904 Ohio League champion, the first in a primarily professional setup, was Massillon, once again. Although rain and difficulty in finding opponents who would risk being slaughtered restricted the Tigers to a 7-0 record, they still were the best team in Ohio. Before the season even opened, the Tigers put a fence around where they played, Hospital Grounds Field, which was located on the grounds of the state mental asylum.

The Tigers rolled through three opponents, beating the Canal Dover Giants 57-0, the Franklin AC of Cleveland 56-6, and Marion 148-0. In the Marion game, Massillon scored 26 touchdowns and 18 extra points. The uneven score was due in part to the rules then in force, which stated that a team that scored received the next kickoff. After Marion punted on its first possession, it did not get the ball back for the rest of the game.

Expecting to have problems with a strong Pittsburgh Lyceum team in their fourth game, the Tigers imported yet another Pittsburgh lineman to join Shiring and Doc McChesney, both of whom had returned in 1904. Guard Herman Kerchoffe (6-5, 235) was perhaps the best lineman in the U.S., and he helped the Tigers to a 44-0 victory. Massillon then defeated Shelby 28-0 and the Sharon Buhl Club, the self-styled champions of western Pennsylvania, 63-0.

On Thanksgiving Day, Massillon took on the Akron AC (which had changed its name from the Akron East Ends) for the state title. By this time, Akron was a pro team as well, featuring virtually an all-star roster. Late in the first half, the Tigers went ahead 6-0 when Emery Powell scored, and Ed Stewart kicked the extra point. Midway through the second half, with the game about to be called on account of darkness, Akron scored to cut the lead to 6-5. Akron had a chance to tie for the state championship, but, under the rules of the time, the extra point had to be made from where the touchdown was scored – in this case the edge of the field. With almost no light, a difficult angle, and a strong crosswind, Joe Fogg missed the kick. The Tigers won 6-5 and were Ohio League champions for another year.

Two consecutive state championships for Massillon were more than its jealous neighbor to the east could stand. Canton hadn't even fielded a major team in 1904, but late that year plans were announced to organize the Canton AC, which would include a pro football team with a pro coach.

Of course, the best way to build a team that could challenge Massillon was to hire all the best players otherwise available. That is exactly what Canton

The 1902 Shelby (Ohio) Blues team was composed entirely of ex-college players and included the first known black professional football player, Charles Follis (middle row, far right.)

tried to do. Canton signed seven players from the Akron AC team, including halfback Eddie Murphy, guard Doc Rayl, and tackle Bill Laub, who became captain and coach. Canton also signed a number of other star players, including quarterback Harry James and guard Buck Hall of Fielding Yost's point-a-minute teams at the University of Michigan. On paper, Canton looked every bit as good as Massillon, although the Tigers added to their already-strong team by signing four players from the Franklin All-Star team that had won the 1903 World Series. Cost obviously was no object to either Canton or Massillon when it came to gaining or keeping the state championship.

For both teams, as well as for most fans in the state, the Canton-Massillon game in late November was the key to the whole season. The other games figured to be just so many warmups. Indeed, through October, Canton defeated its first six opponents by a combined score of 409-0, a point total that would have been even greater if a number of games hadn't been ended early by darkness. Massillon was virtually as dominant in its first four victories.

In early November, in the first important game ever played in Cleveland, Massillon took on the Carlisle Indians, the team that a few years hence would feature Jim Thorpe. Although Carlisle was academically more along the lines of a high school, its football team was big time, playing many of the best colleges in the country. The Tigers, who had been known for their big, bruising line, also unveiled some astonishing speed, as they turned out to be faster than the Indians, who were supposed to have been the fastest team in the country. The result was an 8-4 victory for Massillon, on two field goals to one.

Canton, meanwhile, had traveled to Latrobe to play what was once again the best team in Pennsylvania. When Latrobe kicked off to open the second half of a scoreless game, a botched play on the return resulted in a fumble at the Canton 5-yard line. A Latrobe player recovered the ball and ran it in for a touchdown. John Brallier kicked the extra point, and Latrobe held on to win 6-0.

The Latrobe game was more than a disaster on the scoreboard. Canton also lost Laub, who suffered a career-ending leg injury. An urgent call went out to Charles E. (Blondy) Wallace, a Canton native who had captained Connie Mack's 1902 Philadelphia pro team and had held down a similar position with the 1903 Franklin All-Stars. At 6-2, 240, Wallace was a giant by the standards of the day, and more than Laub's equal on the field. His being named captain would have repercussions in both 1905 and 1906, however.

In the week prior to the Canton-Massillon game, Wallace completely revamped the Canton team. He brought in three new linemen and added three new starting backs, including Willie Heston, a two-time All-America for the point-a-minute teams at Michigan and a player many thought was the best back in college football history. To obtain his services for one game, Canton paid him $600, a figure that would be the highest paid to any football player for one game until Red Grange entered the NFL in 1926. Meanwhile, Massillon kept its regular lineup. Coach Stewart indicated that he felt the Tigers would win, "owing to teamwork and the fact that they have played together all season." It was a good assessment.

The score was 4-4 at halftime, but Massillon took control in the second half when Canton guard Doc Rayl was expelled for slugging one of the Massillon players. From that point on, Massillon was able to move the ball by consistently running directly at Rayl's replacement. The Tigers scored twice on runs by Red Salmon and won the game — and their third consecutive championship – 14-4.

Although the 1906 Ohio League season again revolved around the two giants, Massillon and Canton, the entire football world temporarily was thrown into confusion before the season opened. Late in 1905, U.S. President Theodore Roosevelt, horrified by a sport that had recorded 18 deaths and 149 injuries in the 1905 season, threatened to ban football if those in charge did not clean it up.

In December, 1905, the Intercollegiate Athletic Association of the United States (IAAUS) was organized to assist in the formation of sound

The explosive Massillon Tigers were the most dominant team in the Ohio League, winning three consecutive league championships from 1904-06.

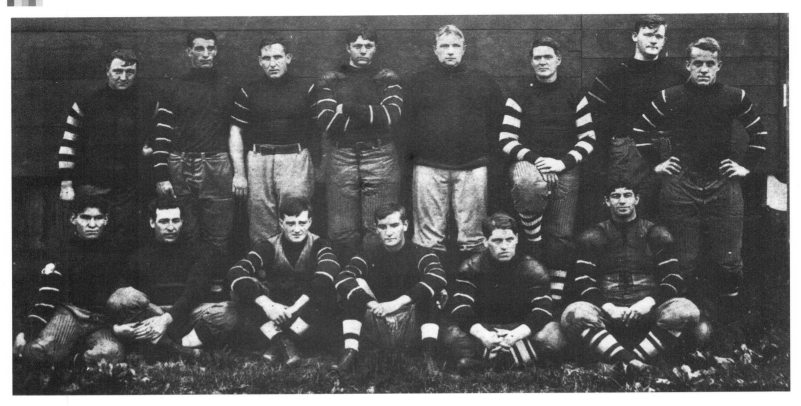

requirements for intercollegiate athletics, particularly football. In 1910, the IAAUS changed its name to the National Collegiate Athletic Association (NCAA).

At a meeting on January 12, 1906, the new rules committee for the IAAUS dramatically changed the focus on the game from that of brute force to an open, quick-striking offensive attack. The rules changes included legalizing the forward pass; reducing the game from 70 to 60 minutes; establishing a neutral zone to separate the teams by the length of the ball; increasing the distance to be gained for a first down to 10 yards; adding a third official; and requiring six (later seven) men to be on the line of scrimmage.

The 1906 changes were just as important for the pro game as for college football, because the pros had not yet developed any independent rules. Although legalizing the forward pass eventually was to be the most important rules change of 1906, those with the most immediate effect were requiring six men on the line, which helped eliminate the popular but dangerous mass plays, such as the Flying Wedge; and the increase from 5 to 10 yards for a first down, which forced the development of outside running attacks, helped lead to the actual use of passing, and increased the importance of the kicking game.

With the new rules and the hopes of a cleaner, less vicious game, 1906 promised to be the greatest pro season yet in Ohio. Instead, it developed into a disastrous season for both pro football in general and Massillon and Canton in particular.

Before the season started, Canton's Blondy Wallace looted Massillon of players. By offering more money, he was able to sign quarterback Jack Hayden, tackle Jack Lang, guard Herman Kerchoffe, and end Clark Schrontz. He also signed a number of outstanding college players.

The Tigers tried to replace the four players who had gone to Canton. To replace Kerchoffe, new coach Sherburn Wightman (who had replaced Ed Stewart, who, in turn, had moved up to manager) signed Bob (Tiny) Maxwell, a 250-pound giant. And to replace Hayden, he signed the enormously talented George (Peggy) Parratt.

Parratt was perhaps the best athlete in Ohio when he attended Case University, which was a major sports power at the time. He was the captain of the baseball team, the star of the basketball team, and he was such an outstanding quarterback that he was pushed as the first All-America from Ohio. In fact, he eventually played all three sports professionally.

Although Canton appeared to be a little stronger than Massillon on paper, some had thought the same thing the year before and had been proven wrong. As both teams knocked off opponent after opponent on the way to their two expected November showdowns, Massillon under Wightman showed more cohesive team play than Canton under Wallace.

After eight games, Canton, which for the first time was being called the Bulldogs, had outscored its opponents 285-0. The only two close games had been 8-0 and 12-0 victories over the Pittsburgh Lyceums. On the other hand, Massillon had outscored eight teams 438-0, including 19-0 and 33-0 victories over the Lyceums.

Three of Massillon's early games proved to have significance later. On October 20, in a 57-0 victory over the Shelby team regarded as the third best in Ohio, the Tigers installed Walter East, an Akron baseball player, at end. East had a big day and his play was publicly commended. A week later, against a combined Benwood-Moundsville team, Parratt completed a forward pass to Bullet Dan Riley, the first authenticated pass completion in pro football history. Then, on November 1, East was released after having a good game in the 33-0 victory over the Lyceums. Although Stewart and Wightman appeared to be ready to sign some big names to replace East, and therefore simply could have been upgrading the team, a more sinister reason for East's departure would be announced later.

In late October, the Tigers and the Bulldogs finally worked out a contract for their November games. The two teams would divide the gate receipts from two games, one in Canton on November 16, and one in Massillon on November 24, the weekend before Thanksgiving. It was "mutually agreed" that both teams had wanted to play on Thanksgiving, but that was impossible because Canton had scheduled a game that day with Latrobe. Another part of the contract stipulated that each team would put up a $3,000 guarantee to insure appearance on both dates.

The lack of trust between the two teams – and specifically between Wallace and Stewart – was underlined in the section of the contract that stated that Massillon's gate receipts from the first game in Canton would be placed in a Canton bank and would be forfeited to Canton if Massillon did anything to spoil the Canton-Latrobe meeting. On the other hand, Canton's half of the receipts from the second game would be deposited in a bank in Massillon. If for any reason other than mischief by Massillon the Latrobe team did not play in Canton on Thanksgiving, Canton would forfeit the money to Massillon. Thus, the fiscal futures of both teams were staked on the Canton-Latrobe game, and both teams' finances were shaky anyway. Although each team's signing the best players in the country increased its chances of winning, it also decreased the chances of finishing in the black. The salaries long ago had doubled or tripled former all-time highs, and the Canton Repository estimated the Bulldogs' payroll to be at $8,700 and the Tigers' at $9,000.

When November 16 finally arrived, nearly 8,000 fans showed up at Canton's Mahaffey Park. Canton played virtually flawless football, building a 10-0 lead before Tiny Maxwell scored on a 55-yard fumble return late in the game. The Bulldogs' 10-5 final margin represented the town's biggest victory ever.

Eight days later, the rematch was held at Hospital Grounds Field. Before the game began, a dispute developed over the selection of a football. Massillon had decided to use a Victor football, one several ounces lighter than the Spalding used by most teams, including Canton. Although Wallace protested, Canton was forced to accept the football or forfeit its $3,000 guarantee.

Once play began, the reason for Massillon's preference became obvious. Peggy Parratt was shifted to end, and Homer Davidson moved to quarterback. Davidson had learned the signals, but his primary responsibility was to kick the daylights out of the ball. The combination of the light Victor and Davidson's powerful leg was amazing. Six times punts sailed over the head of Bulldogs safety Jack Hayden. Davidson's punting and the resulting field position helped the Tigers gain a 5-0 halftime lead. The Bulldogs scored a touchdown to go ahead 6-5, but a blocked punt resulted in a safety (two points for Massillon), and the Canton team was disheartened. The Tigers eventually won 13-6, clinching their fourth consecutive state championship.

But the most important part of the game story was just beginning. Soon after the contest ended, things turned ugly. On the Monday after the game, Ed Stewart charged in his newspaper that not only had an attempt been made to fix the game, but that Blondy Wallace was at the bottom of it. Wallace's plot, according to Stewart, involved splitting the first two games, thereby forcing a third.

To this day, events following the second Canton-Massillon game of 1906 are misrepresented in nearly every book on pro football history. It is widely reported that, under the orders of Wallace, the Bulldogs "threw" the game. Moreover, the consensus is that the discovery of this "fix" destroyed pro football in Ohio for at least five years.

The major source of these misconceptions was the first published history of pro football, Harry March's *Pro Football: Its "Ups" and "Downs"*, a rambling, frequently inaccurate account written in 1934, decades after many of the incidents mentioned. The author was forced to rely on unsubstantiated stories and his apparently faulty memory for many details. These inaccuracies were compounded when later "experts" – which included virtually everyone who wrote a football history during the next three decades – borrowed liberally from March's book, apparently never bothering to check his information for accuracy. Thus, many of the mistakes March made were perpetuated. Of all the mistakes in March's book, none was more significant, nor more difficult to correct, than his report about the 1906 Canton-Massillon game.

At the time, March simply was not interested in hearing about strategy that backfired or in acknow-

Ed Stewart

ledging that Canton residents might have made mistakes in betting on the Bulldogs. The day after Stewart made his charge, a committee drew up a list of 11 questions for Wallace. He answered them all, and most of the committee left satisfied, while the Canton Morning News printed both the answers and an apology for writing negative things about him after the game.

March, who apparently was not satisfied, propagated the "conspiracy myth" in his book. However, March apparently misread the first article by Stewart and then missed some of the important developments of ensuing weeks that helped to clear a muddy picture. First, Stewart had not said the game was fixed. He wrote that an attempt had been made to bribe some of the Tigers players before the first game. This attempt had failed. Walter East, the Akron baseball player, had solicited Tiny Maxwell and Bob Shiring to fix the game, but he had been released after the two players told Stewart and Wightman about the attempt. Thus, it appears both games were played on the up-and-up.

Stewart had said that East had an accomplice, namely Blondy Wallace. But the day after the game, which was the day before Stewart made his accusation, Wallace had told a Canton Morning News reporter that he did not favor another meeting between the Bulldogs and Tigers. Because, according to Stewart, the extra game was at the heart of Wallace's machinations, that statement should have gone long way toward clearing Wallace of any wrongdoing. But Wallace's reputation for liking life in the fast lane did not help inspire the public's confidence. He knew and openly consorted with men and women of shady reputation. He drank too often

and too much. And he rubbed too many conservative Midwesterners the wrong way. There were many who were only too willing, whether there was evidence or not, to believe Blondy Wallace had set up their team and their town for a fall. The facts did not support their beliefs.

On Thanksgiving Day, George Williams, the Bulldogs' manager, publicly gave his version of the story. He stated that on November 16, Stewart had met with him and indicated that East had tried to make a deal with some of the Massillon players and that Wallace was implicated. However, according to Williams, Stewart also stated that the whole plan had been nipped in the bud and that publishing the story would only hurt the game's attendance. Stewart also said that as far as he was concerned the game was going to be played totally on the square.

After Williams's meeting with Stewart, Williams conferred with Wallace and asked him about the story. Wallace gave Williams his assurance that he knew nothing about the bribery attempt and that his team was going to do its best to win the game. Before the second game, Wallace repeated the pledge. Williams must have believed him; he actually went ahead and, through a prominent Canton businessman, bet money on the Bulldogs to win the game. Williams also indicated that a number of players had bet on their own team, after asking for and receiving advance money for that purpose.

The same day as Williams's story was published, the Bulldogs defeated Latrobe 16-0 before a crowd of only 939, less than one-sixth the turnout expected. The Bulldogs were totally broke. In fact, they could not pay their players for the Latrobe game and many

had to play a public pickup game several days later to earn enough to pay for railroad tickets home. Meanwhile, Wallace announced a $25,000 libel suit against Stewart and his newspaper.

A week later, the chief actor in the drama, Walter East, who had been traveling in the east, made a statement to the Akron Beacon Journal. Incredibly, East accused Sherb Wightman of being behind the whole thing. According to East, Wightman had first asked East to solicit Maxwell and Shiring, then had East find a backer who would pay Wightman $4,000. Then, at the last minute, Wightman backed out of the deal.

East exonerated Wallace of any charges, saying that neither Wallace nor any other member of the Canton AA had any connection with the deal. And he stated that the only reason Stewart went public with the story was to hurt the attendance for the Canton-Latrobe game. As proof, East produced a contract in which Wightman agreed to throw the game for $4,000. The document was signed by East, Wightman, and John Windsor, one of the owners of the Akron baseball team.

Shortly after East's confession, Windsor added his, which backed East in all particulars, including the comment that he never had met and still did not know Blondy Wallace. The conclusion from these statements was simple: to all except the most diehard Wallace haters, Blondy had been completely cleared. Wightman now was on the hot seat.

However, Wightman, backed by Stewart, came up with a new story. He explained that he had entered into the contract with East in order to get the goods on the fixers. Once Stewart and Wightman had the names of East and Windsor on a contract, he said,

East could be released, the fixers would see they had been exposed, and the honest Massillon management could keep East and his crew away from the game.

It was left up to the people of Canton, Massillon, and the entire state of Ohio to sort through the contradicting stories. The one thing that had been conclusively shown was that Blondy Wallace had had nothing to do with the shady dealings.

Shortly thereafter, the Canton officials leveled charges against Stewart, stating he had deliberately set out to injure Canton football by destroying confidence in the team and ruining the attendance at the Latrobe game. In retrospect, they may have underestimated Stewart. He might have had an even bigger haul in mind. Had the Canton-Latrobe game been canceled, the Tigers stood to gain all of the gate receipts from the second Canton-Massillon game. There always was a possibility that the Canton players would believe Wallace was not crooked and would quit the team before the Latrobe game. Even more likely, the Latrobe team might decline to involve itself with such sordid business and cancel. That neither of these possibilities occurred was not Ed Stewart's fault.

Regardless, the damage had been done. The Bulldogs were broke and out of business. And the Tigers, although still alive, were considerably in the hole financially.

It has been written that the fix scandal killed pro football in Ohio. But even if there had not been a scandal, pro football could not have continued in the manner in which Canton and Massillon played it. It had become too expensive a proposition to constantly field true all-star teams. The Tigers' 1906 payroll totaled more than $20,000, and the Bulldogs' figure was probably even higher. Attendance did not support the high salaries, largely because virtually all games except those between the two powerhouses were runaways. After several games, fans grew bored and stopped coming.

With the demise of the Bulldogs, an era ended. In 1907, Massillon and the other teams throughout Ohio consisted mostly of local athletes who were paid reduced salaries. On a personal level, most of the best football players scattered to their homes around the country, some retiring, some playing again at lower pay, and some lucky ones finding an occasional large payday. In general, nothing much changed in the lives of most of the key performers in the scandal. However, it did have a lasting effect on one person's place in history.

Neither Wightman nor Stewart lost face in Massillon. In Akron, Walter East generally was thought of as the hapless victim of a crooked coach and a Machiavellian manager.

Apparently, the only one who lost anything more than money was Blondy Wallace, the proverbial innocent bystander. His libel suit never came to trial. He probably settled out of court. Wightman and Stewart were under the gun, and they hardly would have held back facts that could have made them look better. At the same time, Wallace was too deeply in debt to turn down any reasonable cash offer. Perhaps he should have gone to court. Because he didn't, there was no real end to the fix scandal. It just whimpered out in charge and countercharge. But because March and his followers have had the last word for three quarters of a century, the name of Blondy Wallace has lived on in infamy.

The 1922-23 Canton Bulldogs emerged as the NFL's first true powerhouse. The team won the league's first two championship games and compiled a 22-0-3 record during that period.

1907-1914: Keeping the Game Alive

When pro football historians consider the period from 1907-1914, not many think of football in Ohio. Not many people around the United States thought of it at the time, either. The big-name players who had dominated the Ohio professional football scene in 1905 and 1906 scattered around the country and were replaced by local talent throughout most of Ohio. Crowds were smaller and salaries were lower. Yet the game did not totally die. In one way, the games actually were better than they had been. They were less predictable. Talent was so dispersed that each year a half-dozen or more teams seriously contended for the state professional championship.

Without the Canton Bulldogs or Massillon Tigers around to make the accomplishments of the other teams seem Lilliputian, as in the past, the notion of an Ohio pro league – first seriously mentioned in 1904 – again came to the fore in September, 1907. The plan involved a semi-pro arrangement in which teams around the state would share gate receipts instead of receiving regular salaries. Therefore, the players necessarily would be local athletes willing to play on speculation, rather than the high-priced pros who had been imported for several years.

But the plan died in October, because most of the cities involved could not get enough players to take the financial chance.

Although the Bulldogs and Tigers were gone, Canton and Massillon still fielded teams. Canton actually had several teams, although none was very strong. The best was the Canton Indians, an amateur team that twice beat the Alliance AC, but could not beat anybody else. The Canton AC played only one game and then disbanded after losing to the Akron Tigers.

In Massillon, Sherb Wightman put together another strong team with many of the locals who had been integral parts of the Tigers in 1903 and 1904. Fred Haag, Frank Botoner, and Mully Miller all returned and helped the All-Massillons, as they were known, to four consecutive victories before playing a scoreless tie with the undefeated Shelby Blues in November. The next week, the All-Massillons struggled to a 6-4 victory over the Columbus Panhandles, who had been reorganized by Joe Carr after two idle years.

After an easy victory over a local amateur team, the All-Massillons met the Panhandles again on Thanksgiving Day. The game was for the state championship, because Shelby, although undefeated, also had a tie with the Columbus team. Because of the game's importance, Massillon imported several familiar faces – Peggy Parratt, Bob Shiring, and Bullet Dan Riley. The All-Massillons won 13-4 with outside help, and the city celebrated its fifth consecutive state title, which now was commonly known as the professional championship, rather than the independent championship.

Although they lost to Massillon, the Panhandles had become the first pro team from southern Ohio to challenge for the state title. In 1907, the Panhandles were represented by six of the Nesser brothers, and another would play for the team before it folded after the 1926 season. The Nessers, in order of age, were

quarterback John, tackle Phil, coach and halfback Ted, tackle and end Fred, halfback Frank, guard Al, and the youngest, Raymond. All except Raymond had long careers together, and, in the early 1920s, Ted's son Charles also played for the Panhandles, making them the only father-son duo ever to appear in a pro football lineup together.

Although the Nessers played for teams other than the Panhandles, year after year their primary allegiance was to Joe Carr's club. Other players, however, regularly continued to move from team to team. No one was more active this way – or more successful – than Peggy Parratt.

Parratt made his first big splash in the pro football world as the quarterback for Massillon in 1906, but he actually had been a pro the year before while he still was playing for Case University.

Late in 1905, Parratt was accused of playing professionally for Shelby under the name Jimmy Murphy. Although such charges were not unusual at the time, Case officials had no choice but to call Parratt in to answer them. A standard scenario had developed when such incidents took place at other institutions. It went like this: The star athlete was asked about his involvement in professionalism; he denied it; and the school announced its investigation had exonerated the star. It was all very pat.

However, when Case officials asked Parratt if he had been playing pro football, the answer was a little different.

"Sure," said Parratt. "And I intend to keep doing it."

It is an indication of the esteem in which Parratt was held that after being ruled ineligible, he still was awarded a varsity letter by Case, which cited his invaluable leadership on and off the field. He also was selected to the all-Ohio college team for 1905. Oddly, Parratt did not play for Shelby after losing his college eligibility, but signed with the Lorain team for the rest of the season.

After playing for the Tigers in 1906, Parratt started the 1907 season with the All-Massillons before returning to his home in Cleveland, where he played for the Franklin AC and also refereed games. By the end of the season, he was back helping Massillon win the state championship.

In 1908, Parratt rejoined his first pro team, the Shelby Blues. Shelby fans had been vociferous when their team lost the championship to Massillon because it had played one more tie. To help gain the title, Parratt was brought in as coach and star. Shelby already had an excellent quarterback in Homer Davidson, who had gained fame as the punter of the Victor-brand football in the 1906 Canton-Massillon game and who was one of the best kickers around. But the versatile Parratt could play halfback and end.

Parratt also was able to put together a team that won...but also turned a profit. He sometimes was unpopular with his own players because of his tight-fisted ways, but they stuck with him because they could depend on being paid.

With Parratt leading the way, the Blues were undefeated in 1908. Still, Shelby had to settle for second

best again when it could not arrange a game with the Akron Indians. The Indians, who were led by black halfback Charles Baker, won eight games and generally were given the nod as state champions, despite managing only a tie with the cross-town rival Tigers.

Meanwhile, Massillon lost its luster. Sherb Wightman took many of his star players with him to Canal Dover. There, his Giants became one of the state's best teams, destroying the Lorain AC 158-0 and defeating an improving Canton AC team, before being upended 10-0 by the Akron Indians on October 31.

Massillon was not the only traditional powerhouse not to field a representative team in 1908. The Toledo Athletic Association (TAA) had been perhaps the best team in northwest Ohio from 1902 to 1907. The team had been led by Louis Kruse, an outstanding halfback, and 18-year-old Fred Merkle, who later would gain fame – and the nickname "Bonehead" – when his failure to touch second base led to the New York Giants losing the 1908 National League baseball pennant. But the TAA did not return in 1908 – for rather unusual reasons. It may, in fact, be the only football team ever to go out of business due to habitual mud. The TAA played its home games at Armory Park, an unsodded field that inspired the name for Toledo's minor league baseball team – the Mud Hens. Armory Park was bad enough in summer; in the less-than-ideal weather of the autumn, it took an ox team to make a successful end run. The ground was in such bad condition in 1908 that the TAA refused to play there and disbanded.

The 1909 season in many ways was a continuation of 1908, although one major rules change dropped the value of a field goal from four points to three. Once again the Blues and the Indians went through most of the season undefeated, and once again Parratt publicly lobbied for a game between the two powers. This time he got it. The Indians went ahead early 6-0, but Shelby tied the game on Parratt's 45-yard fumble return for a touchdown. When Davidson drop-kicked a field goal

late in the game, Shelby appeared to have a victory, but the Indians turned to desperation passes, and several of them worked, leading to the winning touchdown and another championship for Akron.

Meanwhile, there was a changing of the guard in Canton. When Bullet Dan Riley took over the leadership of the Canton AC in 1909, in appeared to spell the start of a new power. After a good start, however, the team lost its last six games. In the final game of the year, against the cross-town-rival Simpson Tigers, the Canton AC lost without playing a down. The Cantons dressed three players who had not been with the team before. Although they were locals, not out-of-town ringers, the Simpson manager argued that, according to the contract, they could not play. When the Canton AC refused to play without them, the referee ruled the game a forfeit, and the Tigers won 1-0. The game was more important than it seemed, because the victory, no matter how technical, made the Simpsons the city champs. More importantly, it established their young players as the nucleus Canton would use to get back into the race for the state football championship.

Whereas Canton's rebuilding program was just starting, Shelby's finally was culminating in its goal. In 1910, a new team in town, the Shelby Tigers, went 7-0 and received some backing for the state title. However, they still couldn't match their cross-town rivals. Parratt combined his team with a squad from Mansfield, forming the Shelby-Mansfield Blues. Then he signed some of the state's best players, each of whom had gone into coaching. The mixture of football brains and brawn paid off, as the Blues twice upset the powerful Akron Indians, 16-6 and 8-6, to pick up the Ohio title.

Actually, Parratt's team was more than just the best in Shelby, or even Ohio. For the first time since the Massillon Tigers in 1906, an Ohio team probably was the best in the nation. The three previous years, many of the former Tigers and Canton Bulldogs had gone

Despite having Joe Carr (top row, far right) as their manager and five of the Nesser brothers on their roster, the 1921 Columbus Panhandles finished with a 1-8 record.

home to Pennsylvania. There, in an echo of former glory, Pittsburgh produced its last pro football power for more than six decades – the Lyceum team. Doc McChesney, Bob Shiring, and a few other pros returned home from Ohio to join with the Dillon brothers, who had starred at Princeton. The result was a team that was undefeated for nearly three seasons. Their victims included many of the strongest teams in Pennsylvania, West Virginia, and Ohio, justifying a new title – the "Tri-State Champions." With all the area, state, county, city, and even neighborhood crowns floating around, it seemed everyone was champion of something, but the Lyceums' claim was legitimate. They finally were upset by the Dayton Oakwoods in their final game of 1909. After that, the Lyceums broke up, and pro football in western Pennsylvania drifted into the "also-ran" category.

Powerful football teams were disappearing in some places, but Parratt was far from through in Shelby. In 1911, he combined his team with the Shelby Tigers and recruited a number of players from schools outside Ohio, and the Blues won the state championship again, shutting out the tough Akron Indians twice, 6-0 and 3-0.

The sport also came back to Massillon, where a new team challenged Canton's best team to a game for the Stark County championship. Canton easily won the game against Massillon, but it was not as successful in an attempt to wrest the state title from Shelby, which won 1-0 after a dispute over an offside call. Parratt actually had been willing to compromise with Canton over the official's call, in an attempt to ease the ill feelings between the teams, but Canton's captain, Harry Turner called his team off the field in a fit of anger and refused to continue the contest.

In a postgame statement, Turner told the local newspapers, "Right or wrong, no more football for me after this. These old football duds, mud and dirt, go up to the attic. I'm done."

Turner made his vow to quit football on November 26, 1911. He should have kept his word. As it turned out, he so badly wanted to beat Peggy Parratt that he returned to play for Canton against Parratt's teams for the next three years.

Parratt, Canton, and the rules of football all had new looks in 1912. The major rules changes increased the value of a touchdown from five to six points, added a fourth down to each possession, and established end zones, while decreasing the actual playing field from 110 yards to 100.

But from a professional standpoint, even more important were the changes brought about by Parratt, who was more than a player, coach, and manager. He also was a promoter, and he had a master plan for pro football – a parity plan many years ahead of its time.

Parratt had learned from his Massillon days that one-sided victories did not fill the stands. Just being good wasn't good enough. To make money, a team needed close, exciting games against worthy rivals – games that the fans would beat down the gates to see.

After his Blues repeated as state champions in 1911, Parratt moved on to rebuild the Akron Indians. He was careful to leave enough good players in Shelby to keep the team competitive. Some of the leftover talent went to the Elyria AC, putting a third worthy challenger on the field.

Parratt had helped to build three teams. Meanwhile, a new force appeared in Canton. Jack Cusack, who would prove to be Parratt's only serious rival as a promoter, became the secretary and treasurer for a new team that had been built from the best players of the Simpson Tigers and several other Canton teams. Although he had taken the unpaying job only as a favor to team captain Roscoe Oberlin, the 21-year-old Cusack suddenly found himself in the midst of a power struggle before the new Canton Professionals ever took the field. As Cusack himself later recounted the situation:

H.H. Halter, who was the manager at the time, did not take well to the arrangement, giving a rather cool climate to our association. Halter booked the games for the season, a total of nine, with emphasis on Akron. The Akron Indians, owned, coached, and managed by Peggy Parratt...were a real drawing card as an opponent because of the intense rivalry between Akron and Canton, but Parratt was a hard man

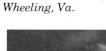

Stats Athletic Club, Wheeling, Va.

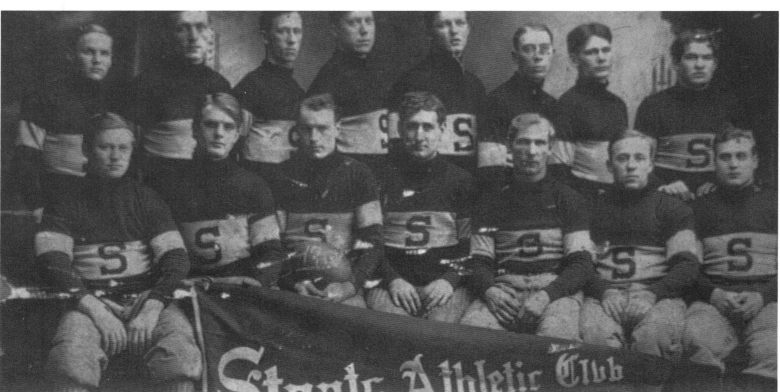

to do business with when it came to dividing the gate receipts. He liked to divide the money half-horse and half-rabbit, his preference being the horse end.

Finally, the two managers had so much difficulty in arriving at an agreement that Parratt refused to meet Halter, but said he would be willing to discuss terms with me. Accordingly, we met in Akron and signed a contract after five hours of talk. The situation naturally displeased Halter, and during my absence in Akron he called a meeting of the team, at which a vote was taken to dispense with my services. I circumvented that by securing a five-year lease on League Park, with an option for five more years, and installed myself as manager. Halter was out and the team continued with the exception of one or two who resigned.

Cusack quickly built the Canton team into a power that went 6-3 its first year, losing only two games to Parratt's Indians and one to Elyria. With those three teams, plus Shelby, the state suddenly had four first-class teams competing, and all of the games among the four were close on the field and profitable off. Parratt's former teammates who had joined the Elyria Athletics won the championship with an 8-0 record.

The 1913 season saw even more parity among the big four teams. In Canton, Cusack quickly realized that to compete for the championship, he would have to have some former college players with more experience. Of course, that meant paying salaries, so with the help of Oberlin he persuaded the players to take salaries instead of splits. He and Oberlin became the owners, with Cusack remaining as manager.

Meanwhile, Parratt brought some of Elyria's championship team to Akron. The result was that the Indians defeated Elyria and Shelby, while tying Canton. Despite a less-than-perfect 8-1-2 record, the Indians won the state title. Perhaps the most important game of the season came in early November when Shelby visited Akron. The Blues hired a number of famous players from eastern colleges, running up a one-week payroll of $700. But the fates

were on Parratt's side. A snowstorm forced a postponement of the game, and when Shelby returned the following week minus a few of their more expensive imports, Parratt's Indians were awaiting with superior talent. Akron won 20-0 to earn the state championship.

Although almost unnoticed in Ohio, there were important rumblings coming west of the state. For several years, pro football had been growing in Iowa, Indiana, and Illinois. Although the teams were not on a par with those in Ohio, they were improving, especially in Illinois, where there were several good teams, including the Rock Island Independents, the Moline Red Men, and the Peoria Socials. In 1913, the little-known Pine Village Pros in Indiana set the stage for a historic move. That year, Pine Village signed a contract with Jim Thorpe, the former football All-America at Carlisle Indian School and the hero of the 1912 Olympics in Stockholm. The sport had its first immortal name. In the summer of 1914, Cusack was summoned to a secret meeting in Massillon, where a group of local businessmen indicated that they intended to field a major team, something that hadn't been done there since 1907. Cusack liked the idea of a team in Massillon, because a Canton-Massillon game would be a terrific payday. But he did not like the group's plan to steal its players from Parratt's Akron team by offering more money. So he reminded the group that it was just such action that helped bring on the 1906 scandal. He said he would refuse to play against any team assembled that way.

"I'd rather fold at Canton than risk losing the confidence of the public, thus destroying the game," he said.

Without Cusack's support, the Massillon group could not field a team in 1914, and Parratt started the season with his regular crew. But for a while it looked like the Indians had lost their edge, anyway. After two victories, they were thrashed 16-0 by the Columbus Panhandles, who put themselves in the thick of the race for the first time since 1909. A week later, the Indians had problems again, and were fortunate to escape with a 7-7 tie with the Youngstown Pros.

The week after the Youngstown-Akron game,

Canton, which had started with four consecutive victories by a combined 209-0 margin, put itself in the driver's seat for the state title by embarrassing Youngstown 31-0. Then, in the last week of October, Cusack's team administered the first loss of the year to the Panhandles, 40-10. On November 1, Akron regrouped with a 14-0 victory over Columbus.

Parratt and Cusack both went all out prior to the Akron-Canton game, beefing up their teams with powerful collegians. Robert (Butts) Butler, a tackle from Wisconsin, was the first All-America to play for Canton since 1906, while the left side of Parratt's line came entirely from Notre Dame, including end Knute Rockne. On November 15, before a crowd of 3,000, Canton took a huge step toward the state championship by defeating the Indians 6-0. However, tragedy marred Canton's victory.

Years later, in his short book *Pioneer in Pro Football*, Cusack wrote about the incident:

Harry Turner, a Canton boy who played center, died of injuries received in the game, which brought our first victory over Parratt's Akron Indians. In making a tackle, Turner's back was fractured and his spinal cord completely severed, but he showed a rare type of courage and spirit. I was at his bedside when he died. He was conscious almost to the end, and his last words left an indelible imprint on my memory.

'I know I must go,' he said, 'but I'm satisfied, for we beat Peggy Parratt.'

The death of Turner, the team captain who had been driven to beat Parratt ever since he forfeited the 1911 game to Parratt's Shelby Blues, turned the season upside-down. Several players quit the Canton team, and the heart went out of those who remained. Cusack, who only that year had been the first to conceive the idea of selling season tickets, considered closing down the whole operation. But he and the

players had spent so much time bringing the team to the point of both profit and a championship that they decided to finish the season.

Although the Professionals did win the next week over Shelby, they had to close out the season on Thanksgiving Day with another game against Akron. The Indians won easily, 21-0. The game turned out to be more than just one defeat, however. It was Canton's only loss in a 9-1 season, but, coming when it did—in the finale—and at the hands of Akron, it dropped Canton behind the Indians in the estimation of most football experts. Although Canton's record was better than the Indians 8-2-1 mark, Parratt had grabbed another championship by winning when he needed to and winning the games that counted.

It was only fitting that Parratt's Indians won the title in 1914. Parratt had helped carry pro football through its toughest times, when many people had given up on it. And this final championship year marked a beginning for the sport. For pro football finally had turned the corner in becoming a bigger and better game. Although the 1914 season seemed—except for Turner's death—much like 1912 or 1913, a closer look at the lineups shows it actually was a transitional year. The quality of play was being upgraded significantly by the importation of more ex-college players from distant and prestigious schools, symbolized by Cusack's hiring of Butler. Similarly, Turner's tragic death symbolized the passing of the sandlot player from the mainstream of action.

It would be several seasons before this transition was completed, but 1915 saw a tremendous acceleration. More than that, 1915 would see the Ohio debut of the sport's first great legend—Jim Thorpe, the man whose feats and personality would help put professional football on the map.

1914 Toledo Maroons

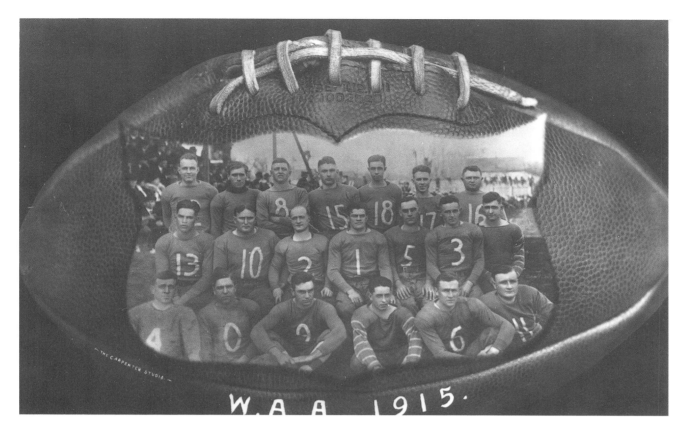

1915-1919: Bulldogs and Indians

It was not a decision that made newspaper headlines, but the personal career choice made by an Ohio gas company employee late in 1914 was a critical event in the development of pro football.

Jack Cusack had worked for a gas company in Canton for seven years, and by 1914 had risen to a position of trust and responsibility. In fact, he was the only employee with the combination to the company safe, and his major duty was to deposit daily cash receipts in the bank. In late 1914, Ralph Gallagher, his general manager, informed Cusack that he either had to give up football or leave the gas company. Cusack promptly resigned.

Cusack did not wait long before taking major steps toward his bonanza. Before the end of 1915, his far-sighted policies had assured his Canton team of fiscal stability and continued on-field excellence.

In 1915, pro football began to reach major-sport status. Cusack had a lot to do with it, but so did the return of the most legendary rivalry in pro football history.

Before the 1915 season, Cusack again was invited to Massillon by businessmen interested in organizing a football team. Unlike that of the previous year, this group, headed by Jack Whalen and Jack Donahue, was successful both in gaining Cusack's blessing and in launching a team, which quickly established itself as one of the best in the state. In a nod to former glory, the Massillon team quickly was christened the Tigers, which encouraged the people of Canton to rename Cusack's Professionals the Bulldogs. Many fans expected the championship to hinge on the two games scheduled between the old rivals in late November.

But 1915 did not develop quite like the fans figured it would. It turned out to be the one season in the history of the Ohio League in which no team was dominant enough to receive consensus acclaim as the champion.

By 1915, football fans had begun referring to the Ohio League by name, as if it were a real entity. However, there never was anything official about it, and its makeup changed from year to year. The Ohio League essentially was made up of those teams strong enough to be considered "major." In any given year, that usually involved three to five teams in northeastern Ohio, and, depending on their fortunes, two or three from Columbus, Cincinnati, Dayton, or Toledo.

When Peggy Parratt decided to take the year off in Akron, his Indians collapsed, and the city championship went to the little-known Burkhart Brewers. Shelby and Elyria also fell on hard times and never were in title contention. The Toledo Maroons opened quickly, but had some key losses. The contending teams narrowed to Canton, Massillon, Columbus, and the surprising Youngstown Patricians.

The Patricians, a team representing a men's club from the St. Patrick's Parish on the south side of Youngstown, had been formed only a year earlier, but they had gone 8-1 in 1914 and clinched the city and Mahoning Valley championships with a season-ending 3-0 victory over the Crescent AC, which had been the local champion for several years.

In 1915, the Patricians put together an even better team that included Ray Miller of Notre Dame, Busty Ashbaugh of Brown, and Elgie Tobin of Penn State (who later would be co-coach with Fritz Pollard of the Akron Pros, champions of the American Pro Football Association). Under the leadership of player-coach Ray Thomas, the Patricians won eight games, outscoring their opponents 271-22. Included in the victories was a 13-7 win over the Washington Vigilants. During the previous nine years, the Vigilants had won 90 games while losing only 3, each to college all-star teams.

The Panhandles' 1915 squad may have been called the best in the club's history. The Nesser brothers all were in top form, and only some tough losses – they went 8-3-1 despite outscoring their opponents 192-37 – kept the team from a potential state championship. The key game for the Panhandles was a 7-0 loss to Canton early in the season.

The Bulldogs wasted no time in establishing

1915 Wabash Athletic Association team

themselves as one of the best teams in Ohio. Before the season began, Cusack, figuring he had to go all out to keep up with Massillon, recruited new stars. When Canton opened the season with a 75-0 victory over a team from Wheeling, West Virginia, they included newcomers Bill Gardner, a tackle and end from Carlisle; Hube Wagner, an All-America end from Pittsburgh; and Earle (Greasy) Neale, the coach at West Virginia Wesleyan. Neale, as well as some of the others, played under an assumed name – there still was a stigma attached to playing professionally and he might have lost his coaching job had his involvement with Canton become public.

Massillon also had some big names in 1915. The Tigers were represented by four former Notre Dame players – ends Knute Rockne and Sam Finegan, tackle Keith (Deak) Jones, and quarterback Gus Dorais – and Ohio State halfback Maurice Briggs.

As the two games between the rivals approached, it was just like old times, with Canton and Massillon appearing to be the best teams in the state. Each had lost only once, and Canton's defeat – a 9-3 loss to the Detroit Heralds – had come while traveling out of state. With fans anxiously awaiting the first game, Cusack, in a move reminiscent of the old Canton-Massillon wars, signed Jim Thorpe.

Thorpe first earned national attention in 1911-1912, when he was an All-America halfback at the Carlisle Indian School under coach Pop Warner. In his final season, Thorpe ran for 1,869 yards on only 191 carries, while scoring 29 touchdowns and 224 points. He received world acclaim when he won gold medals in both the decathlon and the pentathlon at the 1912 Olympics in Stockholm, where King Gustav V of Sweden told him, "Sir, you are the greatest athlete in the world." Thorpe also had played pro baseball, as well as football with the Pine Village team in Indiana. When Cusack contacted him, Thorpe had slid into semi-oblivion and was coaching backs at the University of Indiana. Nevertheless, he still was Jim Thorpe. The great American Indian was a star at any sport he set his mind to, but on a football field he was peerless. Some players could run as well, some could pass as well, a few were on a par defensively, and a very few could kick equally well, but no one combined all these skills to the same degree of perfection. Still when fans heard that Thorpe had been promised $250 for each game, they figured Cusack had lost his mind.

1915 Salem (Ohio) Athletics

But Cusack had the last laugh. The paid attendance for the Bulldogs' games had averaged 1,200 before he signed Thorpe. For the final two games with Massillon, Thorpe helped draw crowds of 6,600 and 8,000. Everyone wanted to see the world's best football player in action.

Unfortunately, Thorpe didn't help the Bulldogs on the field as much as off in the first game, and Massillon won 16-0. Thorpe didn't start, although he did break loose for a 40-yard run to the Massillon 8-yard line, before he slipped trying to avoid Dorais.

Two weeks later, the teams met at Canton, with the Bulldogs winning 6-0. Thorpe dropkicked one field goal from the 18-yard line, and later made a 45-yard field goal from placement. But one of the most exciting finishes ever earned the game its place in history.

This second game was played before a crowd so large that fans stood in the end zones. Ground rules for the game stipulated that any player crossing the goal line into the crowd had to be in possession of the ball when he emerged from the crowd. Late in the game, Massillon drove the length of the field after a winning touchdown. That is when the fireworks really exploded, according to Cusack, who wrote:

Briggs, right end for Massillon, caught a forward pass on our 15-yard line and raced across our goal right into the midst of the 'Standing Room Only' customers. Briggs fumbled – or at least he was said to have fumbled – and the ball popped out of the crowd right into the hands of Charlie Smith, the Canton substitute who had been following in hot pursuit. Referee Connors, mindful of the ground rules made before the game, ruled the play a touchback, but Briggs had something to say about that.

'I didn't fumble,' protested the Massillon end. 'That ball was kicked out of my hands by a policeman – a uniformed policeman!'

That was ridiculous on the face of it. Briggs was either lying or seeing things that didn't happen to be there – for most everybody knew that Canton had no uniformed policemen in those days. But Briggs was unable to accept this solid fact.

'It was a policeman!' he insisted. 'I saw the brass buttons on his coat.'

As the arguing over the call continued, the crowd grew more and more restive. Only three minutes remained in the game that would determine the Ohio professional championship. If the touchdown counted and Massillon either won or tied, they would win the undisputed championship. However, if the score did not count and the Bulldogs won, they might be awarded the title. Fans of both teams who could stand the strain no longer, broke down the fences surrounding the field, and swarmed by the thousands onto the ground. The officials, unable to clear the field, ended the game. However, the officials were not allowed to escape. The Massillon team and its fans demanded that they settle the matter by making a definitive statement about the referee's decision. The officials agreed to make the statement, but only if it were to be opened and read by the manager of the Courtland Hotel at 30 minutes after midnight. That would give the officials time to leave town, thereby avoiding the wrath of either the Canton or Massillon fans.

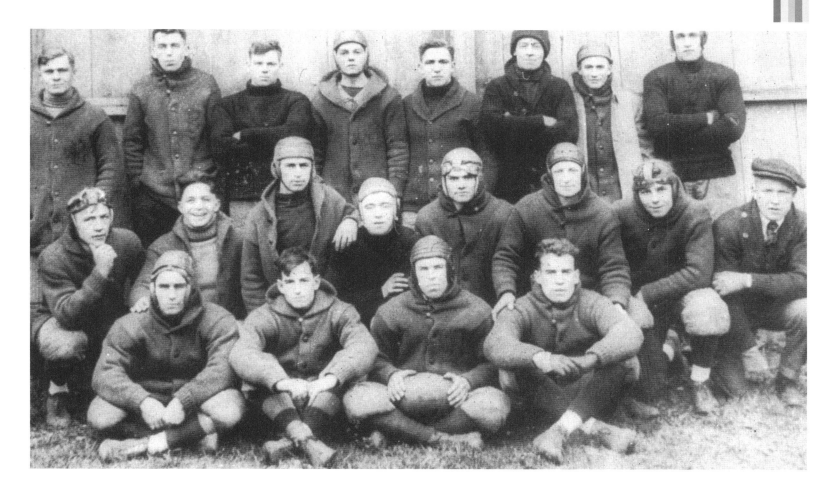

That night the lobby of the Courtland was filled to capacity with both Canton and Massillon fans waiting for the statement to be read. When it was announced, the fans learned that the officials had backed the referee's decision and crowned the Bulldogs winners.

But the last chapter of the season did not end at the hotel. It was not until 10 years later that Cusack solved the mystery of Briggs's fumble and the phantom policeman. As Cusack wrote about it:

While on a visit back to Canton I had occasion to ride a street car, on which I was greeted by an old friend, the brass-buttoned conductor. We began reminiscing about the old football days, and the conductor told me what had happened during that crucial final-quarter play back in 1915. Briggs, when he plunged across the goal line into the end zone spectators, fell at the feet of the conductor, who promptly kicked the ball from Briggs' hands into the arms of Canton's Charlie Smith.

'Why on earth did you do a thing like that?' I asked.

'Well,' he said, 'it was like this – I had thirty dollars bet on that game and, at my salary, I couldn't afford to lose that much money.'

That kick might have saved the conductor $30, but it cost Massillon a consensus state championship. Instead, the Ohio League title race was left in a muddle of three teams – Canton, Massillon, and Youngstown – all claiming the championship. As it happened, the only clear winner in 1915 was Canton, and that was off the field, where the signing of Thorpe helped lead to immediate financial success and gave the Bulldogs a bright future.

Thorpe actually did more than that, giving football a boost throughout Ohio. More important than anything he did in any single game, Thorpe's presence with Canton focused the attention of the entire nation on Ohio professional football. More players of quality began arriving and attendance and salaries both were on the rise. Ohio sportswriters began to trumpet the "world professional championship." True, pro and semi-pro teams could be found from New England to Iowa in nearly every town with 11 able-bodied men and a flat expanse of 100 yards, but they all carried the image of minor leaguers; Ohio held the majors. The annual talk of forming a real pro league – with the Canton Bulldogs of Cusack and Thorpe as the cornerstone – became more vocal than ever before.

One of the top advocates of a pro football league came back into the game in 1916. Peggy Parratt returned to the football wars with a new team in his native city, the Cleveland Indians. Parratt brought together some members of his old Akron team and some former college stars, and the Indians immediately fielded a competitive bunch that split two games with the Columbus Panhandles and tied Massillon. The Indians were not enough to overcome Canton, however, as the Bulldogs took a pair of games from them. Unfortunately, the Cleveland fans quickly lost interest when the Indians fell from contention, and Parratt's team disappeared after a financially unsuccessful season. Likewise, Parratt called it quits at the end of the year, retiring from football until the mid-1920s. Despite the problems, the year did have one highlight. On October 22, in a 9-6 loss to Columbus, Parratt inserted himself at quarterback, playing in his last game.

Parratt's last opponent, the Panhandles, also came up short against the Bulldogs. The Panhandles lost to Canton and to Massillon and finished with a 7-5 record, although they did defeat the Youngstown Patricians 13-0 in the season finale. The Patricians, who had expected to challenge Canton and Massillon, started with five straight wins before losing 3-0 to Massillon, 6-0 to Canton, and 26-0 to Massillon. A 7-4 record left them among the also-rans.

As the season wound down, Canton appeared to be

the strongest team, with Massillon a close second. The Bulldogs won their first eight games, including victories over the Panhandles, the Indians, and the Patricians, while giving up only one score all season, a touchdown to Parratt's team scored on a blocked punt. Massillon also was undefeated, although tied by the Indians.

On November 27, the two teams met before more than 10,000 fans at Massillon. The day was cold with high winds that whipped across the muddy playing field, and the bad weather and slippery footing robbed both teams of much of their offensive might. Canton never threatened, the wind blew two field-goal attempts by Dorais off line, and the game ended in a 0-0 tie. In an effort to avoid being completely stopped again in the rematch with Massillon, Cusack added another star to his roster. The new player was fullback Pete Calac, an American Indian and former teammate of Thorpe's at Carlisle. Calac moved right into a starting position, which allowing Thorpe to switch from fullback to left halfback.

The combination of the two native Americans simply was too much for Massillon. The Bulldogs won 24-0, scoring four touchdowns and missing each conversion. With Thorpe and Calac romping through the Massillon defense, and the 11 starters all playing the entire game, the Bulldogs dominated the contest. They scored on a fumble return by "Fat" Waldsmith, a short run by Calac, a long pass from Milton Ghee to Ernie Soucy, and a short run by Thorpe. Canton, with a 9-0-1 record, finally had won its first undisputed state title.

The situation remained largely the same for Canton in 1917, although it changed dramatically for most teams as the new football season brought with it a stern challenge for the Ohio League. The United States had entered World War I, and not only did the drafting of players into the service make building teams difficult, attendance at games fell off dramatically.

The Youngstown Patricians were particularly hurt by the war. They fielded an almost entirely new squad, including former Notre Dame All-America back Stanley Cofall and Bart Macomber of Illinois. The Patricians won their first four games, but, on November 3, Doc Spears of Canton kicked a field goal while Macomber missed his three attempts. The Bulldogs won 3-0. The Patricians defeated Massillon 14-6 the next week, but then were beaten again by Canton, this time 13-0. The second Canton game abruptly ended Youngstown's season, as a number of players entered the service, Cofall and several of his teammates jumped to Massillon, and the weakened team disbanded for the duration of the war.

The influx of Youngstown players made the Tigers immeasurably stronger. For much of the season, they had matched the mediocrity of most of the other Ohio teams, and they approached their concluding two games against Canton with two losses. Even the Columbus Panhandles, who had fallen to a 2-6 record and had lost 54-0 to Canton, had played the Tigers tough. On November 26, the Bulldogs had little trouble with their opponents from Stark County's second city. Canton took the kickoff and moved to a touchdown, which Thorpe scored on a short run. The Bulldogs' defense totally shut down the Tigers, allowing only a field goal on a dropkick by Charlie Brickley. Canton won 14-3.

A week later, however, the scenario changed dramatically. In a game that turned into a personal duel between Thorpe and Cofall, the younger player had the better of it, kicking 34- and 31-yard field goals for a 6-0 Massillon victory.

Despite the split, Canton was regarded as the better of the two teams everywhere in Ohio except Massillon. Even in the Tigers' victory, the Bulldogs outgained them 186 yards to 35. Although the Tigers argued that their season-ending victory should give them the Ohio League championship, they had lost three times during the season, and no true expert felt their record constituted a legitimate claim to the title. Canton, with a 9-1 mark, retained its Ohio championship.

Although Cusack was able to keep the Bulldogs in the black, the 1917 season had not been as successful at the gate for many Ohio League teams. In Massillon, Whalen and Donahue had lost more than $4,700, while in Youngstown the Patricians had been a financial disaster. The primary reason for the monetary drain was that any team manager who wanted to improve his team at any time during the season usually did so by stealing another team's players for a little more money. As a result of this philosophy, salaries continued to escalate. Although fans and managers alike kept the idea of a league alive – with its ability to rein in the out-of-control salary problems – no one seemed interested in actually joining any formal organization that would be able to establish and enforce rules.

The issue was dismissed completely the next year, however, when thoughts of football took a sabbatical for 1918 as World War I, with its "work or fight" orders, closed down most of the major clubs. Indeed, between the war and a major influenza epidemic, not even Canton or Massillon fielded a team, and Cusack left Canton to try for a fortune in the oil business in Oklahoma.

The Ohio League championship was awarded, virtually by default, to the Dayton Triangles, led by coach and fullback Greasy Neale. The Triangles, the only major Ohio team to play a full schedule, easily won eight games against outmatched opponents to claim a title few cared about. The ease of Dayton's schedule was evidenced by the fact that the Triangles played seven teams from Indiana and only one from Ohio – the Columbus Panhandles. It was the Panhandles' only game of the season.

By mid-1919, in the months before the football season, the will of the team managers to spend money seemed to be waning. As in the past, there were three major concerns facing the teams.

First among these problems was rising salaries. In 1915, Cusack had lured Thorpe to Canton for the unheard-of salary of $250 per game. Thorpe had proved worth it, but his super paydays triggered a spiraling inflation, so that a strong team might now expect to spend about $2,000 per game. That sum was tough to cover with most tickets going for a dollar each. Moreover, most of the small Ohio parks seated only a few thousand and were filled only for the biggest games. By today's standards, the players were paid peanuts. Only top stars earned much more than $100 a game. But this was 1919, and a lot of folks didn't make $100 for a whole week's work. Still, the issue was not so much whether the players were overpaid, but rather whether the struggling teams could afford to pay them.

Another problem was the players' ability to drive up salaries by jumping from team to team. Youngstown's experience in 1917 was one of the worst, but rosters changed for all teams from game to game as the players went from manager to manager in search of the highest bidder. For example, the Nesser brothers claimed to have faced Knute Rockne on five different occasions against five different teams in one season. The managers, of course, were their own worst enemies because they were willing to pay handsomely to have the best possible teams. But they felt that if they did not, someone else would get the best players; because fans would not support a loser, a team would be just as broke as if it had hired the high-paid stars. One could not really blame the players. They had no allegiance to any town, and the only difference between teams was the size of the paycheck.

The third problem was the use of college players. These players often played in college games on Saturdays and, under assumed names, in pro games on Sundays. The use of college players generated a negative image for the professional sport, which was seen by the public as enticing honorable young men with illicit inducements. Meanwhile, no one was sure if the top teams of the 1917 season – Canton, Massillon, Akron, and Youngstown – having taken a financial beating that year and not playing the next,

In the 1939 movie "Knute Rockne – All America," actor Pat O'Brien (seated at desk) portrayed the former Notre Dame coach. Seated before him are real life coaches (left to right) Amos Alonzo Stagg, Howard Jones, and Glenn (Pop) Warner.

would return in 1919. In July, the situation began to clear.

Ralph Hay, a friend of both Cusack and Thorpe, requested permission from Cusack to take over the Canton Bulldogs. Cusack turned the lease to League Park over to him; Thorpe agreed to return from Boston, where he was playing baseball; and, after only one year off, the Bulldogs were back in business. In Massillon, Whalen and Donahue decided to give it one more try, although a suitable field, one surrounded by a fence to keep out gate-crashers, had not yet been found. In Akron, two different groups that were trying to organize teams merged and formed a new edition of the Indians. And in Youngstown, Mickey Stambaugh announced that he would not manage the Patricians, although hope remained in the community that the team somehow could be put back together.

On July 14, the managers of Canton, Massillon, and Akron met at Canton's Courtland Hotel. There they set a wage scale for officials and agreed not to steal each other's players during the 1919 season. However, they failed to agree to a salary limit when Donahue refused to go along with the proposal.

Three weeks later, the managers, having arranged the meeting to include Thorpe, who still was playing baseball, got together at the Pittsburgh Athletic Club to discuss schedules. No one showed up from Youngstown, but the other managers were so convinced that the Patricians would field a team that they penciled them into the calendar anyway.

But scheduling was not why the meeting received publicity. The news was based on some exploratory talk about forming a real pro football league. Such discussions had been common since 1904 with no discernible results. Even so, the Akron Beacon-Journal, in its report of the meeting, saw fit to announce, "A league will be formally organized at the next meeting and officers elected." But no further manager meetings were held in 1919.

At the beginning of September, the Ohio League gained both a new member and an old one. In Cleveland, Jimmy O'Donnell, a minor promoter, leased League Park and hustled the financial backing for a team he named the Tigers. And Hay, after meeting with former Patricians coach Ray L. Thomas, announced that Youngstown would field a team.

Hay also responded to a challenge. In Hammond, Indiana, Paul Parduhn announced that he would raise $20,000 to put together a team that would represent Hammond, but would play its games in Chicago. Parduhn already had signed a number of well-known players, including former University of Illinois end George Halas, the player of the game in the 1919 Rose Bowl (when Halas was with the Great Lakes team). According to Parduhn, Canton would have to accept a game with Hammond or relinquish its claim to the national title. Hay readily scheduled a game.

Some of the Ohio League teams began their season on September 28, while most opened the following week. On October 5, having already defeated the Independents of Wheeling, West Virginia, the week before, the Youngstown Patricians were thrashed by Massillon 17-0. But it was more than an ordinary loss. The defeat proved so overwhelming that the Patricians called it a season and quit. This time the decision stuck.

Otherwise, the season turned out to be one of the best ever for the remaining Ohio League teams. By the end of October, Canton and Massillon still were undefeated, while Akron and Cleveland were hot on their heels. Akron had lost only to Massillon 9-6. Cleveland had upset Hammond 6-0, and had fallen only to Massillon 3-0 when the Tigers kicked a field goal with six seconds remaining. November produced more key matchups. On the first weekend of the month, in Canton, the Bulldogs handed Akron its second defeat 19-7. Meanwhile, Cleveland again played Hammond, and the result was a 0-0 tie. The next week, Akron signed former Brown All-America halfback Fritz Pollard, but the Indians still fell to Massillon 13-6. On the same day, Canton could manage only a 3-3 tie with Hammond.

On Armistice Day, Massillon suffered its first

Columbus's Lee Snoots leads Fred Nesser on a sweep play in a 1916 game that matched the Panhandles against the Cleveland Indians.

1918 Akron Pros

defeat, 3-0 to Cleveland. The next day, a luncheon held for the Cleveland financial backers ended with demands for the formation of a professional football league similar to baseball's, though nothing was done about it right away.

In Canton, Hay responded cautiously, insisting, "We will be on the ground floor when a meeting for the formation of a league is called." But, he added, the Bulldogs wouldn't even consider such thoughts until the present season ended. Hay no doubt was miffed that rank newcomers to the pro football wars had initiated the call for a league without checking with Canton. He also had more immediate worries. Canton's first meeting with Massillon was scheduled for the following Saturday.

On November 16, Canton staked its claim for the Ohio League championship with a 23-0 victory over Massillon. Thorpe again played magnificently, but he was helped by two other native Americans, Calac and Joe Guyon, the latter having signed with the Bulldogs out of Georgia Tech, giving Canton almost certainly the best set of backs in football – pro or college.

All the pretenders to the Bulldogs' throne were eliminated in the next three weeks. Massillon defeated Cleveland 7-0, while Canton ended any title hopes in Akron by beating the Indians 14-0. On Thanksgiving Day, before a crowd of 10,000 in Cubs Park at Chicago, the Bulldogs again met Hammond, which had added yet another high-priced player to its team, former Northwestern star John (Paddy) Driscoll, one of the best kickers and open-field runners in the game. But Thorpe's 80-yard touchdown run and a stingy Canton defense gave the Bulldogs a 7-0 victory. Three days later, the Bulldogs met the Tigers again, with the Massillon players and fans hoping a victory in the season finale could propel them to the national title. But Thorpe took charge; in the third quarter, he kicked a 40-yard field goal for the only points of the game, and, in the fourth period, he punted 95 yards to keep the Tigers away from Canton's end zone. The Bulldogs left the field with a

3-0 victory, a 9-0-1 record, and the state and national professional championships.

Although Canton celebrated its third championship in four years, no amount of cheering for the Bulldogs could hide the fact that pro football in Ohio was in deep trouble. And the loose, unofficial Ohio League could do virtually nothing about it.

Attempts to control the league's problems prior to the season, had been largely successful. Some of the ugliest charges yet of hiring collegians had surfaced in October, including a report that Washington and Jefferson All-America tackle Wilbur (Fats) Henry had played for Massillon. Henry vehemently denied the charge, but it left the Tigers and the other Ohio League teams with another black eye. Moreover, despite the "tacit understanding" about tampering that had been agreed to by the Ohio League teams, players had continued to move from team to team, and salaries had continued to rise. In addition, strong teams, willing to pay large amounts for players, had surfaced in Indiana and Illinois, threatening to lure Ohio's top pros. And almost every Ohio team lost money in 1919.

Indeed, there was potential for a mass exodus from the football business in Ohio in late 1919. The Youngstown Patricians had folded for good. In Massillon, Whalen and Donahue declared that they were unable to absorb any more losses and were out of the game. Attendance had faded late in the year in Cleveland, leaving Jimmy O'Donnell's team in limbo. The backers of the Akron team had pulled out. Even Hay's team had lost money, because Canton had attracted only moderate crowds except for the games against Massillon and Akron, and moderate crowds did not cover the Bulldogs' large salaries.

As the new decade began, many supported the 15-year-old idea of forming a league. Few realized that not only was a true league just around the corner, but the Ohio League – the unofficial organization that had nurtured the game until its popularity demanded the birth of something greater – had just faded into history.

SEVEN DECADES OF THE NFL

*Football goes through a metamorphosis as the years
pass by; from leather helmets and little other protection to the
helmeted gladiators who now patrol the gridiron.*

Here Comes the NFL

Although professional football flourished in its own unregulated and out-of-the-hat style, problems were beginning to arise that bore a striking similarity to those of the current decade – rising salaries … players on the move from team to team … and use of collegians still in school.

The biggest problem was salaries, and here we're talking about $50 and $75 per game for most players, $100 for stars, with the exception of Thorpe. Patrons usually paid a quarter, sometimes less, for admission, and crowds ranged from a few hundred to a few thousand, depending upon the rivalry. Many of the teams in the Ohio League, the real center of professional football at the time, feared bankruptcy. Others, such as the Decatur Staleys and Racine Cardinals from Illinois; the Muncie Flyers from Indiana; and teams from Buffalo, and Rochester, N.Y., looked for ways to remain solvent.

With each team operating independently, and without a league constitution to tie them into a single unit, player movement was rampant because of the "highest bidder" atmosphere. That often included the use of top-flight collegians, but the entire problem of using players under assumed names had given professional football the look of an outlaw organization enticing innocent and impressionable young men to wrongdoing.

On August 20, 1920, representatives of four teams met in Ralph Hay's Hupmobile agency in Canton. Hay and Thorpe represented the Canton Bulldogs; Frank Neid and Art Ranny the Akron Pros; Carl Storck the Dayton Triangles; and Jimmy O'Donnell and Stan Cofall the Cleveland Indians. Teams from Buffalo, Rochester and Hammond, Indiana had submitted letters of application, so the seven participants formed what then was called the American Professional Football Conference. The APFC would be the forerunner of the National Football League (with an intermediate stop in the 1920-21 seasons when it was called the American Professional Football Association). The group had a stated purpose of "raising the standard of professional football … to eliminate bidding for players … and to secure cooperation in the formation of schedules, at least for the bigger teams." The teams also agreed not to sign college players still in school, nor would any of them offer inducements to lure players from fellow member clubs.

A month later, 10 teams answered Hay's invitation to attend a second meeting. The group included six of the originals, as well as the Decatur Staleys, with George Halas representing A.E. Staley's interests; a second Chicago team, the Racine Cardinals; Muncie, Indiana; and Rock Island, Illinois. There weren't enough chairs for all those present, so some of the reps, including Halas, sat on the running boards and fenders of the automobiles. "It was a hot day," Halas once recalled, "and we sat there drinking beer from buckets while we tried to plan the future of professional football."

The owners' agenda began with changing the organization's name to the American Professional Football Association and setting a $100 entry fee. Next came the task of electing a league president. The unanimous first choice for the job was Joe Carr. The owners cited Carr's enthusiasm, his newspaper contacts, and his experience as a successful baseball executive. To everyone's surprise, however, Carr declined, telling the owners that most fans didn't even know who he was. This anonymity would hurt the league's growth, he said, adding that the organization needed the biggest possible name to serve as president. Carr then pointed to Jim Thorpe. The owners all knew Thorpe was not executive material. But he was a national hero, someone who could get space in the newspapers. He was elected.

Opposite: Dick Butkus is considered one of the finest middle linebackers ever to play the game. Butkus played in eight Pro Bowl games in his nine-year career and recovered an incredible 25 opponents' fumbles.

Left: 1921 Dayton Triangles

Above left: *When sponsors could no longer support the Decatur Staleys, player-coach George Halas moved the team to Chicago and led them to the 1921 APFA championship.*

Above right: *Fritz Pollard became the first black head coach in professional football in 1920, when he was named co-coach (with Elgie Tobin) of the Akron Pros. The team finished 8-0-3 and won the APFA title that season.*

Because he simply was not interested in the job, Thorpe lasted just one season. And no team ever paid the $100 entry fee. However, every team agreed to submit a list of its players from the 1920 season so it would have first call on their services in 1921.

On October 3, just before the season began, three more teams joined, bringing the total to 14. The new entries were the Detroit Heralds, the Columbus Panhandles, and the Chicago Tigers. Schedules were left to individual teams – a practice that persisted for several years – so from the beginning there was a disparity in the number of games played by each team. The league didn't keep standings, preferring to choose a champion by consensus. In the first game ever played under this new format, the Dayton Triangles defeated the Columbus Panhandles 14-0. Lou Partlow of Dayton ran seven yards for the first touchdown ever scored in the NFL.

In that first season, two pioneers of the game emerged as stars. Halas, an end who had played for Bob Zuppke at the University of Illinois, was player-coach of the Staleys. Halas always has been considered the "father of the NFL," because of his presence the day the league was born, and his playing an integral part in pro football's growth until his death in 1983 at age 88. The Racine Cardinals soon became known as the Chicago Cardinals. (The original name came from Racine Street on the south side of Chicago, not the city in Wisconsin.) The Cardinals were led by the play of Paddy Driscoll, like Halas a future member of the Pro Football Hall of Fame. Driscoll was a great all-around player, once scoring 27 points in a 1923 game against the Rochester Jeffersons. His forte was the dropkick, the main method of attempting field goals in those days. He scored three against the Bears – from 30, 23, and 12 yards – in a 1922 game after hitting one of 50 yards earlier that season against the Toledo Maroons. In 1924, he drop-kicked 11 field goals for the Cardinals, and soon joined the Bears. Driscoll stayed with them for the remainder of his pro football career, which included nearly three decades as an assistant coach and a two-year stint as head coach after Halas retired for a third time in 1956.

But in the NFL's first season, Halas and the Staleys claimed the championship after defeating Driscoll's Cardinals – the only team to beat them – on December 5, and defended that claim the following week against the unbeaten Akron Pros. Putting aside the agreements regarding player movement,

Halas hired Driscoll for that game. It didn't work: the teams battled to a scoreless tie. Akron finished with an unbeaten season and was acclaimed the first NFL champion.

A postscript from that game: Fritz Pollard made a bit of early history as co-coach of Akron, the first black ever to hold such a position.

The NFL's Growing Pains

While the first season of the APFA may have been an artistic success, it didn't solve any of the problems that had brought about its formation. Salaries continued to rise, players moved from team to team, and collegians still found pro football a means of earning some money away from the campus. Moreover, neither Thorpe, league president, nor Cofall, vice-president, provided any leadership. Cofall was fired as player-coach of the Cleveland team after three games and never was involved with the league, while Thorpe proved he was an athlete who loved to play but had little interest in administration. Thorpe also left the Canton Bulldogs before the 1921 season to join the Cleveland team, taking teammates Joe Guyon and Pete Calac with him. Jim was injured early in the season, and played just one more season when he joined a franchise in LaRue, Ohio, again taking Guyon and Calac with him. That team, the Oorang Indians, was named for the Oorang Kennels, the property of team owner Walter Lingo. Nearing his mid-thirties, Thorpe struggled as the team won just two of eight games. After that, he played very little. In a game against the Bears, he fumbled at Chicago's two-yard line. George Halas picked up the ball and ran 98 yards for a touchdown – still the longest fumble return in NFL history.

The APFA's first meeting of 1921 was postponed until spring. A need for experienced leadership was the first order of business, and this time Carr accepted the post. He had performed a major lobbying effort to keep the league intact, and for his troubles he was paid the sum of $1,000. "It was against my will when I was out of the room," he said later, but it proved an inspired move because he led the league through its tumultuous formative years until his death in 1939.

Carr's biggest achievement was pushing through a resolution, with Halas's strong endorsement,

forbidding any NFL team to sign a college player whose original class had not graduated. It was a public relations masterpiece at the time, because the league was being criticized for "leading poor, young men astray." Carr vigorously enforced the rule, to the point of fining teams a thousand dollars for any violation – big money during those times.

Carr's experience as an administrator paid off. He established a league constitution and by-laws; gave teams territorial rights within the league; restricted player movement; and enforced more stringent membership criteria. He also established the league office in Columbus; issued official standings so there would be one champion; and scheduled more interstate games to build the game's popularity.

Twelve of the 14 teams returned in 1921. They were joined by ten others, including the Green Bay Packers and the first New York Giants franchise. That one lasted just two games but reappeared four

Pete Calac played with Jim Thorpe at the Carlisle Indian School and later joined him in the Canton Bulldogs' backfield, where they led the team to the 1916 championship.

The Oorang Indians were an all-Indian professional team featuring Jim Thorpe, Joe Guyon, and Pete Calac. They won only three games in two years before suspending operations.

1920 STALEY TEAM

JOHNSON · GEPFORD · MAC WHERTER · LANUM · KOEHLER · VEACH · STERNAMAN · DRESSEN

YOUNG · SHANK · MAY · HIGH · ADKINS · CLARK · FEITCHINGER · PEARCE · LOTSHAW Trainer

TRAFTON · JONES · INGWERSEN · HALAS · BLACKLOCK · PETTY · MINTUN

Above: *If it had not been for a scoreless tie in the inaugural APFA title game against the Akron Pros, the 1920 Decatur Staleys would have been league champions. They finished with a 10-1-2 record.*

Right: *Earl (Curly) Lambeau, who played under Knute Rockne at Notre Dame, is credited with having been the first pro coach to utilize the forward pass as an important part of a team's offense. Under Lambeau, the Packers won six NFL Championships, and his 230 career victories are fourth-most in NFL history.*

years later when Tim Mara purchased the rights for a franchise for $2,500. (The team's value today is estimated at well over $100 million.) The Packers, of course, have remained in the NFL since the 1921 season, though the franchise struggled in its early days. The team admitted violating the college eligibility rule after the 1921 season, and withdrew from the league. Five months later, at the summer meeting, manager Curley Lambeau borrowed $500 to repurchase the franchise and then went broke trying to support it because a run of bad weather caused poor attendance. But the city's businessmen, knowing the value of a team to a small community, arranged a $2,500 loan to keep the Packers going. They then set up a public, non-profit corporation to operate it, selling shares for $5 apiece, season ticket included. Nearly 70 years later, the Packers still are a community-owned team and those original shares still are prized possessions. They have been passed down through generations of Wisconsin families.

Other money problems plagued the league during its 1921 season. The Staley Manufacturing Co. was forced by poor business to drop its football operation. But A.E. Staley, the company's owner, suggested to Halas that he move the team to Chicago, then paid him $5,000 to retain the Staleys nickname for the 1921 season. The team moved into Cubs Park (later Wrigley Field) and won its first league championship that year. Halas renamed the team the "Bears" in 1922.

Red Grange and the NFL's Traveling Show

Three years later, in 1925, Halas brought professional football into the public consciousness. For the astounding sum of $100,000 he signed running back Harold (Red) Grange, the nation's most renowned college football player. "The Galloping Ghost" was in the vanguard of America's "hero" stage, as the Roaring Twenties began to hit their peak and the nation reveled in the feats of its athletic stars, now visible for the first time via a new medium, motion picture newsreels.

Grange gave them plenty to watch. During three seasons at Illinois, he had gained more yards – 3,637 – than any collegian in history, but it was the way he did it that fit the flamboyance of those years. In a 1924 game against a Michigan team that Fielding Yost considered his greatest, Grange scored five touchdowns, four of them in the first 12 minutes. He came east and played against the University of Pennsylvania, scoring three touchdowns on a muddy field. Doing that against an Ivy League team in those days guaranteed Grange's fame, because all of the major eastern newspapers covered the game. Only 170 pounds, Grange was a supremely gifted runner with the ability to change pace and cut back, and to pass, punt, and drop kick better than any player since Jim Thorpe.

Halas had the inside track with Grange's Illinois background – he was a native of Wheaton, a Chicago suburb, and Halas had played for his coach, Bob Zuppke. So Halas held secret negotiations with Grange's manager, a character named C.C. (some said that stood for Cash-and-Carry) Pyle. There was no college football draft back then so every player was fair game. Only a couple of weeks after Grange had played his last college game, he was in a Bears uniform with a guarantee of a share of the gate receipts for the last few games of the 1924 season. His first NFL game was on Thanksgiving Day against the league-leading Chicago Cardinals. More than 36,000 people – the largest crowd in pro football history – came out to see him. The game ended in a scoreless tie because Paddy Driscoll's punting pinned the Bears in their end of the field for most of the game.

That hardly concerned Halas, Grange, and Pyle. In early December, the team, with Grange as the featured performer, embarked on an eight-game, 12-day barnstorming tour. In a madcap era when everything was bigger than life, no one in football was bigger than Grange. Five of the games were against NFL opponents, and each was a financial bonanza for hard-pressed team owners. In New York, which appreciated more than any city the drawing power of a star, 73,000 jammed the old Polo Grounds to see Grange and the Bears defeat the New York Giants 19-7. The Giants' share of the gate receipts saved Tim Mara's team from bankruptcy.

The Bears then took a week off – Grange already had played 17 games in less than three months – before embarking on a nine-game tour of the South and West, culminating with a turnout of 73,000 fans, who watched the Bears defeat the Los Angeles Tigers at the Coliseum. America loved it, and with no radio or television to carry the proceedings into living rooms, millions were eager to read every word that circulation-hungry newspapers printed. Professional football finally had established its own niche in the nation's sporting consciousness.

The following year Pyle and Grange were rebuffed by Halas in their efforts to get a five-figure salary. Pyle then requested a New York franchise to showcase Grange, but Tim Mara, who held the

territorial right, objected, and Carr dismissed the request. Pyle then formed the American Football League – the first of three such organizations under that name during NFL history – and the two leagues engaged in a bidding war for players, despite Halas's

Right: *After Red Grange fled to the AFL in 1926, the NFL countered back by signing fullback Ernie Nevers as their gate attraction. Nevers played all but 29 minutes of that season.*

pushing through a landmark decision forbidding any NFL team from having in its lineup any player whose college class had not graduated. The NFL's answer to Grange and the AFL in 1926 was the Duluth Eskimos, one of the most colorful teams in pro football history. First, owner Ole Haugsrud signed All-America fullback Ernie Nevers, star of Pop Warner's Stanford Rose Bowl team of 1925. He got a Grange-like deal with a high salary and a percentage of the gate, leaving Haugsrud little money to spread among the other 14 players on the team. But that was only part of the problem. The Eskimos played at home on September 19, then went on a tour that didn't end until February 5, after 14 league games and 15 exhibitions. Nevers played all but 29 minutes of the season.

Despite the iron-man roles and the Eskimos' ultimate financial success, however, Duluth was not a season-long contender for the 1926 title. Pyle ultimately made it to New York as part of the NFL in 1927, after the AFL had folded. Mara allowed him to enter his New York Yankees team, with the agreement that it would play 13 of its 16 games on the road. Making matters worse for Pyle, Grange injured his knee in the fourth game of the year. This forced him to miss three games, and never was a great player again. Without their most important player, the Yankees sagged, and at the end of the season, the franchise folded.

For Want of a Schedule...

The performances of Nevers and Grange did not help their teams win titles. Instead, for three seasons, 1922-24, the Bulldogs – of Canton in 1922 and 1923, of Cleveland in 1924 – ruled the NFL. The team, led by player-coach Guy Chamberlain and future Hall of Fame tackles Link Lyman and Wilbur (Pete) Henry, posted back-to-back unbeaten seasons. Chamberlain, who started his career with Halas and the Staleys and then played and coached for the Cleveland Bulldogs, Frankford Yellow Jackets and Chicago Cardinals in addition to Canton, was a great end. He was a good receiver, considering the limited use of the pass in those days, but his speciality was running with the ball on end-around plays and playing defense. He also was a strong personality, aloof from his players and single-minded in his ideas, which probably was why he worked for so many teams. While Chamberlain, Henry, and Lyman helped Canton to success on the field, there was little success at the bank. Despite his team's championships, Hay lost money and reluctantly sold the club for $2,500 to Sam Deutsch, owner the Cleveland Indians major league baseball team, prior to the 1924 season. After fielding mediocre teams in 1925 and 1926, Canton disappeared from pro football's map until 1962, when it was selected as the site for the sport's Hall of Fame. Its impressive museum show-

Left: *From 1922-26, Guy Chamberlin served as a player-coach on three different teams – the Canton Bulldogs, Cleveland Bulldogs, and the Frankford Yellowjackets – and helped them win four NFL Championships.*

cases all of pro football's history and attracts hundreds of thousands of visitors each year.

Although the first AFL-NFL war cost both sides, it ultimately benefited the NFL by helping pare the money-losers from a 22-team league in 1926 to a healthier NFL of 12 teams a year later. While the Grange and Nevers traveling football shows had been helping bring professional football into the public's eye, the NFL itself was suffering from organizational ills. Cleveland had won its 1924 NFL

title by decree of President Carr, pointing up the league's single biggest deficiency at the time – lack of a uniform schedule. The Bulldogs seemed to have won the title, but scheduled another game against the Bears and were beaten 23-0. Halas then claimed his team was champion because both had agreed to play for the title. Cleveland said not so, and the issue wasn't decided until a league meeting in January, 1925 when Carr ruled in the Bulldogs' favor, saying the clubs didn't have permission to schedule official games. Anything else was considered an exhibition game.

Matters were even more bizarre in 1925 when another title was decided, not on the field but in an owners' meeting. Again, the issue was independent scheduling, this time involving the Cardinals and Pottsville (Pennsylvania) Maroons. After the problems in 1924, the league extended its playing time to December 20, but scheduled official games only until December 6. At that date, all teams should have played the eight minimum games required to qualify for the championship. Those doing poorly could end the season; others who had a chance for a title, or needed extra money, could continue until December 20. On December 6, the league's top two teams, the 9-1-1 Cardinals and 9-2-0 Pottsville, played each other. Pottsville won 21-7. Had Pottsville won the title? The Maroons thought so, but the Cardinals' owner, Chris O'Brien, had three more paydays in mind, including a season-ending game against Grange and the Bears. His team won the first two but never played the Bears because Grange was out with an arm injury. The Cardinals then had an 11-2-1 record, Pottsville 10-2-0.

Pottsville, meanwhile, had a game scheduled against the Providence (Rhode Island) Steam Roller, then added another one against an all-star team featuring Notre Dame's Four Horsemen backfield. Carr ordered that game canceled because it was to be played within the territory of another NFL team (Frankford being a northern suburb of Philadelphia). When Pottsville disregarded his dictum, Carr suspended it from all rights and privileges, including the right to compete for the NFL title. The president canceled the game against Providence and ordered the Pottsville franchise returned to the league.

When the Maroons appealed, Carr referred the matter to the league's owners. They upheld him and awarded the title to the Chicago Cardinals. But Cardinals owner O'Brien refused to accept it, and the NFL never did formally award a 1925 league championship. (The Cardinals since have been recognized as champions because they had the NFL's best record.)

The process of deciding a champion wasn't standardized until 1932, when Carr arranged for the first NFL Championship Game at the conclusion of that season. Teams continued to play an uneven number of games (and many of the unsuccessful and transitory franchises played less than five games, rarely winning more than one of those played) until a 12-game schedule was played in 1935.

Artistically, the NFL was doing well, particularly in its championship races. In 1927, the Giants and Bears came down to the final weekend. New York beat Chicago 13-7, in a game Giants player-coach Steve Owen, a member of the Pro Football Hall of Fame, called "the toughest, roughest football game I ever played." Owen was a defensive strategist, and

back who played for the Detroit Wolverines. However, Tim Mara had to buy the entire franchise to get Friedman, putting Benny in a Giants uniform and the rest of the Wolverines on the borough of Staten Island as the Stapletons. The move almost paid off in another title because the Giants lost just one game in 1929. But the Green Bay Packers didn't lose any, including a 20-6 victory over the Giants, when Johnny Blood, later known as Johnny Blood (McNally), scored once and set up another touchdown. One of the true legends of the game, and a charter member of the Pro Football Hall of Fame, Blood never met a curfew he liked, a party that bored him, or a situation he considered normal. (The parenthetical pseudonym "McNally" was his dodge when he played professionally while still in college.) He had signed with the Packers as a free agent after his Pottsville team was transferred. His exploits on and off the field still are legends by which other free spirits are measured, such as the time when he drove to a railroad station with a pretty female companion expecting to catch a train taking the Packers on a barnstorming tour. "I got a late start for the depot and discovered the train had left without me," he said. "Either I stopped the train, which was just pulling out of the yard, or I got fined for missing it."

So he stopped the train—after driving full speed for three blocks and swinging the car across the tracks just a few hundred feet in front of the train, which still had not picked up much speed. "I couldn't imagine that the engineer was a callous man and would run the engine through the car," Blood said, "especially since the lady and I still were in it."

The train didn't miss the car by much. Blood turned the wheel over to his companion, gallantly kissed her farewell, and boarded the train. It was just another day in his totally unpredictable life.

After graduating from St. John's College, in Minnesota, Blood played with Milwaukee, Duluth, and Pottsville for five seasons before joining the Packers, where his three best seasons coincided with three Green Bay championships. At Green Bay, he joined tackle Cal Hubbard and guard Mike Michalske, also future Hall of Fame members. Hubbard had

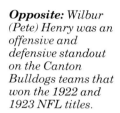

Opposite: Wilbur (Pete) Henry was an offensive and defensive standout on the Canton Bulldogs teams that won the 1922 and 1923 NFL titles.

Left: Joe Guyon was a triple-threat halfback who played with Jim Thorpe at the Carlisle Indian School and on four different professional teams.

his Giants that year won ten of their eleven victories by shutout.

The NFL title game, pre-1932, also had its oddities. The deciding game for the 1928 title was played in the Cycledrome in Providence, Rhode Island, a 10,000-seat oval that had been built for bicycle races, then the rage of the day. The building also served as the home of the Providence Steam Roller. There was so little room to play that tacklers often went careening into the crowd. One end zone was only five yards deep because of the track, and there was just one dressing room—built to accommodate two to four bicycle racers. Somehow, the Steam Roller players found a way to use that room, and also the cramped field. They defeated the Frankford Yellow Jackets 6-0 for the NFL championship on a 46-yard touchdown pass from George (Wildcat) Wilson to Curly Oden.

The floating franchise was another phenomenon that refused to die quietly. The Giants coveted Benny Friedman, the former Michigan All-America tail-

NFL President Joe Carr's strict but fair guidelines helped the league attain financial and organizational stability.

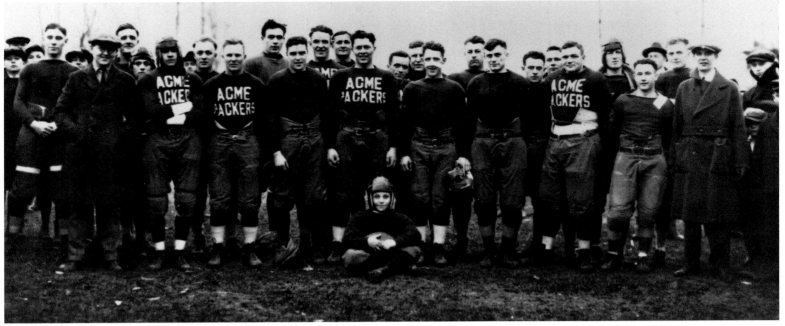

Above: 1919 Acme
Packers, forerunners
of the Green Bay team.

Right: Johnny
Blood (McNally)

first visited Green Bay when he played against the Packers as a member of the New York Giants, and asked to be traded there because he liked the quality of life. Michalske had played with Grange's New York Yankees in the AFL before becoming a free agent, and the three newcomers played with talented holdovers as tailback Verne Lewellen, Red Dunn, LaVern Dilweg, Bo Molenda, and Jugger Earpe. Together they formed the NFL's most versatile offense, and the league's most impressive defense.

The showcase performer was Blood, who not only outsprinted other runners, but was a slashing inside runner as well. He also caught more passes than any other NFL receiver at that time.

In winning three consecutive NFL titles in 1929-1931, the Packers posted a composite 34-5-2 record. The man behind that success was Earl (Curly) Lambeau, a coach who had been an all-pro player during the early days of the NFL. Lambeau put up a borrowed $500, then drove to the league meetings from Green Bay to Canton, saving the franchise. His teams emphasized the forward pass, a weapon Lambeau later would raise to state-of-the-art effectiveness with Cecil Isbell and Don Hutson.

With its first real dynasty, the NFL also was a victim of the Great Depression, which gripped the nation in 1929. Owners of teams in smaller cities soon found they could not compete, and as this miserable time continued, the NFL soon became a league solely comprised of major cities, except for Green Bay. New York with the Giants and Chicago with the Bears already had solid franchises, and other larger cities east of the Mississippi had teams. But the Depression forced a shakedown. Only large population blocks could produce enough customers to keep a franchise alive. In quick succession, cities considered to be off the beaten path – such as Frankford, Dayton, Providence, Buffalo, Minneapolis, Newark, and Pottsville – stopped playing. That also had a positive side effect because the NFL, with the exception of Green Bay, and Portsmouth in 1932-33, now shared cities with major league baseball, at least giving it the look of success. There was little doubt that the game had caught the public's attention. The big challenge would be to keep that attention as the nation prepared to welcome the era of the New Deal and all its hope for the future.

The NFL Grows Up

The Great Depression of the thirties wasn't an atmosphere conducive to prosperity in pro football. But if there were one element of American society that seemed to survive the misery and hardship of this time, it was sports. College football games still attracted millions each Saturday in the fall. Millions more turned out to watch major league baseball during the summer. The motion picture industry, newly welcomed to the sound age, took off. There was one good reason: Americans needed to be entertained and have a few hours a week to try to forget the problems that had gripped their lives.

Even with the uncertain economic situation, the NFL began its so-called "modern era," where football on Sunday afternoons became as much of a way of life in at least eight or ten major American cities as was college football on Saturday afternoons.

That "modern era" began with the 1933 season when the league was divided into eastern and western divisions, and the winners played for the championship. The 1932 season, the last under a single unit format, also had produced a championship game – a controversial one – but the NFL was solidly bulwarked by a group of owners who put the the game ahead of personal interests and were willing to endure the financial hardships. Adding to this good fortune was an influx of new owners who were equally dedicated to the sport. From 1932-42, the NFL welcomed new leadership. Bert Bell, Art Rooney, George Preston Marshall, Charles Bidwill, and Dan Reeves joined Carr, Halas, Mara, and Lambeau, who had established the sport's foundation in the previous decade.

These newer owners were often Runyonesque characters but also interesting and challenging people because they operated within the scope of true American pioneers. Independent, fearless, chance-taking, maybe even a bit zany, they never worried about the unknown. All of this conspired to help nurture the NFL at a time when others, who didn't have their calculating cool or that special flair, wouldn't have survived. Rooney and Bell, who joined the NFL in 1933, became part of a group affectionately known as the "Irish Mafia," because all of them, including Mara, Bidwill, and later Dan Reeves in Cleveland, were of Irish-American descent. They were true sportsmen. Any income they achieved from their other business activities, they poured into pro football. Mara and Rooney were race track devotees and made enough on sporting ventures to get started in pro football. Mara, who owned a coal business in New York City, once was a licensed bookmaker in New York. (He hired his coach, Steve Owen, as a foreman in the off-season because head coaches who were not team owners didn't have year-round jobs with their teams at that time.)

In 1925, Mara tried to buy an interest in boxer Gene Tunney but was persuaded by Billy Gibson, Tunney's manager, to spend $500 for an NFL pro football franchise. Rooney won $2,500 at the race track in 1933, enabling him to buy the Steelers – then known as the Pirates – and won $350,000 at Saratoga one summer to help sustain them.

Bidwill was a wealthy Chicago tycoon and a vice president of the Bears. He had invited David Jones, the owner of the Chicago Cardinals, to a dinner party aboard his yacht one evening in 1933. Jones mentioned that he was looking for just the right person to purchase his team, and when Bidwill asked about the selling price, Jones put out a $50,000 figure. Bidwill immediately pulled $2,000 from his pocket as a down payment, and the deal was soon finalized.

During Saratoga Race Track's annual month-long meeting in August in the upstate New York spa, Saratoga Springs, pro football's Irish Mafia rubbed elbows with the cream of society each afternoon at the track. They spent each evening celebrating – not their wins or losses – but each other.

Bert Bell

Because they were involved as much for competition as for profit, they weathered the ups and downs of their NFL seasons. But despite their sporting sentiments when their teams played each other, they were acutely involved with each other's well-being. Their mutual venture offered all the risks of a six-furlong race, with the same promise of losing money. This formed a bond of self-survival that moved most of them to put selfish interests in the background and act for the good of the game. That, above all else, was the biggest factor in bringing the NFL through this growing period. This group – with the exception of league president Joe Carr, who died in 1939, and Bidwill, who died in 1948 – carried the sport for the next three decades, and were joined by equally outstanding leaders as the game continued to grow.

George Preston Marshall, The Irrepressible

George Preston Marshall, the first of the new breed of NFL owners to join the NFL, never fit the profile of his Irish-American cohorts. He led a four-man syndicate that in 1932 established a franchise in Boston called the Braves. Marshall had to fight two immediate battles – Boston was primarily a baseball and hockey town, and its football preferences were Harvard and Boston College. It was only lukewarm about pro football, and this indifference was accentuated by the Depression. Even a not-so-bad 4-4-2 season and running back Cliff Battles, a rookie from

Left: George Preston Marshall

Right: Cliff Battles

West Virginia Wesleyan who won the league's rushing championship, couldn't keep the syndicate from losing $46,000. That was too much for Marshall's partners and at the season's end, he wound up as the team's sole owner. Marshall was undaunted, one of his overriding attributes over the next 37 years. He kept his team in Boston through the 1936 season, running it with an air of independence. For instance, when the team opened the 1933 season, the owner told his coach, Lone Star Dietz, that if he won the coin toss, he was to kick off. When Marshall reached his seat, he saw the Redskins lining up to receive the kickoff. So he immediately reached for the phone that ran directly to the bench – a weapon that Marshall would use indiscriminately during most of his seasons as owner – and heatedly reminded Dietz of his orders.

"We did kick off, Mr. Marshall," Dietz replied. "But they ran it back for a touchdown."

With Battles as its best offensive weapon, the team won the 1936 Eastern Division title in relative obscurity at Fenway Park. Without notice, Marshall raised ticket prices for the next-to-last game of the season. There was a firestorm of criticism in the press, and only about 5,000 showed up for the final

regular season game. Marshall, incensed at the city's refusal to turn out for his championship team, refused to host the NFL title game. Instead he moved it to the Polo Grounds in New York City, where nearly 30,000 "home" fans watched the Green Bay Packers defeat the Redskins. The following year, Marshall moved the team to Washington.

Marshall's role as a pro football pioneer was considerable. After his first season in the NFL, he had proposed to his fellow owners that the league be split into two divisions, with the winners playing each other for the NFL championship. George Halas got behind the idea immediately, and while they would be fierce rivals for years in the league's inner councils, they convinced their fellow owners the idea had merit and it was adopted. In 1933, the Western Division champion Chicago Bears defeated the New York Giants, champions of the Eastern Division, for the NFL championship.

Marshall also helped to convince the owners to put the goal posts on the goal line, instead of ten yards deep in the end zone as was the case in college football. This was one more feature to differentiate the pro and college games, and the goal posts stayed there until 1974 when a proliferation of field goals forced the rules makers to return them to the end line. But while they were on the goal line, pro coaches used them to every advantage. The uprights became like two additional defensive linemen on goal line stands – or a maddening obstacle to defensive backs trying to cover a receiver going into the end zone. Wily receivers used the posts to "pick" a defender on a perfectly thrown pass to that area.

Away from the technicalities of the game, Marshall understood that pro football was a part of the entertainment business. He did everything to give it a theatrical approach, reflecting some of the frustration he felt in never making it as an actor. If nothing else, he added some color and zest to the game and

made it more appealing for spectators who were used to the hoopla of college football. For most of his time as owner of the Redskins – he changed the team's name from Braves in 1933 – Marshall was one of the best promoters ever, in any sport. His team was the first to have its own band, which still exists, and then he dressed it in lavish Indian garb, complete with feathered headdress. For the band's signature number, he co-opted the melody from an old revival song, "Yes, Jesus Loves Me." His wife, Corrine Griffith, a former star of silent movies, and Barnee Breeskin, who led the orchestra at the Shoreham Hotel in Washington, wrote the words to "Hail to the Redskins," now one of the most recognizable fight songs in football. For more than a quarter century, after the team relocated in Washington in 1937, the band accompanied thousands of Redskin rooters to away games. They came to New York City aboard chartered trains when the 'Skins played the Giants, and Marshall often led a huge parade of Washingtonians out of Penn Station and up Broadway. One New York columnist to observe in print, "George Preston Marshall slipped quietly into town this morning, accompanied by 10,000 Redskins rooters and a 110-piece band, his own."

In Washington, Griffith Stadium was the team's home field until 1960. As a co-tenant, Marshall demanded that it be as spotless as a theatre when his teams used it on Sunday afternoon – even if a college game had taken place the previous day. He argued that this was a dress-up outing in Washington society and he wanted its members who were his season ticket holders, to feel comfortable wearing their Sunday finery to a ball park.

The idea of selling season tickets to Washington society and others was a first in the NFL, one that he borrowed from Ivy League schools. Soon, every NFL team adopted the practice. In 1938, Marshall also sold the idea of matching the best players from the two divisions in an annual post-season all-star game, which has since come to be known as the Pro Bowl. It had a short life before being suspended during World War II, and was revived in 1950.

Mr. Rooney and The Steelers

When the NFL streamlined its product by introducing divisional champions in 1933, it also became a ten-team league, marking the beginning of its "modern era." It now had both form and substance, and it finally was playing to determine a true champion. In so doing it welcomed the Pittsburgh Pirates football team (they became the Steelers in 1940) and its owner Art Rooney, who became the common man's hero. Rooney's father, an Irish immigrant, was a former steelworker who scraped up enough money to open a saloon in an Irish-American neighborhood in Pittsburgh. Young Art was a fine athlete who once had been offered a football scholarship by Notre Dame but preferred to stay in Pittsburgh. He had played professional baseball for five years and qualified for the 1920 U.S. Olympic boxing team. He also played semi-pro football and owned his own team, the Hope Harvey, before he was 20 years old. To purchase his NFL franchise, Rooney parlayed two big assets – the $2,500 that he won at the track, and his knowledge of the imminent repeal of Pennsylvania's Blue Laws, which forbade any public entertainment on Sundays.

Ironically, his team's first game was played just two days before the Blue Laws' repeal. But Rooney wanted to open on time. He secured the cooperation of a police superintendent charged with enforcing the laws, who successfully "hid" himself among the 3,500 fans turning out for that game and never was available to take any action.

For Rooney, pro football then was just another gamble, not unlike his often-successful ventures in the stock and commodities markets, and with the horses that ran through the spring and summer at tracks from Chicago to New York. Rooney often said that he and his NFL friends were involved "for kicks" and thought little of losing thousands of dollars on their teams each season.

"Those were times when the game on Sunday was incidental to making the payroll on Monday," he once said. "When we started making the payroll, the

1934 Pittsburgh Pirates

suspense went out of the game." The suspense lasted for some time, because Rooney never involved himself too heavily with the club's day-to-day operations and admittedly had more interest in his speculative ventures. The team's offices were a suite of rooms at a Pittsburgh hotel. For a time, its scouting staff consisted of one employee who leafed through the sports pages of various out-of-town newspapers looking for stories about college stars and occasionally went to see the local Pittsburgh colleges – Pitt, Duquesne, and Carnegie Tech – when they played against good teams.

This was not unusual for NFL teams at the time. There were no full-time coaching staffs (that didn't happen, in most cases, until the late sixties) and scouting staffs were non-existent, consisting mostly of referrals from coaching friends or former players, and the various annual football magazines. Rooney's main job, he often said, was to notify players who were being cut, but he was such a softy that often he didn't have the heart and kept them on the team. The Steelers fielded some sad-sack teams, but Rooney's players held him in the highest esteem. His relations with his coaches were about the same, though at times he used some of his boxing skills to get his point across. One of those coaches, from 1937-39, was the unpredictable Johnny Blood (McNally). Blood didn't put much stress on fundamentals, and never imposed a curfew during training camp or the season. In the wee hours, players often searched for Blood, rather than the other way around. Once, on a return

Below: Program cover of 1925 game matching the New York Giants against the Columbus Tigers.

Opposite: As a player-coach in 1928, Jimmy Conzelman led the Providence Steam Roller to the NFL championship. In 1947, Conzelman won his second league title, this time as the non-playing coach of the Chicago Cardinals.

PRICE, 10 CENTS

N. Y. FOOTBALL GIANTS
vs.
COLUMBUS TIGERS

Sunday
November 8, 1925

Polo Grounds
New York

trip from a game in Green Bay, thinking his team had an open date, Blood got off the train when it stopped in Chicago. The following week, he showed up at Wrigley Field to watch the Bears play, only to hear the final score of the Pittsburgh game over the public address system. In 1941, Rooney and Bert Bell became co-owners of the Steelers in a complex three-way deal that involved swapping the Philadelphia Eagles franchise. Bell became the head coach, even after a very mediocre record in Philadelphia with better players. Of course, things got only worse with the Steelers. After the team was defeated soundly in its first two games, Bell phoned Rooney and said, "We've got to do something drastic."

"I know," Rooney replied. "You've got to quit." Bell did, and Rooney handed the job to Aldo (Buff) Donelli, who also was the successful head coach at Duquesne University, and allowed him to keep both jobs. Donelli didn't do any better, losing the next five games. But he was able to juggle the Steelers' game-day coaching duties because the Dukes either played on Friday night or their Saturday games were convenient to make the necessary travel connections. However, he ran into a schedule conflict when Duquesne traveled to California to play St. Mary's while the Steelers were scheduled to play in Pittsburgh the next day. Obviously, there was no way Donelli could coach both teams that weekend, so he opted for Duquesne. Rooney then fired him and re-hired Walt Kiesling for the second of his three head-coaching stints.

Though he never was pleased when his team lost, Rooney somehow blithely endured these trials. He had a high tolerance limit for giving people he liked a chance to work for him, whether or not it made sense. He also was attracted to the "characters" of the game but, no doubt, it was an offshoot of his time at the track.

Though not as creative as Marshall, Bell, or Halas in producing dynamic rules changes to help the game's growth, Rooney carried great influence within the league when he pushed legislation that he believed was for the benefit of the game.

Bert Bell, The Eagles and The Draft

Bert Bell's background was in absolute contrast to Rooney's, yet they became dear friends and prime movers in building pro football. Bell was born on Philadelphia's Main Line, home to the city's millionaires. His real name was deBenneville Bell, which he quickly changed to Bert. His grandfather was a congressman, his father the state's attorney general, and his brother its governor.

Yet, the only part of life that ever appealed to Bell was football. For two seasons before World War I, he had played for the University of Pennsylvania as a self-assured, I'll-do-it-my-way quarterback and punter. He enlisted in the Army and served for two years in a field hospital in France, then returned to finish his football eligibility at Penn. As soon as his final season ended, he left school. For most of the next eight years, the only things that counted in his life were part-time assistant football coaching jobs at Penn and Temple in Philadelphia.

Not long after marrying beautiful Ziegfield Follies stage star Frances Upton in 1932, he borrowed $2,500 and, in partnership with Lud Wray and two other former Penn teammates, bought the Frankford Yellow Jackets franchise. The club had last played in the NFL in l931 when it was forced to disband after just seven games.

The league approved the bid of Bell et al but insisted that the group pay 25 per cent of the outstanding debts from the old team. A year later, the Yellow Jackets entered the NFL as the Philadelphia Eagles, named for the symbol of the National Recovery Administration of the New Deal. Bell was the team's general manager. Wray became head coach. The Eagles lost their first three games by the combined score of 116-9, beginning with an opening game loss of 56-0 to the Giants. However, the team righted itself and went four weeks without a loss at one point during that first season.

Bell soon bought out his partners. For the next 12 years, until he was named Commissioner of the NFL in 1946, he did everything possible to help his team survive. He ran the team out of a downtown Philadelphia restaurant that today would be called a "sports bar." He gave the bartender tickets to sell while he haunted newspaper sports departments and radio stations trying to drum up interest in his team. He even sold tickets on the street if someone were willing to buy. Once, when the Philadelphia Athletics American League baseball club and the Eagles both had home games just a few blocks apart, he gave a guy five dollars and a megaphone and sent him to Shibe Park, where the A's played. The assignment: to yell, "No game today, rain!"

After the Eagles lost $80,000 in the first three seasons, Wray lost interest, so Bell bought his share for $4,000 and became the team's sole owner. Bell appointed himself head coach, with mediocre results. However, for three seasons, from 1938-40, he had one of the NFL's most exciting players in quarterback Davey O'Brien who had succeeded Sammy Baugh at Texas Christian University and then vied with him for honors as the NFL's best passer.

The struggle to survive nearly was overwhelming both the Eagles and Pittsburgh Pirates, so Bell and Rooney came up with a plan to save themselves. First, Rooney sold the Pirates to Alexis Thompson, a wealthy Pittsburgh native best described as bon vivant, who sought a challenge to occupy his spare time. Bell and Rooney then became partners in the Eagles before convincing Thompson to swap franchises. Bell and Rooney took control of the Pirates and changed the name to Steelers. Thompson owned the Eagles through some of their greatest seasons after hiring Earl (Greasy) Neale as head coach.

But Bell's most lasting accomplishment during his time as the Eagles' owner was proposing a draft of college players. Teams still were free to sign any players they wished, and the best clubs, such as the Bears, Packers, and Giants, were getting most of the good players who had decided to play pro football. Many college stars disdained the NFL for better paying jobs.

On Bell's part, it also was an idea born of necessity, because his woebegone club wasn't getting much talent. He figured that if the teams with the worst records had first call on the best players, the days would end where the personnel (and financially) rich got richer by getting all the best players, and the worst ones had to scrape for the survivors. The poorer teams would have a better chance to improve – and improvement could mean survival. The league would become more competitive, and the result would be a more attractive product. Again, as a tribute to the group of owners who put the league's survival over

their own self-interests – particularly teams such as Chicago, Green Bay, and the Giants, which were attracting the great players and consistently playing for championships – the college draft was approved on May 19, 1935.

On February 8, 1936, the first draft of nine rounds was held at the Ritz Carlton Hotel in Philadelphia. Appropriately, Bell and the Eagles had the first pick. They chose Jay Berwanger, a talented halfback from the University of Chicago who had just won the first Heisman Trophy (then called the Downtown Athletic Club Trophy), awarded to the best player east of the Mississippi River. Bell traded Berwanger's rights to George Halas and the Chicago Bears, but he never

When a winter storm hit the Midwest in 1932, the first NFL Championship game was moved indoors to Chicago Stadium and featured an 80-yard field.

played pro football. Bell also had the first pick in the second player draft, which had been increased to 10 rounds. He selected Sam Francis, an All-America fullback from Nebraska, and he traded that pick as well to Halas. The college draft, which at one time during the fifties reached 30 rounds, lives on. Now it confers instant-millionaire status on players who are picked in the first round. But the lasting tribute to Bell and his idea – and to the foresight of the owners of the thirties – is that when teams use the draft intelligently, it ensures a balance of competition in every decade.

NFL Football Goes Inside and Upward

The player draft was just one last step in solidifying the sport. The first step had occurred when the 1932 season ended and the Bears and Portsmouth (Ohio) Spartans were tied for first place. NFL president Joe

Carr ordered a playoff to decide a champion, thus introducing the first NFL title game. When a brutal winter storm hit the Midwest, Halas moved the game from Wrigley Field indoors to Chicago Stadium. The arena was primarily a hockey rink, so Halas ordered dirt left over from a just-departed circus to cover the floor. Because the building could not accommodate a regulation football field, an 80-yard gridiron was laid out, but with special rules: once a team passed midfield, the ball was moved back 20 yards. On every play, the ball was spotted 15-yards from the sidelines because the rink walls abutted the playing field. The goal posts were placed on the goal line. With a crowd of more than 11,000 on hand, and with Portsmouth without its best player, Dutch Clark, who had already left the team for his off-season job as basketball coach at Colorado College, Chicago won the game 9-0. The teams were scoreless for three quarters until Bronko Nagurski faked a dive into the line, backed off, and flipped a touchdown pass to Red Grange, who had returned to finish his career with

the Bears. The Spartans protested, claiming that Nagurski had not moved back the then-required five yards behind the line of scrimmage before passing.

At the 1933 league meetings, Halas, with avid support from Marshall, pushed a rules change to allow a pass to be thrown from anywhere behind the line. This, plus an additional rule benefit from that game – setting hashmarks ten yards from the sidelines – opened up the offenses in pro football and opened both sides of the field to runs and passes.

Papa Bear and The Monsters of the Midway, Part I

The Bears may have been the new rules' first direct benefactor. Halas insisted that his naming of Ralph Jones as head coach in 1930 was a giant step forward in giving NFL football more crowd appeal because Jones altered the T-formation by splitting the ends and halfbacks wider and added a man in motion. This gave birth to the "Bears T" as the pre-eminent offense

in the modern era (though it didn't really become widely copied for almost another decade when Sid Luckman became quarterback and added his passing and ball-handling talents). Jones didn't stay around to take advantage of the new rules. After winning the 1932 title, fulfilling a promise to Halas that he would produce a championship, Jones stepped aside.

Halas had named Jones head coach after becoming the team's sole owner when he purchased the shares of his partner, Dutch Sternaman, for $32,000 – a sum he didn't have. But with the help of friends, former players, and a friendly banker, Halas got the money. He said he made a pledged due-date of delivering the money, or losing the team, by just ten minutes. After Jones resigned, Halas returned as head coach. He stayed (except for three World War II seasons, and two others in the mid-fifties) until he finally stepped away in 1967 as the winningest coach in pro football history with 325 victories. No one could be more cantankerous, either as an executive or on the sidelines. Halas bullied officials and tried to intimidate opponents, sometimes even shutting off the hot water in their dressing rooms. He often was accused of bullying his players, though he claimed with some justification that he expected a lot of them and worked only to help them achieve their potential. The tremendous number of former players who became successful is moot testimony to his achieving that aim. Salary hassles were commonplace for nearly all of the time he was Papa Bear, including one with a player named Mike Ditka. That dispute is best remembered for Ditka's final salvo: "Halas throws nickels around like they were manhole covers." Shortly thereafter, Ditka was traded to Philadelphia. But when it came time to hire a head coach in the early eighties for one last run at the glory he still sought for his team, Halas chose Ditka. For all his stubbornness and rigidity, Halas never strayed

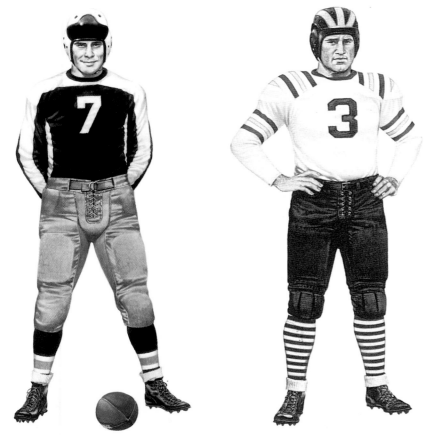

from his pledge to make pro football as exciting and entertaining as possible. This was reflected in two eras: first from formation of his team in Decatur, Illinois, through the short-lived Red Grange era, to 1932-33 when the Bears won their back-to-back NFL titles; second, in a six-year period from 1938-43, when the Bears won three NFL titles and five Western Division crowns.

Bronko Nagurski, Legend and Player

As he showed in signing Red Grange, Halas always had an eye for the charismatic, almost legendary player. In 1929, he did it again, signing Bronko Nagurski, the All-America from Minnesota. When Grantland Rice had picked his college All-America team after the 1928 season, he picked only ten starters, naming Nagurski as both fullback and tackle. The tales surrounding Nagurski already were Bunyanesque. He had run six miles each way to and from high school every day. He had rescued a man buried under a pile of logs at a sawmill. He had single-handedly lifted a truck off a dying man.

Of course, Nagurski was tested at once, perhaps most significantly by Cal Hubbard, one of the greatest tackles ever to play pro football and no small person himself at 250 pounds. During a game against Hubbard's Green Bay Packers, Hubbard told Grange that he wanted a shot at the rookie. The next time Chicago punted the ball, he asked Red to let him through so he could go after Nagurski. "I let Hubbard past me the next time we punted the ball, and then turned around to watch," Grange said. "Hubbard socked the Bronk a good one but the guy who went down was Hubbard. After the game, he said to me, 'I've seen enough. The kid is as hard as they said he was.'"

With the Bears, Nagurski had the strength and stamina to play fullback, offensive and defensive tackle, and linebacker in nearly every game. Everything about the man was bigger than football life, beginning with his size 20 collar, his massive hands with their size 20 ring fingers, and a perfectly proportioned 234 pounds spread over his 6-foot, 2-inch frame – in an era when someone 195 or 200 pounds was considered big. In eight seasons as a running back, from 1930-37, he gained more than 3,000 yards, averaging 4.4 yards a carry.

In his prime, Nagurski carried the ball only 12 to 14 times a game, but he had intimidated defenses. The moment they saw him coming, they rushed to tackle him. Halas made good use of this fear. In the 1933 title game against the New York Giants, Nagurski twice faked line plunges, drawing the defenses to him, then straightened up and threw touchdown passes of 8 and 33 yards as the Bears came from behind in the fourth quarter to win their second straight NFL title, 23-21. Mel Hein, one of football's greatest players, played for those powerful Giants teams. After knocking heads with Nagurski every season, Hein called him "the toughest fullback I ever faced. If you hit him low, he'd run over you. If you hit him high, he'd knock you down and run over you." Clark Hinkle, another great fullback-linebacker for the Green Bay Packers championship teams of those years, said that he took five stitches in his face after the first time he ever tackled Nagurski. "My biggest thrill in football was the day he announced his retirement," Hinkle said.

Beattie Feathers, the First 1,000-yard Rusher

Nagurski wasn't the only star for the Bears during the thirties. In 1934, Halas signed running back Beattie Feathers from the University of Tennessee. In Feathers's rookie season, he became the NFL's first 1,000-yard rusher, gaining 1,004 yards on 101 carries in 11 games. He missed the final two games of the regular season, plus the Bears' title-game loss against the Giants. He averaged 9.94 yards per carry, still a record. Thus, 1,000 yards became the season's benchmark for every rusher. The accomplishment is now somewhat diluted, as teams play 16 games, as opposed to 12 in Feathers's time. But its significance in 1934 is reflected by the fact that it took 14 years before it was equaled – by Steve Van Buren of the Philadelphia Eagles, who bettered Feathers record by just four yards. Linemen such as George Musso, Joe Kopcha, and Jules Carlson led sweeps and sprung tackle traps that propelled Feathers to the record. Kopcha once described the action: "I'd pull and hit the tackle to the outside, and George Musso would hit the guard inside, and the hole would be a mile wide and a mile deep." Then there was the power of Nagurski as a lead blocker. All of the Bears' players from that era said it was impossible to separate Feathers's rushing feats from Nagurski's blocking, particularly on inside plays. Nagurski would simply bulldoze potential tacklers out of the way while Feathers, a 5-10, 180-pound halfback, ran as low to the ground as possible, then just whirled away once he got through the heavy traffic. "Watching him run reminded me of watching a jackrabbit in a cornfield being chased by a hound," Nagurski once said. "He would change his pace and his direction all the time. He would stay with me as long as I could do him some good, then he'd make his cut and go off on his own."

Grange, who made his mark as a cutback runner, said that Feathers was the first pro back he saw who used to use that move extensively. "He could do it right or left, or stop on a dime and go again," Grange said. "He was the finest cutback runner I ever saw."

Sadly, the shoulder injury that cost Feathers the final games of his rookie season hampered him for the rest of his career. He joined the Brooklyn Dodgers and retired after the end of the 1940 season, having gained just 974 rushing yards during his last six seasons.

Sid Luckman,
A Pure T Quarterback

Though the Bears won the 1937 Western Division title (then lost to the Washington Redskins in the NFL Championship Game), their real impact came at the end of the decade. Halas had polished his T-formation, and found that Sid Luckman, an All-America tailback from Columbia University, would be the ideal man to run one of the most explosive offenses in NFL history. In those years, there were no T formation quarterbacks coming from college football. Every team used the single and double wing formations, where a tailback was the chief offensive operator. He stood seven yards behind the center and received a direct snap, then either ran or passed the ball.

When Luckman reported to the Bears in 1939, Halas had no doubts that he could learn an entirely different way of playing offensive football. Luckman's coach at Columbia, Lou Little, had assured the Bears that he never had coached a player of Luckman's ability. "He told us there was nothing that Sid could not do on a football field," Halas said. "'If you are looking to make someone a T-formation quarterback, then Sidney is your man,' Little told me. I had the greatest respect for Lou Little and his word was sufficient because I had seen Luckman play and I knew he certainly had the physical ability."

The initial problem was physical – teaching Luckman to take the ball while standing directly behind the center, then to hand it off to a running back or dropping back to throw. The footwork and the action of handling the ball was intricate but Luck-

man had a superb teacher, Clark Shaughnessy, who then was head coach at the University of Chicago. Shaughnessy, a sort of "mad football genius" who was forever coming up with new plays, formations, and techniques, was an "advisor" to the Bears. He was helping Halas refine and sophisticate his offense. The more Shaughnessy worked with the system, the more difficult it became to run – and later to defend – but Luckman was the perfect person to handle it. He was intelligent and able to absorb Shaughnessy's teaching. Most of all, though, he was physically adept at handling the ball. So much of the offense's success spun off the ability of the quarterback to fake in different directions before releasing the ball, thus keeping a defense off-balance. Luckman began his rookie season in 1939 playing behind incumbent Bernie Masterson, who had quarterbacked Chicago to its 1937 divisional title. Chicago finished second in the division in 1939, and by the end of the year Luckman was the starting quarterback. His supporting cast included fellow rookie Bill Osmanski, who led the NFL in rushing, and such holdover veteran linemen as George Musso, a huge 270-pound tackle and middle guard on defense, Danny Fortman, Aldo Forte, Ray Bray and Joe Stydahar, as well as backs Joe Maniaci, Jack Manders, and Ray Nolting.

Papa Bear and The Monsters of the Midway, Part II

In 1940, Halas put the final pieces into place, drafting Clyde (Bulldog) Turner, a 6-1, 235-pound center from Hardin-Simmons College, end Ken Kavanaugh of LSU, running back George McAfee of Duke, and tackle Ed Kolman from Temple. Those rookies,

In the 1940 NFL Championship Game, Chicago fullback Bill Osmanski (with ball) rushed for 107 yards on 10 carries, including a 68-yard touchdown on the second play of the game, as the Bears recorded the most lopsided victory in NFL history, 73-0 over Washington.

together with the great veteran players, earned the nickname, "Monsters of the Midway." Luckman, McAfee, Fortman, Stydahar, and Turner later were accorded Hall of Fame honors. Osmanski, Kavanaugh, and Maniaci also made great offensive contributions. But the spirit of this team was centered in Musso, another Hall of Fame player who, as a rookie, had played with Grange and Nagurski on the 1933 championship team. Musso had earned 12 varsity letters at Millikin College. Halas was so impressed with his football skills that he offered him a salary of $90 a game (par for rookies of that time, and perhaps half of what starters received), plus five bucks to get to training camp – three for a train ticket and two dollars for incidental expenses. Musso accepted because the New York Giants had offered him only $75 a week. He almost didn't make the Bears as a rookie but always claimed that his threats to leave the team for promised roster spots in both New York and Green Bay caused Halas to counter with an offer of $45 a week until he proved himself.

Musso became a starter before his rookie season ended, and for nine of his 12 seasons with the Bears, he was the team's captain. He became a great pulling guard two years after winning all-league honors at tackle in 1935, and no one was better at getting out of the line to lead interference, a great feat for a player of Musso's girth. "There is no secret," he once said. "I am blocking for Nagurski and he waits for no one."

Musso also set the tempo for the Bears' style of play, which in turn mirrored the fiery nature of their coach. After a 2-2 start in 1940, the team roared to six victories in its last seven games and won the Western Division. (The loss was 7-3 to the Washington Redskins three weeks before the season ended.) But that team is remembered mainly for what it did in the 1940 NFL championship game against the Redskins – a 73-0 thrashing that stands as the largest winning margin in NFL history. On the game's second play, Osmanski ran around left end for a 68-yard touchdown. Washington came back down the field and would have scored, but Charlie Malone dropped a perfect pass from Sammy Baugh. Asked later how that might have affected the outcome, Baugh said, "It would have made the score 73-7."

The Redskins never were competitive after that.

Chicago rolled up a 21-0 lead after one quarter, and 28-0 at the half. As the Skins tried to come back with a flurry of passes, the Bears' defense sat back and picked off eight of them, three going for touchdowns in a 26-point third quarter. Three others were turned into quick, easy touchdown drives. By that time referee Red Friesell had asked Halas not to kick any more extra points because there were only two footballs left for the game. The rest of the supply had disappeared into the crowd. Though the Bears rolled up 501 yards, Luckman had a modest day, completing four of six passes for 102 yards and a touchdown (the Bears only threw 10 times). But Chicago rushed the ball 52 times, and three backs averaged more than 10 yards a carry.

That game, more than any other to that time, changed the face of football at every level. Halas' T-formation proved that finesse was going to be as important as speed and power. The days of the various wing formations began to diminish. "Hundreds of coaches from all over America wrote to me for details and diagrams," Halas said later.

The Monsters of the Midway dominated the NFL for the next three seasons, winning titles in 1941 and 1943, but losing to the Redskins in 1942, 14-8,

Above: George Halas and his players celebrate the 1940 NFL Championship Game victory over Washington. The game showcased the Bears' T-formation.

Left: 1940 NFL Champion Chicago Bears

CHICAGO BEARS
NATIONAL CHAMPIONS
~1940~

spoiling a perfect season. In 1941, the Bears became a deeper, even more talented team after drafting fullback Norm Standlee and halfback Hugh Galarneau from Stanford's Rose Bowl champions. At Stanford they had been coached by Shaughnessy, so they were familiar with the Bears' style of offense. The two rookies alternated with Osmanski and McAfee, and Chicago led the NFL in both rushing and passing offense, averaging more than 36 points a game. They tied Green Bay for the Western Division championship, then romped to a 33-14 victory in a division playoff game. Gallarneau began the scoring with an 81-yard punt return. A week later, on a bitter cold day, the Bears broke open a battle of field goal kickers in the third quarter. Standlee led the running game, scoring twice in a 37-9 victory over the Giants for Chicago's second straight title.

In 1942, many of the Bears' stars joined the armed forces. Halas himself spent more than three years as a naval officer, turning the coaching duties over to Luke Johnsos, Hunk Anderson, and Paddy Driscoll. The Bears lost all three fullbacks – Standlee, Osmanski, and Maniaci – but Famiglietti became the main runner, leading the league with eight touchdowns as the team went 11-0. But in a bit of sweet revenge for their 1940 title game embarrassment, the Redskins cost the Bears a perfect season, stopping Chicago's running game and winning 14-6. The Bears' only score was a 52-yard fumble return by Lee Artoe in the first quarter.

In 1943, the Bears staged one of the most dramatic curtain calls in NFL history, bringing Bronko Nagurski out of retirement. Nagurski had left pro football in 1938 when he asked for a $1,000 raise to $6,000, was turned down by Halas, and went home figuring the Bears would eventually call him with a new contract. No one ever did until 1943, when he was 34 years old – not old by today's NFL standards but considered almost ancient back then. By the time Nagurski returned, Chicago's line had lost Stydahar, Kolman, Artoe, Fortman, Chuck Drulis, and Ray Bray.

In the final game of the regular season, against the crosstown Cardinals, the Bears needed a victory to edge Green Bay for the Western Division title. The Cards were ahead 24-14 early in the fourth quarter when co-coach Hunk Anderson told Bronko to take over his old fullback position. Seven plays later, Nagurski ended a 62-yard drive with a touchdown. Later in the quarter, on fourth-and-two, he got six yards, setting up Luckman's clinching touchdown pass to Harry Clark. Though he hadn't touched a ball in six seasons, Nagurski finished the game 84 yards in 16 carries. He said afterward, "That game gave me the greatest kick out of football."

In the NFL Championship Game, the Bears won their third title in four seasons with a 27-point second half, defeating the Redskins 41-21. Luckman threw five touchdown passes, and Nagurski scored the final touchdown of his career. Earlier that season, Luckman had become the first NFL quarterback to gain more than 400 yards in a game, with 443 yards and seven touchdowns (the latter still a shared NFL record and a Bears team mark) in a 56-7 victory over

Bronko Nagurski is brought down by the New York Giants' Ed Danowski in the 1934 NFL Championship Game. The Giants rallied for 27 points in the fourth quarter to overcome a 13-3 deficit in what has come to be known as the "Sneakers Game."

the Giants. He finished the season with 28 touchdown passes, another team record that has survived nearly a half-century.

A Giant Love Affair Began in New York City

Yielding 443 passing yards to Luckman was one of the few bad moments the Giants endured during the first decade of the NFL's new look. New York vied with the Packers, Redskins, and Bears for the power positions. During a 13-season period from 1933-1945, the Giants won seven division titles and two NFL championships. Perhaps their most memorable title came in the famed "Sneaker Game" at the Polo Grounds against the Bears in 1934. The field was frozen. Conventional cleats gave players no footing, as they slipped and slid like ice skating beginners every time they tried to run. But the Giants' trainer, who also worked for Manhattan College, about two miles from the Polo Grounds, suggested to coach Steve Owen that he get some sneakers from the school's gym so the players would have better traction. Owen immediately sent a couple of volunteers in a taxi to the college, and they brought back every available sneaker.

Though physically overmatched by the Bears and trailing 10-3 at halftime, the Giants stunned Chicago when they came out for the second half wearing the gym shoes. "Step on their toes," Halas told his players, but the Bears simply could not stay with the sure-footed New Yorkers, who won the cham-

Left: Tim Mara's purchase of the Giants in 1925 put a NFL team in New York, which gave the league some much-needed notoriety.

pionship game 30-13. Halas always said that one of his greatest regrets while coaching the Bears was not thinking to bring sneakers for his team that day. Ironically, he allowed himself to be victimized again

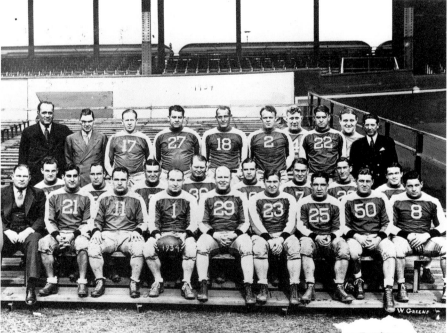

in almost similar circumstances when the Giants routed the Bears 47-7 in the 1956 NFL title game on a frozen field at Yankee Stadium. Andy Robustelli, the Giants' all-pro end, owned a sporting goods store, and he had brought a supply of sneakers to the game on the chance that field conditions might call for their use. The Bears had theirs ready, but decided not to use them.

The Giants of the Thirties had a splendid coach in Owen, who had been a great tackle during the twenties and then a player-coach for the Giants for several years. His coaching philosophy was simple: "Body contact is the basis of the game." Owen was an exacting coach. Once, after the Giants had lost a

Left: Steve Owen directed the New York Giants to two NFL titles and made them one of the league's toughest defensive teams.

Above: 1934 NFL Champion New York Giants

game at the Polo Grounds, he told them, "Don't bother to take off your uniforms. We're going back out there and work on a few things." He then put them through a full-scale practice. His teams always were tough defensively. From 1931-1945, the defense was led by Mel Hein, a linebacker and center who still is considered the best all-around player in Giants history. Hein was a two-way, 60-minute player during most of his 15 seasons. In 1938, following his sixth straight selection to the all-pro team, he was named the NFL's first Most Valuable Player. When New York beat the Packers in a regular season game that year, Hein intercepted a pass and ran 50 yards for the only touchdown of his career. He was among the earliest enshrinees of Pro Football Hall of Fame.

Owen's Giants played conservatively on offense, often punting on third down. He had great punters and figured that if he could back up an opponent in its end of the field and keep it there with his defense, it would be easier to score with such great kickers as Ken Strong and Ward Cuff. That happened in the 1938 title game against the Packers. New York's defense blocked two punts, the first leading to Cuff's field goal and the second setting up Tuffy Leemans's six-yard touchdown run en route to a 23-17 victory. In 1936, the Giants drafted Alphonse (Tuffy) Leemans from George Washington University in Washington, and he won the NFL rushing title that year. During Leemans's eight-year career, the Giants had a 53-27-8 record, three division titles, and an NFL championship. Wellington Mara, president of the

Giants, signed Leemans to his first contract in 1936. Mara says that he was the team's greatest offensive player, even though he wasn't fast and was predictable, most of his runs going off-tackle. But Leemans started quickly and, at 6-1 and 210 pounds, was a big back for those years. He also had extraordinary leg strength. The best way to get him down was to tackle him around the shoulders. Greasy Neale even threatened to fine any of his Eagles players if they tried to tackle Leemans below the waist.

Rules at that time said that a runner were tackled only if he was pinned to the ground and not able to move. Otherwise, he could get up again and continue to run. Leemans often got first downs by crawling along the ground until opposing tacklers jumped on him. He did his best in clutch situations. He wasn't a great passer but always seemed to complete a pass for a touchdown when it was needed. He wasn't fast, but if he broke free, few ever caught him from behind.

In 1934, the Giants picked tailback Ed Danowski, the star of Fordham's great teams. Danowski became part of a group of 17 rookies that formed the backbone of the Giants' 1938 NFL title team. Danowski was a better passer than Leemans, but not as good a runner. So Owen devised a two-backfield system, using the Leemans group in the first and third quarters, and the Danowski group in the second and fourth. In the 1938 championship game, against Green Bay, the Giants trailed 17-16 until Danowski's passing and Hank Soar's running keyed a 61-yard drive for the winning score.

Philadelphia Eagles coach Greasy Neale threatened to fine any of his players if they tried to tackle Tuffy Leemans (4) below the waist.

Curly Lambeau's Packers, A Winning Tradition

Despite that setback, the Packers won three other NFL championships during the 1932-45 era, when they and the Bears dominated the Western Division. Curly Lambeau, who had founded the team, helped to nourish it through the beginnings of the NFL, and won three straight NFL titles in 1929-1931. He had been a fine passer as a player and believed the passing game was an integral part of a team's attack. Lambeau's willingness to throw from any part of the field gave the Packers a dimension most other NFL teams lacked.

Of course, Lambeau picked players who gave him this extra dimension, beginning with Arnie Herber in 1930, Clark Hinkle in 1932, and Cecil Isbell in 1938, and a fine all-around player in Tony Canadeo in 1941. All but Isbell are members of the Hall of Fame.

Herber led the Packers to four NFL titles. He won the passing title in 1932, the first season the NFL began keeping official statistics, and added two in the next three years. But the Packers gradually became a team deep in tailbacks with the acquisition of Hinkle in 1933, Isbell, and Canadeo. The work load was spread around to a point where no one player ever became a dominant force. Hinkle was the NFL's top rusher with 3,519 yards from 1933-41, five times leading the Packers. Isbell and Herber teamed with end Don Hutson. Isbell led the NFL in passing yardage in 1941 and 1942, and was tops on the

Left: Don Hutson and Earl (Curly) Lambeau

Below: Green Bay's Clarke Hinkle carries for a 4-yard gain in the 1938 NFL Championship. The Packers outgained the Giants 378-212 in total yardage, but the New York defense blocked two punts that led to nine points and a 23-17 win.

Packers during his five seasons with the team. He abruptly retired for college coaching in 1942 while at the peak of his career because he feared Lambeau's telling him that he no longer was capable of playing at top form. Canadeo, nicknamed "The Gray Ghost" because of his prematurely gray hair, was the best all-around player of the group and still ranks second among Green Bay's career rushers with 4,197 yards. On defense, he was one of the league's top safeties. But no player was better than end Don Hutson, a star at the University of Alabama (he was the "other" end with Bear Bryant on those teams). Lambeau fought off attempts by the Brooklyn Dodgers to sign Hutson in 1935. For the next 11 years, Hutson set every NFL pass receiving and scoring record. The most celebrated – 99 career touchdown passes – finally was

62

broken in 1989 by Steve Largent of the Seattle Seahawks, some 45 seasons after it was established. Hutson also played defense – he led the NFL with six interceptions in 1940 – and was an excellent placekicker. He was a spindly 6 feet, 1 inch, and weighed 180 pounds. But his hands were soft and resilient. Arguably the best receiver ever to play pro football – and in an era when the pass was not a featured weapon, even by the Packers – Hutson was virtually impossible to cover. He was a master of using a head fake and a change of pace. Teaming with Herber and Isbell for most of his career, Hutson established a slew of records. The following still exist:

Led the NFL's receivers in eight (of his 11) seasons, five of them consecutive.

Caught 488 passes for 7,991 yards.

Led the league in receiving yardage for a record seven seasons, four of them consecutive.

Led the league in touchdown passes eight times, four consecutive.

Led the league in scoring five consecutive seasons from 1940-44.

Is the all-time scorer among receivers with 833 points, from place-kicking and running.

On the second play of the first regular season game Hutson ever started, he caught an 83-yard touchdown pass from Herber. He caught a season-high 74 passes in 1943, when his 1,211 yards made him the first receiver to break the 1,000 yard barrier. Hutson's single greatest game may have come against the Detroit Lions in his final season, 1945, when he scored 29 points on four touchdown passes from Roy McKay. The longest was 59 yards, the shortest 6. That day, he also kicked five extra points in the second quarter.

In 1936, the Packers defeated the Boston Redskins 21-6 at New York's Polo Grounds. As noted earlier, Boston owner George Preston Marshall had taken the game from Boston because of what he considered poor support. Hutson scored the game's first touchdown on a 43-yard pass from Herber. Then Johnny Blood got into the act with a 52-yard reception that set up Herber's second scoring pass. After losing to New York in the 1938 championship game, the Packers twice beat them for NFL titles. But Hutson's only significant role seems to have been as a decoy. He didn't catch a pass in Green Bay's 27-0 victory in the 1939 game, and he caught only two in the Packers' 14-7 victory over the Giants in 1944. In the 1939 game, the Packers' defense kept New York in its own territory for most of the game while Herber threw a seven-yard touchdown pass to Milt Gantenbein and Isbell threw one of 27 yards to Joe Laws. Green Bay ran the ball 51 times.

Sammy Baugh's Aerial Circus

Green Bay's rise to excellence in the Hutson years coincided with the emergence of another proponent of the passing game. In 1937, Washington welcomed Sammy Baugh, a lean, raw-boned player from Texas Christian University. Baugh had led an attack at TCU dubbed the "Aerial Circus." For 16 seasons, he recreated it in the NFL, leading the league in passing six times. In his rookie season, he led the Redskins to the first of two NFL championships and five Eastern Division titles.

Baugh had a fine supporting cast, beginning with Cliff Battles, who won his second NFL rushing title in 1937 and then retired from the game after just six seasons. End Wayne Millner and tackle Turk Edwards were other future Hall of Fame players who helped the team turn Marshall's $80,000 deficit in his final season in Boston to a $20,000 profit in his first year in Washington. In the next decade, the team had 40 consecutive home sellouts.

Baugh was the big draw. He was a single-wing tailback in his early career in Washington a much better thrower than a runner, and a superb punter and defender. Baugh still holds the NFL season punting average of 51.4 yards per kick, and shares the record of making four interceptions in one game.

Following Marshall's instructions, Baugh arrived in Washington wearing a 10-gallon hat and cowboy boots. He never had worn such a traditional western outfit. In fact, he had grown up in a traditional house

Top: The Packers' quarterback-halfback Cecil Isbell was an accurate passer who led the league in passing yardage in 1941 and 1942.

Bottom: Though the 1937 NFL Championship Game was played in chilly 15-degree weather, Washington rookie quarterback Sammy Baugh caught fire and completed 18 of 35 passes for 354 yards and three touchdowns in leading the Redskins to a 28-21 victory over Chicago.

in Sweetwater, Texas. In his backyard, he hung an old tire and achieved his great accuracy by throwing a ball through it day after day, from every possible distance, and often with the tire swinging back and forth. He was the best passer of his era, and one of the greatest of all time. He threw the ball overhand, sidearm, or even underarm when he got into deep trouble from pass rushers, with a touch unmatched by any passer, including Luckman.

Baugh made a tempting target for the "headhunters" of the day. In one game, he had received a going-over from an opposing lineman's elbows and knees. Finally, one of Baugh's own linemen, Wee Willie Wilkin, suggested that he take care of the culprit. "Leave it to me," Baugh told Wilkin. On the next play, the lineman came piling in on him as usual. Players didn't wear facemasks in those days, so Baugh waited until the last instant, then drilled the football right between the player's eyes. He toppled over like a felled tree.

In his first NFL game, Baugh completed 11 of 16 passes against the defensive-minded Giants, and went on to take Washington to its second straight division title. This time, the Redskins got their crown, beating the Chicago Bears 28-21 as Baugh threw two touchdown passes in the third quarter to overcome a 21-14 Chicago lead. He completed 17 of his 34 passes for 358 yards and three touchdowns. The Bears came back with that 73-0 victory in the 1940 championship game. But Baugh got some sweet

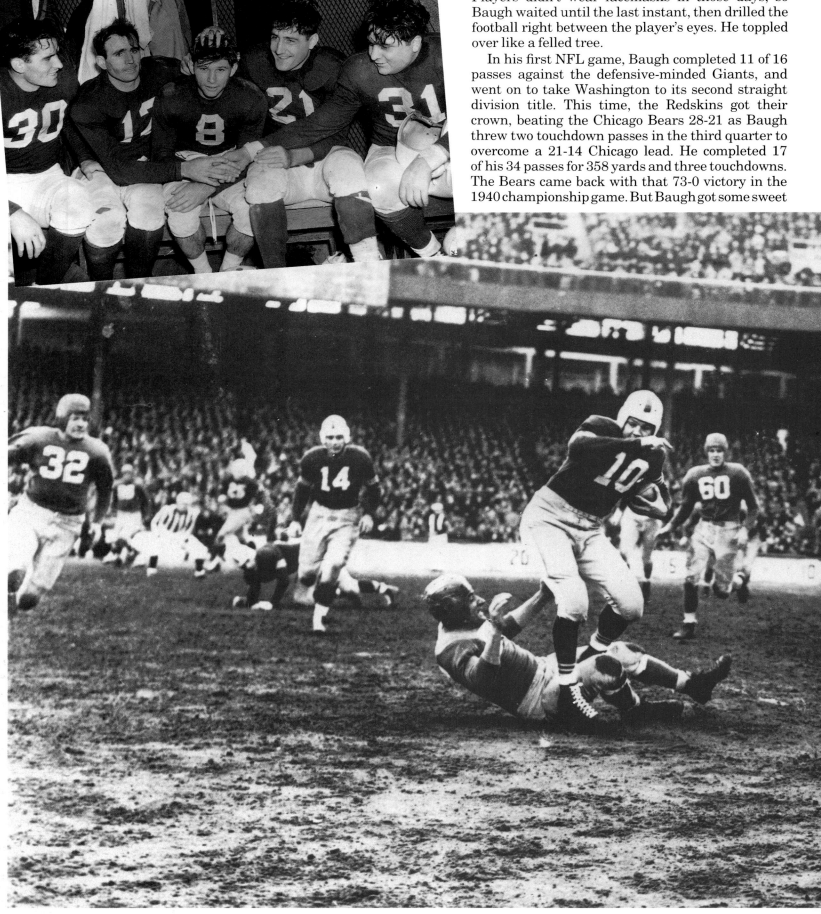

revenge of his own in 1942, spoiling Chicago's bid for a perfect season by beating the Bears 14-6 in the championship game.

Here, Baugh showed his excellence as an all-around field leader. With Chicago leading 6-0, he boomed an 83-yard punt that put Chicago deep in its own territory. Washington quickly intercepted a pass by Sid Luckman, and Baugh right away threw a 32-yard TD pass to Wilbur Moore for a 7-6 lead. Chicago then spread its defense to try to stop Baugh's passing. He responded with a 12-play drive entirely on the ground, ending with Andy Farkas's one-yard scoring plunge.

Times, They were a-Changin'... But for the Better

While players such as Baugh, Luckman, Hutson, Leemans, and Herber were bringing more attention to pro football, other stars were coming into the league. In 1938, Art Rooney had signed Byron (Whizzer) White, an All-America running back from Colorado, who had led the nation in rushing and scoring. Many believed White would forego pro

football to accept a Rhodes Scholarship. Against the wishes of his player-coach, Johnny Blood, Rooney drafted White. "I'll offer him so much money he can't refuse," Rooney said, then offered his rookie the unheard-of sum of $15,000.

White turned down the offer, first made on a visit to Colorado by Blood, and continued with plans to attend Oxford University in England. But late in August, he changed his mind –not for the money he said, but because he had become so fascinated with Blood as a person that he wanted to get to know him better. The two became life-long friends, and Blood once led a campaign to nominate White for the Presidency in 1972. Pittsburgh was a poor team in White's only season there, but he led NFL rushers with 567 yards. He left to attend law school at Yale University. Needing some money to continue his studies, he returned for two more seasons with Detroit after Rooney sold his contract to the Lions for $5,000. White was named to the United States Supreme Court by President John F. Kennedy in 1962.

The NFL got its first commissioner, Elmer Layden, in 1941. Joe Carr had died in 1939, and had been replaced on an interim basis by Carl Storck, one of the NFL's founding fathers. Layden had been one of the members of Notre Dame's famed Four Horsemen backfield and had been a college coach. The owners had sought a man with a football background and instant visibility. Then, to elevate their game to the status of major league baseball, they adopted the title of "commissioner."

During this time, the NFL also started some of its time-honored traditions. In 1934, George Richards had purchased the Portsmouth franchise for $15,000 and moved it to Detroit where it became the Lions. Late in the season, the team had two games scheduled against the Bears, one on Thanksgiving Day. Every ticket was sold. Richards offered the game for nationwide radio broadcast, and 94 stations signed up carrying Graham McNamee doing the play-by-play. It was the first time an NFL game ever was broadcast, and a Lions' Thanksgiving Day game remains a part of the NFL schedule.

The broadcast medium began to expand. By the end of the decade, every team had its own radio outlet. The Bears' lopsided victory over the Redskins in 1940 was the first NFL Championship Game to be broadcast nationwide. A year earlier, a game between the Brooklyn Dodgers and Philadelphia Eagles had been televised from Ebbets Field to the approximately 1,000 sets then in New York City. As the nineties begin, NFL Games now are televised to hundreds of millions around the world.

A new game also was added to pro football's schedule. In 1934, a team of College All-Stars was scheduled to play the defending NFL champions at Chicago's Soldier Field. Promotion-minded Arch Ward, the sports editor of the Chicago Tribune, also had recently introduced the major league baseball All-Star Game. The first game, matching the Bears and the All-Stars, was a scoreless tie, but the prestige of college football still was so high at the time, that this annual event actually enhanced the reputation of pro football. The game drew huge crowds for most of its first quarter-century, sometimes exceeding 100,000. The All-Stars weren't always overmatched, either: the NFL champions won only one of the first five games, and just eight of the first 15. Gradually, the game became one-sided in favor of the pros, but it

Top: In his final game, Philadelphia Eagles quarterback Davey O'Brien (8) completed 33 passes against the Washington Redskins in 1940 to set an NFL record. Teammate Don Looney (30) also set a record in the game with 14 receptions.

Bottom: George Kracum (10) of the Brooklyn Dodgers is tripped up after making a long gain in a 1941 game against the New York Giants. The 55,051 fans in the stands were unaware that the Japanese had attacked Pearl Harbor during the game.

continued until the mid-seventies, when scheduling difficulties forced its cancellation.

Relative popularity and prosperity also arrived in 1939 when the NFL attracted a million spectators for the first time. In 1943, individual winners' shares in the NFL title game passed the $1,000 mark when each Bears player received $1,146 for defeating Washington. That compared to the $210.34 each Bears player had received ten years earlier when Chicago defeated the Giants and players were given a cut for the first time. Players on the San Francisco 49ers Super Bowl XXIV championship team each received $36,000.

World War II Takes its Toll

All of this good news was muted, though. On December 7, 1941, the first public inkling of the Pearl Harbor disaster came during a game between the Giants and Brooklyn Dodgers at the Polo Grounds. That Sunday afternoon, the public address announcer began an almost constant paging of various armed forces personnel. Pro football really didn't feel the impact of World War II until 1943, when it was stripped of most of its talented players. That there was pro football at all was due to President Franklin D. Roosevelt's decree that all American sports, college and pro, would continue in whatever fashion possible. The President saw them as necessary recreational outlets for a country that was running 24 hours a day in a wartime economy, and which needed some respite from war news. For the first year or so, war news was mostly depressing.

News also was depressing in the NFL. Each team had only 26 players. Most of them worked in war plants, took weekend leave from military service, were draftees waiting for a call-up date, were 4-F (physically unable to serve), or were involved in war-related civilian jobs. Sammy Baugh was one of those because he was raising beef cattle on his ranch

Bob Waterfield led the Rams to the NFL championship in his first pro season; something no other rookie quarterback has accomplished.

in Texas and that was considered a war industry. So Baugh was obliged to be at his ranch some of the time, and on those occasions he would fly to join his team, provided he could secure space. It was not unusual for a player to practice only on Saturday afternoon, play on Sunday, and then perhaps not show up for a game for another couple of weeks, if at all.

League stability also was a problem. The Cleveland Rams, whose owner Dan Reeves was in the Navy, were allowed to suspend operations in 1943. To offset an awkward nine-team scheduling problem, Commissioner Layden forced a reluctant merger of Pittsburgh and Philadelphia, forming a team called the Steagles, with Greasy Neale of Philadelphia and Walt Kiesling of Pittsburgh as co-coaches. The team played four games in Philadelphia and four in Pittsburgh and just missed tying for the Eastern Division title. Most of the players were Eagles and either were stationed nearby in the service or working in Philadelphia-area defense plants. They practiced at night at Philadelphia's Shibe Park. When the Steagles were disbanded after the season. The Rams returned. Ted Collins, an entertainment promoter, was awarded a new franchise in Boston called the Yanks. Once again there was an uneven number of teams for scheduling, so Layden persuaded Rooney and Charlie Bidwill, two old friends, to merge the Steelers and Chicago Cardinals into a team simply called Card-Pitt. Kiesling was a co-coach this time with Phil Handler of the Cardinals but the team lost every game. Fans jokingly called the team the "Carpets". Rooney called it the worst team ever put together.

One Last Gasp

The war ended before the start of the 1945 season, but was not soon enough to return the NFL to top-flight competitive status. But a new star, tailback Bob Waterfield from UCLA, had joined the Cleveland Rams. The Rams had come into the league in 1937 when Homer Marshman and a group of sportsmen were awarded a franchise. Dan Reeves, who owned a stock brokerage firm, and Fred Levy, Jr. gained control of the team in 1941. The Rams came of age competitively in the 1945 season, Waterfield's rookie year, when they won the Western Division title.

Baugh led the Eastern Division-champion Redskins into their fifth NFL title game in nine years. The game was played on a cold day in Cleveland. Players sat huddled under mounds of straw that had been used to cover the field and keep it playable. Early in the game, Baugh disdained a punt from his own end zone and called a pass to end Wayne Millner. The play completely fooled the Rams' secondary and Millner was running in the clear as Baugh released the ball. It hit the crossbar and bounced backward into the end zone. Under NFL rules at the time, that was an automatic safety, so instead of taking the lead 7-0 Washington were behind by 2-0. Baugh was forced out of the game in the second quarter after re-injuring his ribs. Waterfield threw a pair of touchdown passes and kicked the winning point–the ball hit the crossbar and bounced over–as Cleveland won the title 15-14. Within a few weeks, the Rams, who hadn't drawn 70,000 fans all season in mammoth Cleveland Stadium, were en route to their new home in Los Angeles. The NFL was ready for a new frontier.

The NFL Expands and Excels

Early in 1946, National Football League owners elected Bert Bell, co-owner of the Pittsburgh Steelers with Art Rooney, as commissioner. "He understood our problems and what it was like to run a club back then," Rooney said many years later. Bell's experience in pro football dated back to 1933, when he brought the Philadelphia Eagles into the league. His tales of survival were pointed lessons for every owner, new and old. They liked him personally because he got along with their divergent personalities. Never cowed or pushed to any rash decisions, Bell could bring people together.

Bell's summer home in Margate, on the New Jersey seashore, became a retreat for many of the owners. Around the kitchen table, the NFL's problems were discussed, solutions forged, and future courses of action planned. The owners trusted Bell's judgment. They admired his problem-solving ability, and they knew that he was ardently dedicated to pro football's prosperity – which meant their clubs' survival.

NFL owners had visions of new and richer horizons. Dan Reeves's decision to move his Cleveland Rams to Los Angeles was not the first move in that direction, just the first to succeed. Actor Don Ameche, a great sportsman, had sought a team for Los Angeles, and lumber tycoon Anthony Morabito had applied for a franchise in San Francisco. Jim Brueil, an oil company magnate in Buffalo, had deposited $25,000 with the NFL for a franchise – in Buffalo or anywhere else. Mickey McBride, owner of the Yellow Cab Company in Cleveland as well as several other ventures, was another avid sportsman who longed to join his friends Art Rooney, Tim Mara, and Bert Bell as an NFL owner. McBride had been turned down by Reeves in his bid to purchase the Rams.

Reeves had tried to move his team to Los Angeles before 1946 but always was confronted with the travel barrier. Every team traveling to the West Coast went by train over three or four days. In pro football, that was too disruptive for practice schedules. And the majority of players had to work second jobs during the season (most football salaries still were well under $4,000). Teams could travel overnight on a train from the East to the Midwest, or vice versa, or on short trips in the same region.

But after World War II, air travel made all points of the nation accessible in short periods of time. There no longer was any need to do business in just one corner of the country. Moreover, radio had linked the country from coast to coast. Games could be broadcast to every city.

The All-America Football Conference

When World War II ended, there not only was an excess of prospective owners and cities, but three years' worth of good football players, collegians and professionals alike. By 1946, thousands of young men were ready to return to college football, or, in many instances, just content to restart their professional football lives. There was room in the NFL to absorb some of this talent, but there also was a rich, powerful, and far-sighted new participant in the sport: the All-America Football Conference.

The AAFC actually was born a year before World War II ended, thanks to Arch Ward who had initiated the College All-Star game against the NFL champions. Ward believed that pro football, sport's "other" major league, beside baseball, should be similarly structured. He wanted a companion to football's "National" league and set about creating an "American" counterpart, envisioning an eventual "World Series" playoff for pro football's championship.

Ward, at one time a top choice to succeed Joe Carr as NFL commissioner, had great power at the midwest's

Left: Rams owner Dan Reeves was responsible for making the NFL a coast-to-coast league when he moved his team from Cleveland to Los Angeles in 1946.

Below: In 1947, Orban (Spec) Sanders of the AAFC's New York Yankees rushed for 1,432 yards and passed for 1,442.

most influential newspaper. His promotions produced both prestige and cash. In 1944, he laid out plans for a new league, with all the "world series" inducements. Representatives from Buffalo, Chicago, Cleveland, Los Angeles, New York, and San Francisco all pledged entries. Miami entered a year later. And in the only case of a team's moving intact to a rival league, the Brooklyn Dodgers of the NFL moved to the AAFC and became the New York Yankees. The AAFC then added its own Brooklyn Dodgers franchise. That team even had its own comic strip in one New York City newspaper, a potpourri of "how to" tips from its coach Mal Stevens, with the dialogue written in "Brooklyn-ese". The league called itself the "All-America Football Conference" because it linked the entire country. It signed an air charter contract with United Air Lines to fly all its teams to and from the West Coast, breaking the "train barrier" forever. Then, in a move to match the NFL, it named Jim Crowley as its commissioner. A teammate of then-NFL commissioner Elmer Layden in Notre Dame's Four Horsemen backfield, Crowley also had coached great teams at Fordham before the war. When Layden was asked if the NFL would join with the AAFC in a baseball-like structure, his answer, boiled down for public consumption, became a rallying cry for the new league: "Tell them to get a football first."

It wasn't the names, or even its sites, that made the AAFC so impressive. Many of its owners had financial resources far deeper than many NFL owners whose primary business was football. For example, the Los Angeles Dons franchise was headed by Ben Lindheimer, a Chicagoan who owned both the Arlington and Washington Park race tracks in that city, and who had tried without success to become a part owner of the Bears and Cardinals. Lindheimer was joined by Don Ameche and fellow show business figures Bing Crosby, Bob Hope, Pat O'Brien, and Louis B. Mayer, head of

Hollywood's largest movie studio, Metro-Goldwyn-Mayer. For three of the team's four years of existence, the Dons were far more popular in Los Angeles than the Rams.

McBride got Cleveland's franchise even while the Rams were struggling to attract customers. In Chicago, the Rockets were owned by John Keeshin, a trucking company owner and operator of the city's other race track, Sportsman's Park. Brueil withdrew his deposit with the NFL, got the Buffalo franchise, and named the team the Bisons before changing it to the Bills. Topping, who also owned the New York Yankees baseball team as well as storied Yankee Stadium, was wealthier than any of the NFL owners. Morabito got his San Francisco franchise and named it the 49ers.

And the players to stock these teams? "There were enough players to stock a dozen leagues," Crowley said, and he wasn't far wrong. The AAFC did not even hold a draft for its 1946 season. In retrospect, Crowley always believed that was a mistake because a draft would have equalized talent among all eight AAFC teams, giving the conference a better chance for long-term survival instead of ultimate domination by the Cleveland Browns. But the Browns resisted. Their coach, Paul Brown, had signed many great players, both from his Great Lakes Naval Training team as well as former collegians. Brown knew his roster would be depleted in a common draft. Yet, for the AAFC's first three seasons, it was a more talented league overall than the long-established NFL—a level of quality, something no new league, before or since, ever could match. In addition to good football players, the league tapped non-traditional sources such as the large military bases, which had provided the best football competition during the war. Chicago Rockets coach Dick Hanley, a former coach at Northwestern, brought most of his team, including future Hall of Fame receiver Elroy

Baltimore Colts halfback Bill Hillenbrand (82) tries to pick up additional yardage in a 1947 battle against the Brooklyn Dodgers. These were the two losingest teams in the AAFC's Eastern Division that season.

(Crazy Legs) Hirsch, from El Toro Marine Base in California. Several of the 49ers came from Fleet City, a giant Navy enclave near San Francisco, while the Dons were built with players from the Fourth Air Force at March Field in southern California. Both the Dodgers and Yankees drew players from Sampson Naval Training base in New York state.

Of the 67 players on the 1946 College All-Star team that defeated the NFL champion Rams, 40 including eight starters, signed with the AAFC. More than 100 NFL players whose contracts had expired when they were in the service freely negotiated with AAFC teams. Members of the Bears and Redskins title teams switched leagues for higher wages. Frank Sinkwich, the NFL's MVP in 1944 with Detroit, signed with the New York Yankees. Three all-pro players – Ace Parker, Bruiser Kinard, and Pug Manders – stayed with the Dodgers team that moved from the NFL. Even coaches Ray Flaherty (Yankees) and Dudley DeGroot (Dons), who had won NFL titles with the Washington Redskins, joined the new league.

Former college players whose eligibility had expired wanted an opportunity to play pro ball. So did many who had eligibility remaining. There was one big reason – money. When Paul Brown agreed to coach the Cleveland team, McBride made it clear that money was no deterrent to producing a winner. Brown paid healthy monthly bonuses to such future stars as quarterback Otto Graham and tackle-placekicker Lou Groza for signing with his team. Salaries of $150 or $175 a game disappeared forever, and players signed for many times that amount, getting bonuses for joining the new league.

The NFL was stunned at this economic upheaval. Some of its owners could not respond in kind on such short notice. In those years, there were no millions from television or other ancillary revenues, only gate receipts and an owner's own resources. The NFL-AAFC rivalry lasted four years, and millions of dollars were spent on both sides. Some NFL teams, such as Green Bay, Pittsburgh, the Boston Yanks, and Detroit Lions, barely survived. The toll also was heavy in the AAFC. Chicago Rockets owner Keeshin was hard-pressed to compete with the Bears and Cardinals. Both of Chicago's NFL teams were either of championship (Cardinals) or near-championship caliber. Harvey Hester's Miami Seahawks team was comprised mainly of southern players.

Hester believed this would make the team popular throughout the south. Prior to playing the league's premiere game in Cleveland, he said to Paul Brown, "I feel sorry for you trying to compete without too many southern players." The Browns won 44-0 before 60,000 fans, more than the Cleveland Rams had drawn at home during the entire 1945 season. Hester hadn't counted on talented southern players, being attracted to Yankee dollars throughout the AAFC, nor could he foresee a rash of tropical storms that always seemed to rake Miami when his team played at home. The Seahawks folded after 1946, and were replaced in the league by the Baltimore Colts.

Paul Brown, Pro Football's Most Influential Force

One man and the team that was named for him – Paul Brown and the Cleveland Browns – made the four-year All-America Football Conference the same kind of smashing artistic success as George Halas and the Chicago Bears had for the National Football League. Brown's influence continues after founding a second pro football team, the Cincinnati Bengals. He still serves in the NFL's inner council. But in 1945, Arthur McBride, along with his partner Dan Sherby, knew

Paul Brown directed the Cleveland Browns to league championships all four seasons of the AAFC's existence. After the AAFC merged with the NFL in 1950, the Browns continued their dominance and played in the NFL's title game six consecutive years.

little about the game's top coaches. McBride at first sought to hire Notre Dame coach Frank Leahy, then serving in the Navy, but Leahy demurred and later returned to Notre Dame. McBride then sought the opinion of John Dietrich, Cleveland's foremost football writer. Dietrich immediately recommended Brown, and this opinion was seconded by Ward. McBride didn't know Brown or much of his football background, though Brown had been Ohio's most famous high school football coach during nine seasons at Washington High School in Massillon, where his teams won 80 games. Brown also had won the national collegiate championship at Ohio State in 1942, prior to entering the Navy in 1944.

Brown was head coach at Great Lakes Naval Training Center, outside of Chicago, when McBride and Ward approached him about the Cleveland job. At the time, he was dedicated to returning to Ohio State when his service commitment ended. However, he also had great trust in Ward, and when the sports editor laid out the details of his new league, Brown was intrigued. The pro job offered greater immediate riches, but he never had been a devotee of pro football, even growing up in Massillon, a cradle of the sport.

When Brown called Lynn W. St. John, the athletic director at Ohio State, and told him of the offer, St. John did not discourage him from accepting it. The Buckeyes had just finished an unbeaten season under Carroll Widdoes, and St. John was in a dilemma about replacing him when Brown returned from the service

because anyone who had left for military duty was guaranteed a job upon his or her return. St. John's lukewarm response hurt Brown's pride. He agreed to take the football post in Cleveland.

Brown's team dominated the AAFC during all four years of its existence, winning every title. In 1948, it became the first pro football team ever to win every game, including the league championship game. Only the 1972 Miami Dolphins of the NFL have duplicated that feat. One of the keys to Brown's success, beside attracting fine players, was establishing a different kind of atmosphere. "I wanted a college atmosphere where kids played for the love of beating the other team," he said. "I wanted our players to represent their city and their team with dignity, not look like some of the pot-bellied, cigar-smoking guys I had seen on other pro teams."

Brown invited two black players to the Browns' first training camp in 1946: Bill Willis, who had been an All-America guard for him at Ohio State, and fullback Marion Motley, who had played for his Great Lakes team. At the same time, the Los Angeles Rams invited tackle Woody Strode and running back Ken Washington to their camp, the first blacks to play in the NFL since 1933. Motley and Willis became immediate stars. The AAFC soon gained such black stars and future Hall of Famers as Joe Perry of the 49ers and Len Ford of the Dons and Browns, as well as running back Buddy Young, who served in the National Football League office after a great career with the Yankees and Colts.

Brown's players wrote everything in notebooks, from why and how they did calisthenics to the plays they used in a game, so they could study their football away from the field. Brown was the first to use intelligence tests as a guide to a player's learning potential. He believed that mistake-free players were one of the keys to success. His other innovations included: setting up complete statistical studies from game films, and grading each player; calling offensive plays from the sideline by sending a guard into the game on each down; developing the first pass offense designed to go to the open areas of a defense, and then designing defenses that could counteract the same very kind of pass offense. Brown was the first to keep players in a hotel the night before a home game to lessen their distractions.

His greatest talent was selecting talent, then getting the most from it. Six Hall of Fame players – Graham, Groza, Motley, Willis, end Dante Lavelli, and center Frank Gatski – started their careers with Cleveland in the AAFC. Brown was the first to take offensive stars from college and make them defensive players with the Browns, taking advantage of their athletic skills so that his team always had its best players on the field in every situation.

He revolutionized pass offense by developing a system of precision timing patterns. The receiver ran a precise number of yards before making a turn. The quarterback, knowing precisely where the receiver would run, threw the ball before the receiver turned to catch it. With receivers such as Lavelli, Mac Speedie, and Dub Jones, and an accurate quarterback, Graham, the Browns set new standards for the passing game. Even George Halas once took his Bears coaching staff to watch them play.

Graham was the biggest star of the All-America Football Conference. Brown always has called him the greatest quarterback ever "because he got us to the championship game every year he played, and he won more of them than any other quarterback in history."

Above: *In each of Otto Graham's 10 seasons with the Cleveland Browns, he led them to a championship game.*

Right: *Marion Motley, who was the career rushing leader in the AAFC, combined with Otto Graham to "invent" the draw play.*

Graham was the first player Brown signed because he had recalled Graham's great ability to run and throw against Ohio State when he played as tailback for Northwestern. He particularly recalled Graham's great peripheral vision, a necessity for any T-formation quarterback. A big, fast fullback was the key to Brown's offense. The strong inside running of Motley, a 246-pounder who also was a great linebacker, made it easier for Graham when he wanted to pass. The two of them also combined to "invent" the draw play, during a game when Motley momentarily forgot his assignment on a running play and didn't run forward to take a handoff from Graham. So Graham took the ball back, accidentally fooling the defense into thinking the play was a pass and that Motley had stayed back to block. In the instant the defense spread out to defend against the pass, the middle of the Browns offensive line opened a large hole for Motley. From that time on, the draw play has been an ideal maneuver against defenses that overplay on an apparent passing down.

Too Much Cleveland Browns

Combining all of their coach's innovations, his acquisition of talent, and the precision of his system, the Browns nearly were unstoppable. They had a 47-4-3 record in four AAFC seasons. In 1947, they trailed the Yankees 28-0 at halftime and came back to gain a 28-28 tie. Branch Rickey, then president of baseball's Brooklyn Dodgers, suggested football

schedules could mirror some of baseball's methods by including more than one game a week. In 1948, the Browns defeated the Yankees in New York City, then flew to Los Angeles and defeated the Dons four days later on Thanksgiving Day. Then, with a division title at stake against the 49ers, they had to play in San Francisco three days later – their third game in a week.

Graham injured his ankle against the Dons and was not expected to play against the 49ers. Several other players were badly bruised from two games in four days. So Brown canceled practice in San Francisco and had his team take hot mineral baths for the next two days. Graham said he would give his injured ankle a try, and then played the entire game, leading the Browns to the division title.

The continued domination of the Browns and the economic pressures took a toll on the AAFC. So did a lack of consistent leadership at the top. Bert Bell, who never once called the AAFC anything other than "the other league," marshaled the NFL owners and kept them together through tough times. The All-America Football Conference, on the other hand, had three commissioners in four seasons. Its biggest job seemed to be patching and filling the rosters of teams that were poorly managed. While the AAFC had consistently outdrawn the NFL during the first three years of its existence, hope of ever beating the Browns dimmed in the other cities. Fans began to give up. They even began to stay away in Cleveland,

Los Angeles Dons halfback George Taliaferro runs behind teammates Art Hodgers (75) and Knox Ramsey (32) in a 1949 game against the San Francisco 49ers.

where crowds of 60,000 to 80,000 slipped to 20,000 and 30,000. In New York, four teams – two in each league – simply couldn't prosper. In Chicago, ownership problems compounded the competition with the Bears and Cardinals and crippled that franchise. The Los Angeles Dons were kept alive by Lindheimer's endless bankroll (he also helped support Chicago) until illness forced his withdrawal from day-to-day business. San Francisco and Buffalo had begun to prosper as their teams improved, but Baltimore barely hung on.

Moreover, salaries had continued to escalate – on both sides – and in 1949 merger talks began. The talks resulted in the NFL's acquiring the Browns, 49ers, and, reluctantly, the Colts. The players of the other teams were placed in special allocation drafts held among the NFL teams and the AAFC survivors. Two days after the resolution, the AAFC played its final title game. Cleveland defeated Buffalo, whose owner, Jim Brueil, then became a 25 per cent owner of the Browns.

The New-look NFL

Bell was ecstatic. The NFL now had the strongest product in its history. It consisted of the six-team American Conference, comprised of five NFL clubs plus the Browns; and a seven-team National Conference, which included the 49ers, Colts and New York Yanks. The latter was an amalgam of the AAFC's Yankees (the new Yanks divided that team's players with the Giants), the New York Bulldogs (nee Boston Yanks) of the NFL, a team disbanded after the 1949 season; and players from the AAFC allocation draft.

The final structure wasn't what Arch Ward originally had had in mind, but the NFL maintained its own distinctive format. While the NFL had been busy waging a war of survival with its rival league, it also had grown on its own. Two long-dormant franchises, the Eagles and Cardinals, became the two strongest teams during the second half of the forties, and split a pair of title games against each other. The Cardinals – under veteran coach Jimmy Conzleman and led by the "Dream Backfield" of Paul Christman, Elmer Angsman, Pat Harder and All-America Charlie Trippi – won the 1947 Western Division title. The Eagles, under head coach Earl (Greasy) Neale, had the game's finest runner in Steve Van Buren and a powerful T-formation attack. They beat the Pittsburgh Steelers, whose coach Jock Sutherland had designed a complex single-wing offense – in a playoff for the division title. But in the NFL Championship Game in Chicago, the Cardinals defeated the Eagles 28-21. In a return match in 1948, the Eagles beat the Cardinals 7-0 on a snow-covered field in Philadelphia, on Van Buren's fourth-quarter touchdown.

A year later, in 1949, Rams head coach Clark Shaughnessy had two talented quarterbacks, Bob Waterfield and rookie Norm Van Brocklin. He also had three outstanding receivers in Hirsch, Bob Shaw, and Tom Fears, who led the league with a record 77 passes. In the 1949 championship game, the final game of the old NFL format, a drenching rain limited Shaughnessy's attack to the ground. Van Buren slogged through the mud for a record 196 yards on 31 carries and helped Philadelphia to its second straight NFL title in a 14-0 victory.

Browns Dominate the NFL

All of the claims and counter-claims about which league and which teams were best could now be settled. Bell scheduled the AAFC champion Browns to play in Philadelphia against the NFL champion Eagles on the night before the rest of the NFL began its 1950 schedule. In Bell's mind, it truly was a "game of the half century" – two of the greatest pro teams in history in a game to decide of "bragging rights." The Browns had remade much of their 1950 team from the AAFC allocation draft without suffering a loss of efficiency. They had the psychological (if not physical) advantage because they and the AAFC had received little respect except from their most ardent followers. Eagles coach Neale didn't help his cause when he compared the Browns to a basketball team "because all they do is throw the ball." He also was at a disadvantage because his starting backs, Van Buren and Bosh Pritchard, had been injured in the College All-Star Game and couldn't play. Still, the Eagles had other good runners and a fine passing game, with Tommy Thompson, a one-eyed quarterback, and receivers Pete Pihos and Jack Ferrante. Pihos later led the NFL in receiving for three seasons en route to the Hall of Fame. Neale also had the "Eagle Defense," which featured a five-man line: two ends often checked receivers at the line of scrimmage or dropped off on pass defense with the four backs, while the two linebackers supporting the linemen.

This was expected to disrupt the Browns' well-timed pass offense, but Cleveland totally dominated the NFL champions in a 35-10 victory before more than 70,000 fans. Brown called it the most emotional

game he ever coached because his players were eager to answer the taunts of four years. The Browns returned the opening kickoff for a touchdown, every Eagles player was knocked down, but a penalty nullified the play. Soon, though, Graham riddled the Eagles secondary with his passes and Brown neutralized the Eagle Defense by gradually spreading the gaps between his offensive lineman after every play until Philadelphia's defensive giants, linebacker Alex Wojciechowicz, and all-pro middle guard Bucko Kilroy, suddenly found themselves isolated and being pinballed by blocking linemen. Motley led a ground game that produced 21 second-half points. "We just wanted to show them we could run the ball better than they could," Graham said afterward.

The Giants were the only team that gave the Browns trouble in their first NFL season. New York coach Steve Owen came up with what he called an "Umbrella Defense" to stifle Cleveland's passing attack. On the first day of preparation for his team's first game against Cleveland, Owen drew a rough outline of his Umbrella concept on the blackboard,

then tossed the chalk to a young defensive back named Tom Landry, who had played against the Browns for one season with the AAFC Yankees. "You figure out how to get it done," Owen told Landry.

The Browns lost their only two games that season to the Giants, and the teams tied for the conference title. In a playoff in Cleveland, Lou Groza kicked two field goals and the defense added a safety but the game's biggest play came when Willis caught the Giants' Choo-Choo Roberts from behind at Cleveland's four-yard line to preserve an 8-3 victory and an American Conference title. In the National Conference, Los Angeles and Chicago also finished in a tie – the only time in NFL history that both conference titles were decided by a tie-breaking playoff. The Rams defeated the Bears 24-14, and returned to Cleveland five years after winning the NFL title there.

The Rams jumped to a 7-0 lead on the game's first play when Waterfield threw an 82-yard touchdown pass to Glenn Davis. It was just the start of a sensational game for Waterfield, who completed 18 of

Above: Van Buren and Philadelphia head coach Greasy Neale are surrounded by smiling Eagles players after their 7-0 win over the Chicago Cardinals in the 1948 NFL Championship Game. The Cardinals had defeated the Eagles for the title in 1947.

Right: Cleveland Browns ends Mac Speedie (left) and Dante Lavelli were a pair of dangerous receivers in the late forties and early fifties.

22 passes for 312 yards. Graham responded. In 18 minutes the teams scored four touchdowns. The Browns missed an extra point during that sequence, but they went ahead 20-14 in the third quarter on Graham's touchdown pass to Dante Lavelli. The Rams then scored twice within 25 seconds for a 28-20 lead. But Graham, who completed 22 passes for 298 yards and ran for 98 more yards in the game, hooked up with Lavelli for five straight completions en route to a touchdown that still left Cleveland trailing 28-27. On the next possession, though, Graham fumbled in Rams territory. The Browns held firm, and regained possession at their own 32-yard line with less than two minutes to play. Graham ran for 14 yards, then completed three straight passes to the Rams' 11-yard line, all in 82 seconds. Lou Groza, nicknamed "The Toe," calmly kicked a 16-yard field goal with 28 seconds to play for a 30-28 victory. The team from "the other league" had won an NFL championship in its first year. More important, it had established a new standard of excellence for professional football.

Top: Lou (The Toe) Groza not only was a great kicker (1,349 points in his career), but also was an excellent offensive tackle who was selected all-pro six times.

Left: Browns quarterback Otto Graham (60) wore sneakers on the frozen field at Cleveland Stadium in the 1950 NFL Championship Game. Lou Groza's 16-yard field goal with 28 seconds to play lifted the Browns to a 30-28 victory in their first season in the NFL.

Pro Football, Hollywood Style

The following year in Los Angeles, the two teams met again for the title. This time the Rams won 24-17 on another dramatic play 73-yard fourth-quarter touchdown pass from Norm Van Brocklin to Tom Fears. Van Brocklin had just replaced Waterfield at quarterback. The Rams were a team ideally suited to the expanding area of southern California. Their wide-open, exciting style of football, always played in ideal conditions, fit so neatly with the aura of nearby Hollywood. Scores of show business personalities, who understood best of all the team's great entertainment value, turned out to support the Rams. In turn, Rams players became part of the entertainment scene. Elroy Hirsch, for example, starred in a movie about his life called, "Crazylegs." And Waterfield married screen actress Jane Russell.

Waterfield was the consummate player. He ran, passed, kicked extra points, punted, played defense, and even kicked off. He was cool and quiet and unquestionably the Rams' leader. Van Brocklin, the Dutchman, was just the opposite in temperament – outgoing and gregarious in calm times, but often defiant and challenging on the field. He was no less a team player, though not as athletically gifted as Waterfield. But he still was the game's best passer at that time, accurate and capable of piling up yardage, as he did in one game against the Yanks when he passed for 554 yards, still an NFL record. Waterfield and Van Brocklin finished 1-2 among the NFL's passers in 1951. The Dutchman would have been No. 1 had not coach Joe Stydahar benched him late in the season for refusing to run a play he had sent into the game. The Rams' supporting cast was equally capable. There were two different backfields. One was the "Bull Elephant Backfield": 225-pound Deacon Dan Towler, 220-pound Paul (Tank) Younger, and Dick Hoerner. Each averaged more than six yards a carry. When the Rams wanted a speed game, in came their "Pony Backfield" – former Army Heisman Trophy winner Glenn Davis, Tom Kalminir, and Verda (Vitamin T.) Smith. Add receivers Hirsch, Fears, and Bobby Boyd, and it was no wonder the team averaged more than 32 points a game in 1951.

Even with all of this offense, the Rams were an enigma throughout the first half of the fifties with quarterback controversies and coaching battles. The Waterfield-Van Brocklin controversy was settled

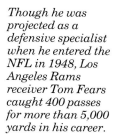

Though he was projected as a defensive specialist when he entered the NFL in 1948, Los Angeles Rams receiver Tom Fears caught 400 passes for more than 5,000 yards in his career.

when Waterfield retired after the 1952 season. A coaching flap between Stydahar and his assistant Hampton Pool, early in the 1952 season, saw the Rams off to a stumbling start. Stydahar was fired and Pool became head coach, leading his team to eight straight victories. But the Rams lost a conference playoff game to the Detroit Lions. Van Brocklin had the quarterback job to himself in 1953 until Bill Wade came along a year later. The quarterback controversy boiled again. Pool was gone after the 1954 season, replaced by little-known Sid Gillman, who had been head coach at the University of Cincinnati. The team won the conference championship in 1955. In the NFL Championship Game, before a record crowd of 85,693 at the Los Angeles Coliseum, the Rams yielded seven interceptions to the Cleveland Browns — six of them thrown by Van Brocklin — and lost 38-14.

The NFL's Blue Collar Team

The team that dogged the Rams, the Detroit Lions, was just the opposite of flashy and glitzy — a blue-collar outfit coached by Buddy Parker. The Lions featured quarterback Bobby Layne, who was as hardnosed as he was talented. Layne already had played with little success for the Bears and New York Yanks. In Detroit, he not only became the focal point of his team's offense — one season he led it in rushing and passing — but set the tone off the field for a diverse group of players. Most of them, like Layne, were not especially talented. Yet each seemed to make the right play at the right time. The Lions had two Heisman Trophy winners, Doak Walker from SMU, who won the NFL scoring title in 1950, and Leon Hart, a giant tight end from Notre Dame who often lined up as a fullback in short-yardage situations and simply plowed over tacklers. The key to the team's success was the NFL's best secondary: future Hall of Famers Jack Christiansen and Yale Lary, joined by Jim David and Bob Smith. Parker later acquired two other Hall of Fame defenders, cornerback Dick (Night Train) Lane and linebacker Joe Schmidt. After the Lions beat the Rams in the 1952 National Conference playoff, they were decided underdogs against the Browns in the NFL Championship Game. But Walker's 67-yard touchdown run late in the game helped them to a 17-7 victory and the team's first NFL title since 1935. Layne led Detroit to a 10-2 record in 1953, and the Lions defeated Cleveland

Top left: Elroy Hirsch (40) got the nickname "Crazylegs" because of his unusual running style. The acrobatic receiver teamed up with Tom Fears to form a record-setting receiving duo for Rams quarterbacks Bob Waterfield and Norm Van Brocklin.

Bottom left: In his first year at the helm, Sid Gillman coached the Rams to the Western Division title.

Below: Norm Van Brocklin led the NFL in passing three times and in punting twice. In 1951, he passed for a record 554 yards against the New York Yanks.

again for the NFL title on a late, game-winning touchdown pass from Layne to end Jim Doran. Just when it seemed that Cleveland finally had met a team it could not handle, the Browns beat Detroit 56-10 for the 1954 title.

Coach Parker was as enigmatic as his quarterback. He battled to get a two-year contract with the Lions, and when it finally was agreed to, he pulled a switch. At a "Meet the Lions" civic dinner only two days before the team's first pre-season game in 1957, Parker announced his resignation. He later spent eight seasons as head coach of the Pittsburgh Steelers. George Wilson, his assistant in Detroit, was named Lions head coach. Wilson made two important acquisitions – quarterback Tobin Rote from Green Bay, who took over when Layne broke his ankle, and future Hall of Fame running back John Henry Johnson, a fiery player who absolutely resented anyone attempting to even tackle him, and often fought to prove his point.

Rote and Johnson combined to help Detroit to the 1957 championship, but only after defeating the San Francisco 49ers 31-27 in a conference playoff game that still is recognized as one of the greatest comeback victories in NFL history. The 49ers of those

Above: Detroit head coach Buddy Parker gets a victory ride after his Lions defeated Cleveland 17-16 in the 1953 NFL Championship Game.

Right: After acquiring quarterback Bobby Layne in a trade in 1950, the Lions signed Heisman Trophy winners Leon Hart (82) and Doak Walker. Walker led the NFL in scoring that season with 128 points.

years were known for their offense, had a great offensive team, led by quarterback Y.A. Tittle, receivers Billy Wilson and R.C. Owens, and two eventual Hall of Fame backs, Joe Perry and Hugh McElhenny. Nicknamed "The King," McElhenny befuddled opponents with his broken-field running, often covering 40 or 50 yards to gain 20. Wilson had won his second straight pass catching title in 1957 (he finished second in 1954-55). Owens, a 6-foot, 5-inch rookie, developed an "Alley Oop" move with Tittle. He ran to a point in the end zone where Y.A.'s high-arc pass would come down, then outleaped the defenders to catch it.

In the 1957 playoff game at San Francisco's Kezar Stadium, the 49ers led 24-7 at halftime, as Tittle threw three touchdown passes. But the teams' dressing rooms were adjacent to each other at Kezar, and the walls were thin. During the halftime break, the Lions could hear the 49ers prematurely celebrating a win. The Detroit players were infuriated. Shortly after the second half began, McElhenny put on his greatest running feat of the day, with a 71-yard run. Films showed that he ran more than 200 yards, cutting across the field to avoid tacklers. He didn't make it to the end zone. Lary managed to catch him,

and the Lions held, and the 49ers settled for a field goal and a 27-7 lead. From that point, the 49ers tried to protect rather than increase their lead. The Lions scored 24 straight points in just 21 minutes for the victory. A week later, the Lions romped past the Browns 59-14 for their third NFL title of the decade. Rote threw four touchdown passes.

Another Great Brown Named Brown

The Cleveland team that lost the 1957 title game to the Lions was a rebuilt version. With the exception of Groza, the veterans who had carried the Browns from the All-America Football Conference to NFL dominance all had retired. Their last moments of glory came in a smashing 56-10 victory over Detroit in the 1954 title game, after the Lions had defeated them 14-10 the week before. The Browns players had begun to grumble about Detroit's domination, and their dissatisfaction with Paul Brown's game plan. They had agreed beforehand that if things weren't going well early in the championship game, they would call their own plays. There was no need for that, because Graham threw three touchdown

San Francisco's Joe (The Jet) Perry (with ball) was a member of the 49ers' "Million Dollar Backfield," which also included quarterback Y.A. Tittle, and running backs Hugh McElhenny, and John Henry Johnson.

passes and scored three others, then announced his retirement.

In 1955, Paul Brown sought to replace Graham in training camp. But the coach wasn't satisfied with the heirs apparent, so he persuaded Graham to play one more season. Graham finished with a second NFL title, the 38-14 victory over the Rams before a record crowd at the Los Angeles Coliseum and a nationwide television audience. A major network (NBC) televised the NFL Championship Game for the first time ever, having paid $100,000 for the rights. Graham passed for two touchdowns and ran for two others. As he trotted off the field for the last time, the Rams partisans gave him a standing ovation. Brown walked over to the man he still considers the greatest quarterback in pro football history and simply said, "Thank you." In 1957, the Browns drafted fullback Jim Brown, a new star who would stamp a special style on pro football for all time. Brown was then, as now, a brooding, moody man who kept to himself as a young player. He had been an All-America in football and lacrosse at Syracuse University, and had played varsity basketball and won the school's boxing title as well. He stood 6 feet, 2 inches and weighed 220 pounds. He could run in and out of a pile of players, but no one ever quite figured out how. Sometimes his tremendous power just burst a pile of defenders. Other times, when tacklers grabbed him, he gave a "limp leg" as if he were going down. The instant he felt their grip relax, he exploded and zoomed away. A halfback in fullback's clothing, he was more powerful than any of the game's bigger fullbacks. Yet he combined near-world-class speed with great open field running ability. He rarely was caught from behind. Brown never was popular with his teammates and resented his coach's iron-clad authority, but he never gave less than his best on Sunday, often carrying the ball 25 or 30 times while absorbing ferocious punishment. He rarely spoke on the field, even after the most violent collisions or less-than-legal tackling. He often got off the ground as if he could hardly walk, only to run for a huge gain on the next play.

When he retired after the 1965 season, he had set an all-time rushing record of 12,312 yards in nine seasons. It took Chicago's Walter Payton 13 years to break the record. Two other still-existing marks: Brown led the NFL in rushing eight seasons, five of them consecutive, and he finished with an average of 5.2 yards per carry.

Brown's running style forced a change in the way defense was played in the NFL. In 1956, Tom Landry, the New York Giants defensive back who devised the mechanics of the Umbrella Defense, had come up with another strategic innovation: the 4-3 defense. But Landry had to fine tune it in 1958, specifically to cope with Brown, whom the Giants faced twice each season. The 4-3 was designed primarily to shut down a running game by controlling the eight gaps along the line of scrimmage where plays are run, then to send four big, mobile linemen after the quarterback before he could throw the ball.

The Browns' offensive line always did a fine job of opening up holes for fullback Jim Brown (32). Here, guards Gene Hickerson (66) and John Wooten (60) pull on a sweep for the man whose running style changed the way defense was played in the NFL.

The Name of the Game Became Defense

In 1956, the year before Jim Brown came to Cleveland, the Giants acquired future Hall of Famer Andy Robustelli, a perennial all-pro defensive end from the Rams. They got tackle Dick Modzelewski in a trade with Washington. The two joined two draftees – Roosevelt Grier, a 6-4, 285-pound defensive tackle, and end Jim Katcavage. Robustelli brought leadership to the young Giants. He was quick and aggressive player and led the team in quarterback sacks in most of the nine seasons he played in New York.

The Giants also added middle linebacker Sam Huff, who almost was cut in training camp as a rookie offensive lineman before he got one last chance at

linebacker. Huff became the national symbol of the Giants defense when he was the subject of a half-hour, prime-time network show, "The Violent World of Sam Huff." During a game, he was wired with a microphone. The turbulent sounds of the game were matched with pictures of smashing tackles, crunching blocks, and head-on collisions. The black-and-white-television screens of the nation for the first time conveyed pro football from a player's perspective. Huff made the cover of Time magazine. The Giants' defensive unit played a major role in the team's winning the 1956 NFL championship. Chants of "DEEEEEE-FENSE" cascaded through Yankee Stadium, the team's new home venue. The Giants' defense made goal-line stands and sacked quarterbacks with regularity. Thousands of fans each Sunday paid more attention to defensive play. They never had seen it with such ferocity. For the first time

in the sport's history, a defensive unit heard most of the cheers. An inter-team rivalry evolved. During a game in which the Giants' offense was doing little and the defense had scored the only points, the two units passed each other after the ball changed hands. One of the defensive players cracked to the offense, "Try to hold 'em,".

Pro Football, At Last The Nation's Game

The rivalry between the Browns and Giants, stemming back to 1950, triggered the surge of pro football's popularity. New Yorkers love good theatre, and dramatic tension needs a villain. The New York media gleefully portrayed Paul Brown's teams as cold, meticulous, unfeeling automatons and Brown himself as the cruel, stern-faced manipulator who called all the plays and never showed emotion. At precisely the time that Jim Brown appeared as an offensive force, the Giants had assembled their "DEEEE-FENSE". The media boiled it down to the Giants vs. Jim Brown.

As a rookie in 1957, Brown won the NFL rushing title. In 1958 he led the Browns to the brink of a second straight Eastern Division title. In the final game of the season, Cleveland needed a victory for the outright division championship and New York needed to win to tie for the lead and force a playoff. The game was held at Yankee Stadium. On the game's first play, Jim Brown ran 65 yards for a

Left: *Jim Katcavage*

Below: *The television special "The Violent World of Sam Huff" helped Huff (70) and other defensive players gain the public notoriety that was usually accorded only to offensive players.*

Right: *Pittsburgh Steelers coach Chuck Noll began his playing career as a guard with the Cleveland Browns in 1953. The team shifted him to linebacker in 1955.*

Centre: *Excellent personnel moves, like the drafting of fullback Alan (The Horse) Ameche (35) and the signing of former semi-pro quarterback John Unitas (19), helped Weeb Ewbank transform the Baltimore Colts into title contenders.*

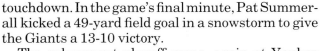

touchdown. In the game's final minute, Pat Summerall kicked a 49-yard field goal in a snowstorm to give the Giants a 13-10 victory.

The subsequent playoff game, again at Yankee Stadium, was shown on national television. Millions saw the Giants hold Brown – who had set an NFL season rushing mark of 1,527 yards – to just 8 yards, also shutting down his supporting cast, to win the championship 10-0.

The Baltimore Colts and Johnny Unitas

The 1958 NFL Championship Game involved a newcomer – the Baltimore Colts. This team was a product of the NFL's growing pains during the early fifties. The first Colts franchise had folded after the 1950 season, and the New York Yanks quit after 1951. The league then awarded Yanks' spot to Dallas. It was named the Texans, and it failed, too. The league took control of the team before midseason, and at the end of the year canceled the franchise – the last time any NFL team failed.

In 1953, commissioner Bert Bell answered Baltimore's plea to return to the NFL by promising a franchise if it could sell 15,000 season tickets. That took a month, and the Colts were reborn with Bell guiding all the moves. First, he approved a group headed by Carroll Rosenbloom, a long-time friend who had played football at Penn when Bell was an assistant coach there. Next, the club hired Don

Kellett, a former Penn coach and friend, as the team's general manager. Former Dallas players, including future Hall of Famers Gino Marchetti and Art Donovan, became key players on the Colts' defensive teams.

A year later, Rosenbloom signed head coach Weeb Ewbank, who had been an assistant coach at Cleveland. Ewbank began building the Colts by drafting fullback Alan (The Horse) Ameche, halfback Lenny Moore, tackle Jim Parker, and a near-sighted, short-legged end named Raymond Berry. But his most important act cost him less than a dollar: a phone call to a sandlot semi-pro quarterback, of Lithuanian descent, in Pittsburgh who had played at the University of Louisville before being cut by the Steelers in 1955.

Johnny Unitas came to the Colts sporting a crew cut, the toughness of a Marine drill sergeant, and a desire to excel. Unitas always was in command. He didn't have the strongest arm in the game, and he wasn't a fancy runner. But his passes went to receivers with bull's-eye accuracy and he ran well and often enough to worry every defense. He also had daring. Perhaps his greatest attribute was his ability to turn games apparently lost into last-second victories. No game ever was considered lost as long as Unitas still was on the field. It didn't take long for an aura of invincibility to build around him and to rub off on his teammates. For most of the next 18 seasons, he set the standards by which all quarterbacks are measured.

Left: Art Donovan

The Greatest Game Ever Played

Ewbank promised Rosenbloom he would build a champion within five years, and the Sunday after Christmas in 1958, he brought his team to Yankee Stadium prepared to meet that deadline. By now, the drama of the Browns and Giants had piqued the country's imagination and millions tuned in for the sequel. The 1958 NFL Championship Game, still called "The Greatest Game Ever Played," was no technical masterpiece. The Giants fumbled and bumbled themselves to a 14-3 halftime deficit. It looked as if the physical and emotional strain of their two games with the Browns had at last taken a toll. Early in the second half, though, New York's defense turned matters around with a goal line stand that prevented the Colts from scoring a critical touchdown at that point of the game, one that would have put Baltimore ahead 21-3.

Instead, the defense's heroics seemed to energize New York's offense. On a third-and-two situation, quarterback Charley Conerly passed to end Kyle Rote at Baltimore's 40-yard line. As he was being tackled, Rote fumbled. Halfback Alex Webster of the Giants, scooped up the bouncing ball and ran to the Colts' one-yard line. The Giants scored on the next play, and on their next series, they took a 17-14 lead as Conerly passed 15 yards to Frank Gifford for a touchdown. The Giants' defense shut down Unitas and the Colts until two minutes remained. Baltimore got the ball one last time, 86 yards from the Giants'

end zone. In the next 113 seconds, Unitas drove the Colts within field goal range. With seven seconds to play, Steve Myrha kicked a 20-yarder that tied the score 17-17.

For the first time in NFL history, a game that counted was played in "sudden death" overtime: the first team to score would win. The Giants had first possession but couldn't move. Unitas took over, methodically taking his team down the field against the NFL's best defensive unit. The Colts mixed big runs by Ameche with Unitas's passes to Berry at key times. Finally, from the one-yard line, Ameche ran off right tackle with 8 minutes and 15 seconds of that overtime period expired, giving Baltimore a 23-17 victory and the NFL title.

In 1959, the Colts repeated as champions, again defeating the Giants in a game not nearly as dramatic (though Unitas again brought his team from behind in the fourth quarter to win). But then, what could top "The Greatest Game Ever Played"? On that December Sunday afternoon in 1958, an entire nation had watched the drama that raised professional football to heights of public acclaim and acceptance.

The 1958 Giants-Colts game opened the way to prosperity from television revenues. Millions had witnessed for the first time the ideal marriage of pro football and TV. No one, including commissioner Bert Bell, understood the impact the medium could have on the game until that afternoon–although Bell had laid some of the necessary foundations. In 1956,

CBS had televised selected games into specific market areas. The Redskins, for example, were seen throughout the South. The Browns had large areas of the midwest, and in the early fifties had extended their coverage throughout New England before the Giants became popular and blanketed that area and most of New York state. Mindful of the need to fill stadiums, Bell convinced the owners not to allow any of their home games to be televised by stations within 75 miles of the stadium site. Even those three season-ending Giants games were blacked out in New York City. A newspaper strike prevented New Yorkers from even reading about the Colts game. Thousands of people drove to Connecticut and southern New Jersey, where the game was available from other cities. During the early part of the sixties, when the Giants still had powerful teams, the exodus to Connecticut to watch home games was just as great. Motels close to New York state had special rates, sold hot dogs and soft drinks, and even staged halftime shows, complete with marching bands, to give their patrons a taste of "the real thing". The total blackout rule stayed in effect until 1973, and home games now are televised only if the team's stadium is sold out 72 hours before kickoff.

It wasn't until the American Football League came into existence in 1960 that one network was allowed to televise all the games of one league. In 1962, the NFL followed the AFL's lead. Television revenues soon began to escalate – $615,000 from NBC to televise the 1961 NFL title game; $14.1 million from CBS for all NFL regular season games, and an additional $1.8 million for the title game, in 1964, $18.8 million from CBS for all regular season and playoff games in 1965; and $2 million for the NFL title game in 1966. Nearly a quarter-century later, television revenues now are close to a billion dollars a season. How powerful was this medium? In 1968, the New York Jets were playing an exciting game against the Oakland Raiders. NBC carried the telecast nationwide. However, the game's fourth quarter overlapped the network's scheduled start of the children's movie Heidi. NBC went to the movie. Within minutes, the volume of calls from irate viewers jammed the network's New York switchboard. Heidi continued, and at a poignant moment in the story, NBC irritated many of its filmwatchers by superimposing the news of the Raiders' come-from-behind 43-32 victory. Never again was a game cut off until it had finished.

Right: New York Giants kicker Pat Summerall's 49-yard field goal sails through the uprights with less than a minute to play and gives his team a 13-10 victory over the Cleveland Browns in the final regular season game of 1958. The win enabled the Giants to tie Cleveland for first place in the Eastern Conference.

Opposite top: In what many consider "The Greatest Game Ever Played," Baltimore's Alan Ameche gets a good block from halfback Lenny Moore (24) and bulls his way to score the winning touchdown in the 1958 NFL Championship Game.

Opposite bottom: Defensive tackle Gene (Big Daddy) Lipscomb (76) anchored a strong Baltimore pass rush.

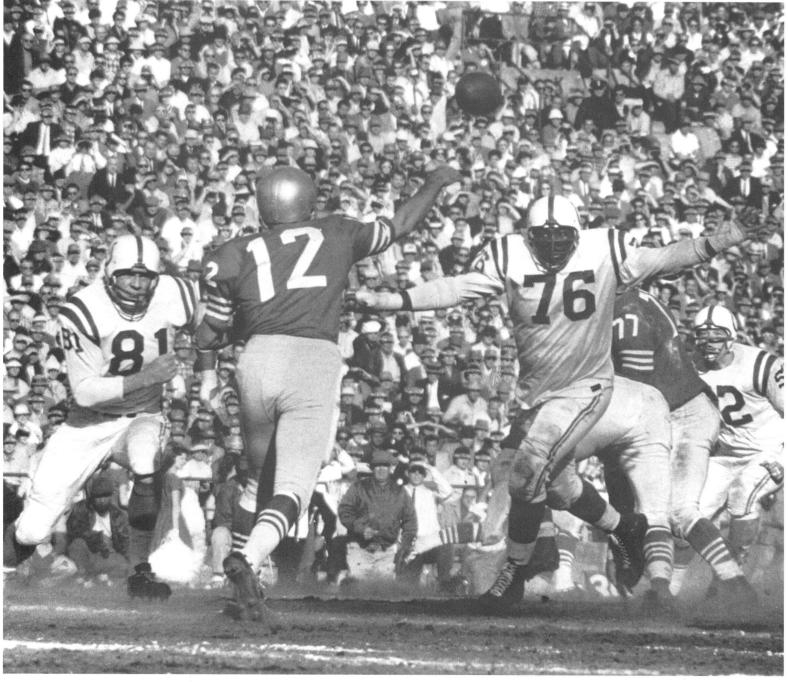

Pete Rozelle Gets The Call

Bert Bell died in 1959 while watching his two favorite teams, the Eagles and Steelers, play each other at Philadelphia's Franklin Field. Ironically, he was planning to abdicate the job as commissioner and become owner of the Eagles, returning to the roots that brought him into the game. Bell felt that he had carried the game as far as he could, and that it was time to turn over direction to younger people, who better understood the changes beginning to confront pro football.

The NFL owners elected Pete Rozelle, the 33-year old general manager of the Rams, as Bell's replacement a few months later. For the next three decades, Rozelle led the league through the most dramatic, and at times most difficult, period of its existence. Under his guidance, the NFL not only survived three serious challenges by rival leagues, more than doubled its size, and reached an all-time high as a saleable product. When Rozelle became commissioner, the league was averaging nearly 47,000 spectators per game. When he retired during 1989, the average was up to 65,500, to a season total exceeding 17 million for its exhibition, regular, and post-season games. Rozelle expanded and improved the television policies established by Bell. The Super Bowl became the single biggest one-day sports event in the nation, and now is an international event. NFL teams now play preseason games in the Far East, the United Kingdom, and Europe. Each week during the season, a number of foreign countries receive live NFL telecasts. Rozelle also established entities within the league that helped broaden its base of appeal, such as NFL Films, NFL Properties, and NFL Charities. The key to Rozelle's success lay in his

ability to bend the league's owners to his will, by persuasion when possible, by stern action if necessary. It helped that the game prospered under his direction. He also dealt successfully with thorny problems, such as suspending for a year Packers star running back Paul Hornung and Lions defensive lineman Alex Karras, after they admitted that they had bet on NFL games. And to his disappointment, Rozelle fought some losing battles in trying to keep teams from moving without league approval.

Lombardi Brings Back the Pack

In 1960, few foresaw the NFL's growth, or the challenges it would create. Instead, most eyes focused on the revival of an old team, the Green Bay Packers. Their relatively unknown coach, Vince Lombardi, had been the right guard on Fordham's famed line, the Seven Blocks of Granite in 1936. He had been the Giants offensive coach from 1954-58, and before that a five-year assistant at West Point under Earl (Red) Blaik. The Packers had gone 11 years without a winning record, and had won only one game in 1958.

Lombardi changed that with his fiery, demanding, intimidating style that could bully or coax with equal effectiveness. He was forceful and emotional, often bellowing across the field in a deep, rough voice, or bellowing point-blank into the face of a player twice his size. Players who did not respond to his ways, were cut or traded. Those who did respond stayed and became proud champions. Lombardi's theme was: "Winning isn't everything, but making the effort to win is the only thing." Like the man himself, Lombardi's football was strong, forceful, with few frills. He adopted the power of the single wing system he had learned at Fordham to his Pro-T system, and drilled his team so that it would pound an opponent into submission. His ground game featured the famed "Packers Sweep." The play went around either end. Linemen such as Forrest Gregg, Fuzzy Thurston, Jim Ringo, Bob Skoronski and Jerry Kramer mowed down potential tacklers to form an alley for a running back. Fullback Jim Taylor battered opposing defenses and battled tacklers who had the temerity to tackle him with equal zeal.

But it was Lombardi's ability to transform two players – quarterback Bart Starr and running back Paul Hornung – that keyed his team's offensive success. Hornung had won the 1956 Heisman Trophy at Notre Dame, but his professional career had been a mild disappointment. He occasionally had played quarterback for the Packers, alternating with Starr. Lombardi made an instant decision. Hornung would make it as a running back, or he was gone. Starr would stop being a jittery, insecure quarterback, or he, too, was gone.

Both succeeded. Starr, now a Hall of Famer, became one of the most effective passers in NFL history, a nearly mistake-free player who learned to absorb Lombardi's forceful ways. Hornung, for whom Lombardi had an almost fatherly affection,

87

was a renowned playboy off the field but an unselfish player who blocked, ran, and kicked. He also is a member of the Hall of Fame. The Packers won the Western Division title in 1960, Lombardi's second season, but lost the NFL title to the Philadelphia Eagles. Eagles quarterback Norm Van Brocklin finished his career with a superb championship season, helped by an inspirational performance by Hall of Famer Chuck Bednarik, who played both center and linebacker in nearly every game that year. Lombardi vowed that he would never lose another championship game again. In five more appearances, he didn't. The string began with the Packers' first NFL championship since 1934, a 31-0 victory over the Giants in 1961, and ended with Green Bay's victory in Super Bowl II over the Oakland Raiders at the end of the 1967 season.

Green Bay's defense mirrored the toughness of coach, shutting down a great Giants offensive team in both 1961 and 1962. Quarterback Y.A. Tittle had come to New York in the early sixties for four seasons of record-setting passing performances with receivers Del Shofner, Joe Walton, and Frank Gifford. With the continued excellence of their defense, the Giants won three more conference championships. The 1962 title game at Yankee Stadium was played in 31-degrees-below-zero wind chill conditions. Tittle's high tech offense was ineffective in the swirling winds and rock-hard field. In a hard-hitting contest, the Packers won 16-7 because, as one of them said afterward, "We were afraid to lose and have to face Lombardi afterward." Five years later, under strikingly similar conditions, the Packers defeated the Dallas Cowboys in the famous "Ice Bowl" game in Green Bay, where the actual temperature during the game was 13 below zero. The Packers won on their final offensive play, Starr's quarterback sneak for a touchdown, with just 13 seconds remaining.

After missing titles in 1963 (the Bears won and defeated the Giants in Chicago on another icy day) and 1964 (the revitalized Baltimore Colts, coached by Don Shula, were upset by the Browns in Cleveland) the Packers began their final run of glory in 1965, with a little bit of luck. They tied the Colts for the conference title and prepared for the playoff in

Green Bay. Baltimore had lost all of its quarterbacks to injuries, and was forced to use running back Tom Matte, who had been a quarterback at Ohio State, as its emergency signal-caller. Matte had the plays taped to his wrist for reference in the huddle. The playoff game was settled on a pair of field goals by Green Bay's Don Chandler. Films later showed that his first one had missed. (The uprights on NFL goal posts later were raised to their present height of 30 feet above the crossbar to help officials make correct judgements on high kicks.) Chandler's second field goal, came at 13:33 of overtime and gave Green Bay a 13-10 victory. The following week, on muddy Lambeau Field, Green Bay won the NFL championship 23-12 over the Cleveland Browns. Blanton Collier had replaced Paul Brown as the Browns' head coach. Following the 1962 season, Brown was fired in a dispute with the team's new owner, Art Modell. In the next two seasons, the Packers won two more titles, in Super Bowl I and II, after twice defeating the Dallas Cowboys for the NFL championship. In 1966, Tom Brown's end zone interception in the final seconds saved a 34-27 victory and paved the way for the Packers to represent the NFL in the first NFL-AFL Championship Game. Green Bay defeated the Kansas City Chiefs, 35-10. The Pack needed Starr's quarterback sneak in the "Ice Bowl" to win the NFL title the following year. Two weeks later in Lombardi's final game as Green Bay's head coach, they beat the Oakland Raiders 33-14 in Super Bowl II. After Lombardi, Green Bay struggled and won 10 games once only in the following 20 seasons.

The American Football League Forced Another Change

For most of the sixties, the NFL and the new American Football League battled for recognition, players, and a share of the ever-growing financial pie that the game was producing. The new league was formed in 1959 by Lamar Hunt, a wealthy Texas oilman who had unsuccessfully sought to purchase the Chicago Cardinals, in hopes of moving the team to Dallas. Turned away but never discouraged, Hunt decided to form his own league. In quick order, he got responses from such wealthy young entrepreneurs as oilman Bud Adams in Houston; Bob Howsam, a veteran baseball executive from Denver; Barron Hilton, whose family owned the nation's largest hotel chain; famed sportscaster Harry Wismer from New York; and Max Winter and Bill Boyer of Minneapolis.

Hunt's thinking was similar to Arch Ward's a quarter century earlier. He foresaw the AFL operating alongside the NFL, with an eventual competition to decide a champion. In August, 1959, the fourth American Football League was formed, with that nucleus of owners. Later additions included Billy Sullivan, heading a 10-man group from Boston, and Y.C. (Chet) Soda of Oakland, replacing the Winter-Boyer group after it had withdrawn to accept a franchise in the NFL.

In fact, when word spread of the serious new competitor, the NFL set its expansion wheels moving, first offering new franchises to Hunt in Dallas and Adams in Houston. The NFL then added

the twin cities of Minneapolis-St. Paul and Buffalo to its list.

Though tempted to cross over to the NFL, Hunt and Adams nonetheless kept their group intact. "The Foolish Club," as Chet Soda nicknamed them, began a war for the nation's pro football affection. The new league named Joe Foss, the governor of South Dakota and a much-decorated fighter pilot during World War II, as its commissioner, believing his image would be favorable for public acceptance. Foss then endeared himself to his owners by negotiating a five-year, $1.785 million contract with the American Broadcasting Company, to televise all of the league's games. It was a revolutionary deal because each team shared equally, ensuring some form of financial stability. With that move, the AFL did what the AAFC could not do –

winning over Boston in 1963, 51-10; the Houston Oilers went from a high school field, to 76,000-seat Rice Stadium to the Astrodome. The Patriots wound up playing in four Boston stadiums before finally settling into their permanent facility and renaming the franchise "New England" in 1971. There also was plenty of turmoil, including wide-open conflicts with the NFL to sign college players. The player war began in late 1959 when Rozelle, then general manager of the Rams, signed Heisman Trophy winner Billy Cannon of Louisiana State University to a contract in a Philadelphia hotel room, though the Tigers still had to play in the

Right: Houston won the first two AFL championships behind the passing of quarterback George Blanda (16) and the running of Heisman Trophy-winning halfback Billy Cannon (20).

Above: The AFL owners that made up the "Foolish Club." Standing (from left to right): William H. Sullivan Jr. (Boston Patriots), Calvin Kunz Jr. (Denver Broncos), Ralph Wilson Jr. (Buffalo Bills), Lamar Hunt (Dallas Texans), Harry Wismer (New York Titans), Wayne Valley (Oakland Raiders), and Barron Hilton (Los Angeles Chargers). Seated: K.S. (Bud) Adams (Houston Oilers) and AFL Commissioner Joe Foss.

lock in a precise revenue flow during its growth period. The league later added two other teams – the Miami Dolphins in 1966 and the Cincinnati Bengals, formed by Paul Brown, in 1967. By the time the Bengals were established, the AFL and NFL had agreed to merge.

The league began play in 1960, with early growing pains. The aesthetic lowlight was the vertical stripes on the stockings of the Denver Broncos. The strategic gaffe of gaffes: a memorable double overtime championship game in 1962 in which Abner Haynes, the captain of the Dallas Texans, won the toss to begin overtime and announced, "We'll kick to the clock," effectively forfeiting the hoped-for wind advantage, because Haynes's words asked for two choices. Houston found itself with the ball and a tailwind. But the Texans hung on to beat the Oilers 20-17 on rookie Tommy Brooker's field goal at 2:54 of the second overtime period.

Like any new league, the AFL also had plenty of movement. The Los Angeles Chargers moved to San Diego after the first season and became the league's only true dynasty, appearing in five of its first six championship games. The Chargers, named not for medieval steeds but after Barron Hilton's just-out Carte Blanche credit card, and

Sugar Bowl on New Year's Day. When that game ended, Houston signed him to an AFL contract, literally on the field, practically under the goal posts. A judge ruled the AFL contract valid, as was the case with two other celebrated collegians, Mississippi fullback Charlie Flowers and LSU halfback-safety Johnny Robinson, giving the AFL some immediate stars.

The player war sometimes was frantic, always expensive, finally reaching $25 million in 1965 for both leagues to sign their top players. The NFL started a group that "babysat" prospective high draft picks to keep them out of contact with the AFL.

Sometimes, the players and their escorts moved to three or four hotels in the same city in the same day. Inducements to sign always included big bonuses, and occasionally "extras" such as a honeymoon for one player, and a rear-window defroster on a new car for another. In 1962, Hunt pursued quarterback Roman Gabriel, his No. 1 draft pick. Finally getting an answer on the player's phone, Hunt laid out all of the contract's features, except the salary. The conversation somehow skirted that issue. The voice on the other end was not Gabriel's but that of Elroy Hirsch, the general manager of the Rams, who was about to sign the quarterback to a contract.

The AFL Succeeds Where Others Failed

The survival and eventual success of the American Football League settled on four events:

(1) Hunt reluctantly abandoned Dallas, where his Texans fought a losing battle with the NFL's new Cowboys for the same fans. He moved to Kansas City, where the Chiefs were an immediate success.

(2) Al Davis was hired as head coach and general manager of the Oakland Raiders in 1963 and turned the team into a winner. He stabilized the franchise, beginning by moving the team's home games out of San Francisco.

(3) The league sold the bankrupt New York franchise to David (Sonny) Werblin for $1 million. Within a year, Werblin had established the AFL's most successful operation in the nation's media center. He moved the Jets' home games into new Shea Stadium and drew record crowds. A year later, Werblin signed Alabama quarterback Joe Namath for a record $427,000 contract, and the AFL had public credibility.

(4) In 1965, the AFL signed a five-year, $36 million contract with NBC.

The league also developed its own stars, some of them "old" NFL names such as George Blanda, who led Houston to the league's first two championships by accounting for every point in both games on four touchdown passes, four extra points, and two field goals. Jack Kemp, who later became a Congressman, a presidential candidate, and a member of President George Bush's cabinet, was another NFL reject. But Kemp became the AFL's top passer and led Buffalo to two AFL championships. Carlton (Cookie) Gilchrist, who once sought a tryout with the Cleveland Browns when he was just 18 years old and later had a great career in the Canadian Football League, was the AFL's first 1,000-yard rusher, gaining 1,096 with Buffalo in 1962. Wide receiver Charley Hennigan caught 101 passes for Houston in 1963, the same year that the Patriots' Gino Cappelletti, a wide receiver and kicker who had been shooed away from NFL camps because he was too small and too slow, started toward the all-time AFL scoring lead with 113 points. Cappelletti added a record 155 the following season.

Below: The Oilers lured quarterback George Blanda (16) out of a one-year retirement in 1960, and he promptly directed Houston to two consecutive AFL titles. Blanda was voted the AFL's most valuable player in 1961, after he led the league in passing with 3,287 yards and a record 36 touchdown passes. He also kicked a record 55-yard field goal that season.

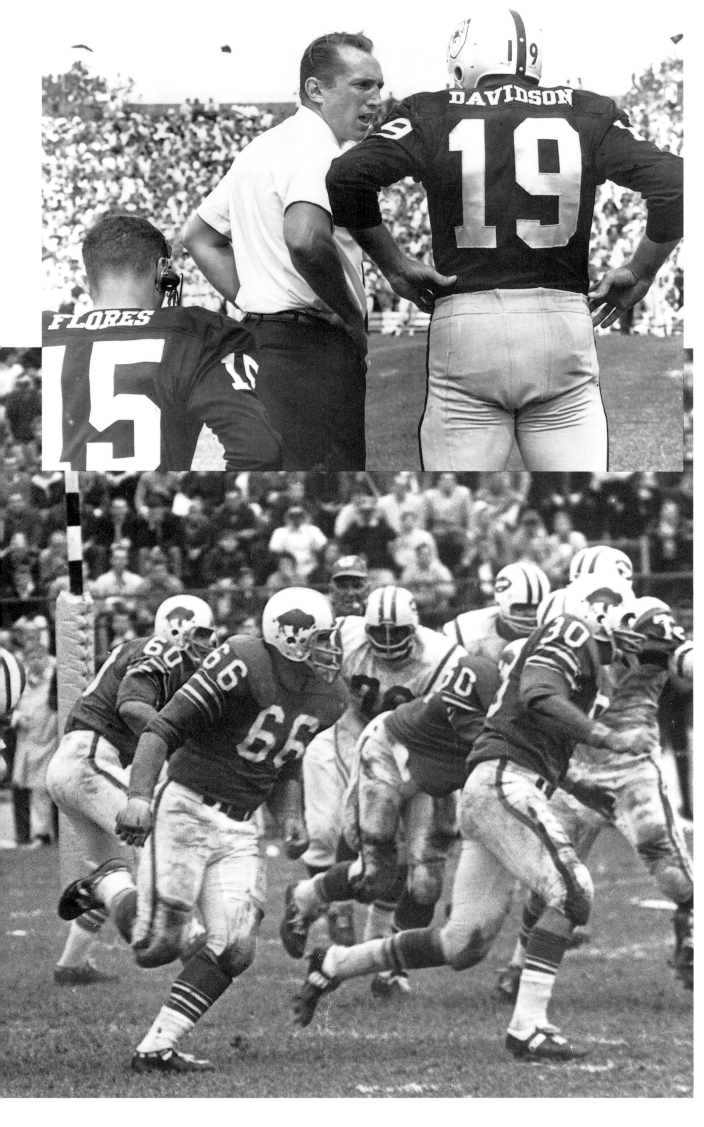

Top: *Oakland's hiring of Al Davis as their coach and general manager helped stabilize the AFL because he turned the team into winners and moved their home games out of San Francisco.*

Bottom: *Buffalo spent only a $100 waiver fee to acquire quarterback Jack Kemp (15) from San Diego. The current United States Congressman led the team to two AFL championships.*

catches, including two seasons when he caught 100 and 92. But there was no receiver in all of football better than Lance Alworth of the Chargers. Both Alworth and Maynard now are in the Hall of Fame. Alworth would glide almost effortlessly downfield, often leaping, ballet-like, to catch the ball. He caught at least one pass in 96 consecutive games until the league merged with the NFL. In each of his seven AFL seasons, he gained more than 1,000 yards.

While Blanda and Kemp were the early quarterback stars of the AFL, Joe Namath became its cult hero. He became "Broadway Joe" in New York City's fast lane. He didn't have movie star looks—his nose protruded and he walked slope-shouldered. Nor was he humble about his achievements. But Namath had the strongest arm in pro football, a quick release that allowed him to wait until the last possible second before throwing, and a knack for reading defenses. With receivers such as Maynard, George Sauer Jr. and Pete Lammons, and running game built around backs Emerson Boozer and Matt Snell, Namath finally brought the team to its first playoff in 1968.

For the Baltimore Colts, who had fired Jets coach Weeb Ewbank after the 1962 season and hired Don Shula, 1968 also was the greatest season in their existence — even without Unitas, who had torn his Achilles tendon. Prior to the season, they had acquired journeyman Earl Morrall. He was superb as the Colts rolled through the season with just one loss, and so dominated the Cleveland Browns in the NFL championship game that they became 18-

Above: San Diego Chargers wide receiver Lance Alworth (19) led the AFL in receiving three times (1966, 1968-69) and gained more than 1,000 yards receiving in each of his seven seasons in the league.

Right: In 1962, Buffalo Bills fullback Carlton (Cookie) Chilchrist (34) became the AFL's first 1,000-yard rusher, gaining 1,098 yards on 214 carries (5.1 avg.)

In the AFL, swift, experienced receivers such as Lance Alworth, Lionel Taylor and Don Maynard generally went against so-so defensive backs. Maynard gained over 10,000 yards during his 10 AFL seasons. Taylor led all receivers with 567

point favorites to beat the Jets in Super Bowl III.

New York had won its league championship game with Oakland, as Namath threw the winning touchdown pass to Maynard in the final minutes. Before the Super Bowl, Namath guaranteed victory. The Jets won 16-7.

The AFL's final season as an entity was 1969, and it once more proved that its best team – the Kansas City Chiefs – was as good as anything the NFL could offer. In Super Bowl IV, the Chiefs scored a 23-7 victory over the Minnesota Vikings, led by quarterback Joe Kapp, the NFL's most valuable player, and their famed Purple People Eaters defense. Chiefs quarterback Len Dawson, another NFL refugee, led an attack that his coach Hank Stram called "the offense of the seventies". It included Heisman Trophy winner Mike Garrett, a 1,000-yard rusher, and wide receiver Otis Taylor, who once climbed out of a motel window to escape his NFL "babysitters" and sign with the Chiefs. Stram had a group of "mini-backs" like Garrett who almost hid from the defense behind a huge offensive line until the play was well underway. The Chiefs' defense featured three future Hall of Famers – tackle Buck Buchanan and linebackers Willie Lanier and Bobby Bell.

That there was a Super Bowl at all was the result of merger talks that began back in 1965 and finally reached fruition about 18 months later. Carroll Rosenbloom, owner of the Baltimore Colts, and Ralph Wilson, who owned the AFL's Buffalo Bills but had been a part-owner of the Detroit Lions, actually laid down the points that eventually became part of the merger agreement. However, they did not resolve the thorny issue of indemnities the AFL would pay to the NFL. Those points formed the basis for talks that Tex Schramm, president of the Dallas Cowboys, and Hunt conducted for nearly a year, often meeting secretly in airport parking lots and hotels to avoid public word of any formal discussions.

The entire issue was pushed to a settlement when Pete Gogolak, pro football's first soccer-style kicker, who had played out his option with the AFL's Buffalo Bills, was signed by the New York Giants. This signalled to the AFL that it was open season on anyone who was in a similar situation. It also became the principal strategy that Al Davis brought to his brief reign as AFL commissioner. Davis began signing agreements with some of the NFL's top players, with bonuses already paid, to jump to his league when their contracts expired. Rather than see either their rosters depleted or salaries increased even more, the rival leagues finalized an agreement. Rozelle was named commissioner of a merged NFL. A world championship game, to be called the Super Bowl, was established. A combined player draft was organized. Two new franchises were added (New Orleans and Cincinnati). Inter-league pre-season play began. And the AFL paid an $18 million indemnity to the NFL over 20 years.

Almost 20 years after the All-America Football Conference had begun the post-war era with a challenge to pro football that helped its growth, the American Football League helped to broaden its popularity and reach more people than ever.

In the 1962 AFL Championship Game, the Dallas Texans (white) defeated the two-time champion Houston Oilers 20-17 in double overtime. The game was played before a record AFL championship crowd of 37,981 in Houston's Jeppesen Stadium.

Pro Football – The People's Sport

Below: Wide receiver Don Maynard, who was the first player to sign with the Jets (then known as the Titans) in 1960, was selected to the all-time AFL team in 1969.

Opposite: Paul Brown's desire to get back into pro football led him to Cincinnati, where he became the head coach and general manager of the expansion Bengals in 1968. Within three years, the Bengals won their first division title.

When the 1970 season began, the National Football League was realigned for the third time. It wasn't easy. The battle between the NFL and the American Football League had officially ended in 1966, but the feelings of league pride between the two groups of owners remained as strong as ever. AFL owners were feeling feisty following the stunning victory of their champions, the New York Jets, over Baltimore in Super Bowl III. They once had longed to become integrated within the 16-team NFL, but now there was a surge of feeling within their ranks to keep their league intact. The feeling was reciprocal among the NFL owners. They had the largest television markets, the common draft gave them 16 of the 26 picks in each round of the draft, and they knew they only could get stronger with more stars and more money than could the smaller AFL.

One man demurred. Paul Brown, who had returned to pro football in the American Football League when he founded the Cincinnati Bengals prior to the 1968 season, insisted that the original terms of the merger agreement be honored. He argued that his group had been assured that the fans who supported their team would see NFL teams every year. Further, he pointed out the folly of weakness which the AFL was advocating for itself—less money in smaller TV markets and fewer potential stars from a lesser draft. Thus began a

stalemate in both camps that lasted until the league's meeting in the spring, when Brown was able to convince his fellow AFL owners that they must demand equality. He then tossed out to the NFL owners, the possibility of testing the legality of the agreement in court. That threat stirred attention, though it took Commissioner Pete Rozelle's famed "lock up" to settle things. He locked the 26 owners in two meeting rooms at the NFL offices in New York City and kept them there until the issue was decided. The object was to design two 13-team entities. Neither group wanted to break up, and none of the NFL teams wanted to join the AFL group. For nearly 48 hours, each of the groups wrestled with the problem until Al Davis, the managing general partner of the Oakland Raiders, suggested that three NFL teams move to join the ten AFL teams and be compensated $3 million apiece. "It was like barracudas going after raw meat," one owner said later in describing the NFL teams' reaction to that proposal.

Three of the proudest, most respected NFL teams – Pittsburgh, Cleveland, and Baltimore – agreed to join the 10 AFL teams to form the American Football Conference. The problem seemed to be solved until Davis then turned around and vetoed the proposal – it required unanimous consent by all the AFL owners – until he was given veto power over the eventual realignment of the NFL. When another uproarious meeting ensued, Wayne Valley, the majority owner of the Raiders, then cast his team's vote for the new 13-13 split, negating Davis's veto threat, and the new structure of the NFL was in place: two 13-team conferences, with the same basic pre-merger structure with the exception of the three old NFL teams joined with the AFL. In 1976, the Seattle Seahawks and the Tampa Bay Buccaneers joined the NFC and AFC respectively, then switched conferences for good in 1977. While it took nearly four months to form the two entities, the thorniest problem was placing teams in their respective divisions. Always at issue were such elements as stadium size, TV market size, weather, historical rivalries, travel. The alignment question finally was resolved when Rozelle came up with five possible options, then asked his secretary, Thelma Elkjer, to pull one of them from a hat. The owners agreed beforehand that the one she selected would become official. That one still exists, though the formula for scheduling and deciding playoff slots has been changed.

As it turned out, the decision to divide the league evenly ensured a competitive balance. Since the merger, teams from the old NFL have won 15 championships in this new format, to just 5 by two original AFL teams, Miami and Oakland. However, Pittsburgh, with 4, and Baltimore, with the first one under the new setup, have won five NFL championships for the AFC. As the league prepared for the Silver Anniversary of its Super Bowl championship, the two conferences each had won 12 games.

Welcome to Monday Night Football

In 1970, a new phenomenon swept the nation – Monday Night NFL Football. The league's rich new television package called for one game to be televised nationally every Monday night by the American Broadcasting Company. Suddenly, the manner in which Americans spent that evening changed dramatically. Bowling leagues and civic and social meetings were rescheduled; movie houses showed a marked decline in business; the streets of cities became more deserted. Even the crime rate declined. CBS had televised three Monday night games the previous season to test the market, but without such positive results. ABC, on the other hand, hyped its new Monday night schedule. More important, the network found a new star in Don Meredith, the former Cowboys quarterback who was pure "country." Meredith had a wit that delighted millions whenever he punctured the pretensions and pomposities of his co-commentator, Howard Cosell. (Veteran Keith Jackson handled the play-by-play.) Suddenly, there was a game within the game.

It all worked with superb show business results, and though the broadcasters have long since changed, Monday night NFL football is the longest running network series in the history of American television.

As Washington Goes, So Goes the NFL

Some of the nation's most important viewing habits had been long established in Washington D.C., where many members of Congress were rabid fans of the Washington Redskins. The Nation's Capitol had been turned on to the team since the early sixties, when coach Bill McPeak helped to break the team's color barrier by obtaining running back Bobby Mitchell, a sensational outside runner from the Cleveland Browns, and switched him to wide receiver. A year later, McPeak teamed Mitchell with quarterback Sonny Jurgensen, who was a veritable passing machine – long, short, medium, but usually long. A team that had lain dormant for more than 15 years began to excite fans again. The Redskins drafted Arizona State running back Charley Taylor in 1964 and switched him to wide receiver. Washington suddenly had the most entertaining passing game in the NFL.

Even with this exciting offense, the Redskins always lacked a complete team until 1969. Vince Lombardi, frustrated with his decision to step away as head coach of the Green Bay Packers, came to Washington that year as head coach and general manager. Lombardi's name was magic. So were the

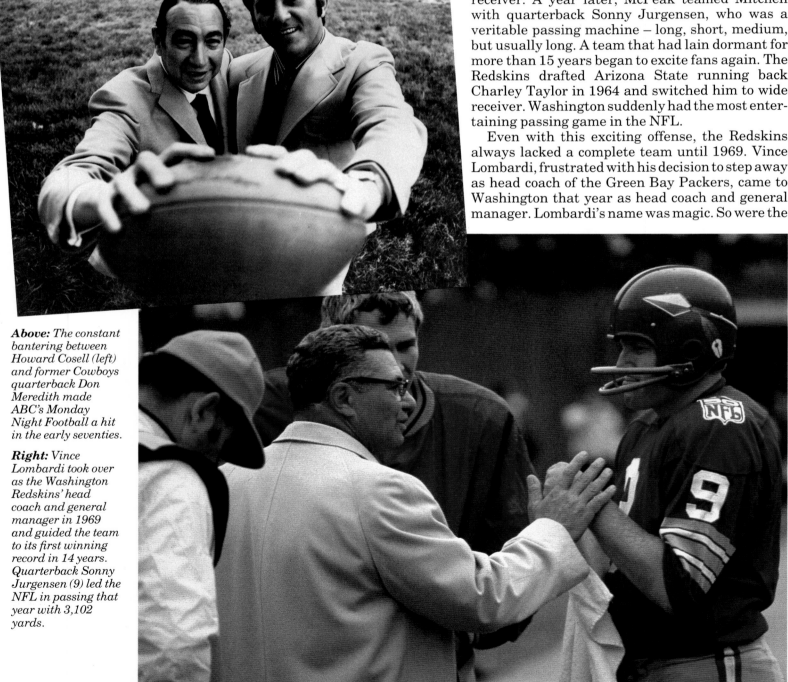

Above: *The constant bantering between Howard Cosell (left) and former Cowboys quarterback Don Meredith made ABC's Monday Night Football a hit in the early seventies.*

Right: *Vince Lombardi took over as the Washington Redskins' head coach and general manager in 1969 and guided the team to its first winning record in 14 years. Quarterback Sonny Jurgensen (9) led the NFL in passing that year with 3,102 yards.*

results. He brought the team its first winning season in 14 years. By then, Redskins Fever had swept Washington, including the Halls of Congress.

Sadly, Lombardi died of cancer before he could coach a second season. Two years later, in 1971, George Allen became the team's head coach. Redskins Fever intensified. In just five seasons as head coach of the Los Angeles Rams, Allen had earned a reputation as a players' coach. Everything was a "Them vs. Us" situation. "Us" always was Allen and the players. He had been defensive coach of the Chicago Bears under George Halas when the Bears won the 1963 NFL title. Following the team's championship game victory over the Giants, Allen, not Halas, had been awarded the game ball. Allen was equally successful on the field in Los Angeles, but he rankled owner Dan Reeves, and Reeves fired him after the 1968 season. Rams players protested so vehemently that Reeves reluctantly hired Allen a week later. Allen made great demands on his players and did it with an old-fashioned, rah-rah style. The team's first winning seasons in seven years made it all palatable. It was no different when he became general manager of the Redskins and directed all the team's financial resources, ("that money can buy a new movie projector for game films"), be funneled to his team. Club president Edward Bennett Williams, Jr., remarked, "We gave George an unlimited expense account, and he exceeded it before the year was over."

Allen's motto in Washington was "The future is now." He preferred talented, veteran players to draft choices, and he accumulated so many that the Redskins were known as the "Over the Hill Gang." Yet, he won, and took Washington to Super Bowl VII after a tight race with the Dallas Cowboys in the National Conference. The rivalry had its genesis in a string of games during the mid-sixties, when Jurgensen and Meredith staged one of the greatest individual personal duels in NFL history. In 1965, Jurgensen brought the Redskins from a 21-0 deficit to a 34-31 lead with 37 seconds to play, but Washington had to block a field goal with seven seconds to preserve victory. The following season, Meredith moved his team 97 yards without a timeout and Dallas won on a field goal in the final seconds. A month later, the numbers were the same, the results the opposite. Jurgensen's touchdown pass to Taylor tied the score 31-31. In the final two minutes Jurgensen drove the Redskins to a winning field goal. The next time the two teams met, in 1967, and Meredith took the Cowboys 71 yards in just 43 seconds, ending with a game-winning 36-yard touchdown pass to running back Dan Reeves. In 1972, when Allen chose Billy Kilmer as his quarterback, a Kilmer vs. Jurgensen controversy swept the city. It never affected the two players, who became close friends and kindred souls in their quest for nighttime adventure. Washington loved it, and Robert F. Kennedy Stadium again became the entertainment palace that George Preston Marshall, who had died in 1969, had envisioned.

The NFL's blackout policy of home games forbade Washingtonians from watching their favorite team. The action moved to the Halls of Congress – no small fan base – where the NFL was threatened with a review of its anti-trust exemption, which made such practices as the blackout rule possible. The result was the provision that a local blackout would be lifted if a stadium was sold out 72 hours in advance. Though the measure originally was to last only three years, the Redskins success ensured continuous sellouts and the NFL never has budged toward changing its policy.

George Allen was a players' coach who had immediate success in Washington. The Redskins finished with a 9-4-1 record in 1971 and made their first playoff appearance in 26 years.

1970 – A Most Amazing Season

The Redskins weren't the only comeback story during the first season of the NFL's merger. Quarterback George Blanda, who had begun his pro football career with the Chicago Bears in 1949, and later had led the Houston Oilers to a pair of AFL titles. In 1967, he joined the Oakland Raiders, primarily as a placekicker. But the Raiders revived his quarterbacking skills during a five-game stretch of the 1970 season. Blanda, now 43, replaced the injured Daryle Lamonica with the Raiders and Steelers tied 7-7 and threw three touchdown passes in a 31-14 victory. The following week, he kicked a 48-yard field goal against the Chiefs with eight seconds to play to produce a 17-17 tie. In Week 3 of his revival he again replaced an injured Lamonica and, with Oakland trailing 20-13, threw a game-tying touchdown pass with a minute and a half to play, then won the game with a 52-yard field goal as time expired. Blanda wasn't finished. The following week against Denver, in another relief appearance, he drove the Raiders downfield in the final minute, completing a winning 20-yard touchdown pass to Fred Biletnikoff in the final seconds. Blanda finished this amazing five-week run against San Diego with a last-second 19-yard field goal for a 20-17 victory.

Blanda wasn't the league's only field goal-kicking star that season. Tom Dempsey of the New Orleans Saints, whose kicking foot, his right, was deformed at birth, made a record-setting 63-yard field goal. Still the longest in NFL history, it came on the final play of a game against Detroit and gave the Saints a 19-17 victory.

When the season ended, three-year-old Cincinnati became the first expansion team ever to make the playoffs so early in its history, but lost to the Baltimore Colts. Before he retired from coaching for good after the 1975 season, Paul Brown got the Bengals into the playoffs twice more. Quarterback Ken Anderson, who made the jump from college football's Division III to the NFL, became one of the most accurate and consistent passers in pro football history. Anderson became the only player ever to complete 20 consecutive passes in one game. He once completed 40 in a game against San Diego – and lost!

The Colts, after losing to the Jets in Super Bowl III, made it to Super Bowl V. Johnny Unitas got them off to a 7-0 lead, but was forced out of the game with a rib injury. On came Earl Morrall, the "goat" of the Jets loss, and he achieved some redemption in a 16-13 victory that was decided in the final five seconds on Jim O'Brien's 32-yard field goal.

Don Shula's No-Names With Butch and Sundance

That 1970 season produced one more big surprise. The Miami Dolphins, a four-year-old expansion team, stunned the NFL by making the playoffs, thanks in large measure to their new head coach, Don Shula, who played for the Browns, Colts and Redskins before coaching. He built the great Colts team of the Sixties, including the one that lost in Super Bowl III. Shula's boss, Carroll Rosenbloom, took that defeat personally. Their relationship deteriorated to such a point that after the 1969 season, Shula signed to coach the Dolphins.

In Miami, Shula inherited a wealth of talent. Using basically the roster he found when he arrived, Shula took the Dolphins to three straight Super Bowls (VI, VII, and VIII) winning two (VII and VIII). In his first five years as the Dolphins' head coach, their record was 57-12-1.

The pass offenses of the early 1970s slowly were being shackled by new defensive concepts. Responding quickly, Shula geared the Dolphins' offense to a strong ground game, first by molding one of the best offensive lines in the game's history – guards Larry Little and Bob Keuchenberg, tackles Norm Evans and Wayne Moore, and centers Bob DeMarco and Jim Langer. All six had been cast off by their original NFL teams. Behind them, he built a backfield of fullback Larry Csonka and halfbacks Jim Kiick and Mercury Morris. Morris was the speed back who mainly ran outside. Csonka and Kiick adopted the nickname, "Butch Cassidy and the Sundance Kid," after a popular movie at the

Opposite inset: Tom Dempsey (19) kicks his record-setting 63-yard field goal in the Saints' 19-17 victory over Detroit in 1970.

Opposite: George Blanda's incredible five-week run in 1970 included two game-winning, last second field goals and a game-winning touchdown pass.

Left: Don Shula stunned the NFL in 1970, when he guided the Miami Dolphins to the playoffs in his first year as their head coach. Shula took the Dolphins to three straight Super Bowls (VI, VII and VIII), winning two (VII and VIII).

Above: Members of the "No-Name Defense" take a rest. From left to right: middle linebacker Nick Buoniconti (85), defensive tackle Manny Fernandez (75), and defensive ends Vern Den Herder (83) and Bill Stanfill (84).

time that glorified a couple of old western rogues. Csonka, now in the Hall of Fame, was a 6-foot, 3-inch, 235-pound line-smasher who correctly capsuled his role as "a power back whose assignment is to establish an inside running game." He never was a quick starter with the ball, and a tribute to the Dolphins' line was their ability to hold off blockers just a bit longer so that Csonka could get started. He led his team in rushing in five seasons and set rushing records in the team's two Super Bowl victories.

Shula's quarterback, Bob Griese, was the perfect director for this offense. Griese didn't have the flair of Unitas, nor was his arm as strong as some other NFL quarterbacks at the time, but he knew how to take advantage of all of his receivers, particularly future Hall of Fame member Paul Warfield. Griese always found Warfield at just the right time – when defenses had their hands full with Csonka, Kiick, and Morris.

Shula also put together the "No-Name Defense." The group was coached by assistant Bill Arnsparger but had Shula's unmistakable stamp. Its "No Name" tag came because it worked so well as a unit and had no real stars, except for its leader, linebacker Nick Buoniconti. No physical giant, Buoniconti directed Arnsparger's schemes. When injuries cut down available defensive linemen in 1972, Shula and Arnsparger resurrected a scheme they had used in the fifties when they were assistant coaches at the University of Kentucky. The alignment used three linemen and four linebackers, one of whom also could be used as a pass rusher. Bob Matheson, nominally a defensive end, played this role for Miami. His jersey number, 53, became the name of the defense. In reality, Shula had reintroduced the 3-4 defense. It still is commonly used at all levels of football – high school, college, and professional.

After losing to the Colts as a wild card team in the 1970 playoffs, Miami won its division title in 1971, then survived the longest game in NFL history – a two-overtime playoff game thriller against the Kansas City Chiefs. On Christmas Day, in the opening round of the playoffs, Griese threw a tie-making 5-yard touchdown pass to tight end Marv Fleming with less than two minutes left in regulation. The Dolphins won the game on Garo Yepremian's 37-yard field goal after seven minutes and 40 seconds of the second overtime quarter. The Dolphins then upset the Colts for the AFC title but lost to the Cowboys in Super Bowl VI.

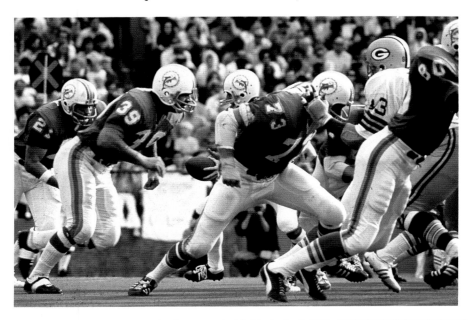

Above: The Dolphins' backfield of fullback Larry Csonka (39) and halfback Jim Kiick (21) adopted the nickname "Butch Cassidy and the Sundance Kid," from the popular movie of the same name.

Right: Oakland's Clarence Davis (28) catches an 8-yard touchdown pass from Ken Stabler with 26 seconds remaining to give the Raiders a 28-26 victory over the two-time defending Super Bowl champion Miami Dolphins in the 1974 AFC Divisional Playoff Game.

The NFL's Crown Jewel – A Perfect Season

In 1972, Shula's Dolphins had a perfect season. It wasn't easy. Midway through the season, Griese went out with an injury. But as he had done in Baltimore in 1968 after Unitas went down, Shula had acquired Earl Morrall as a backup quarterback. Miami stayed unbeaten through Super Bowl VII, in which Griese returned to start in the Dolphins' 14-7 victory over the Washington Redskins.

Although the Dolphins' defense stifled Washington and Csonka's running controlled most of the game, Shula had one awful moment. With Miami ahead 14-0 in the last quarter, the Redskins blocked a field goal attempt by Yepremian. The Dolphins' diminutive kicker picked up the loose ball and tried to pass it – there were no receivers downfield – and had the ball knocked loose and returned by defensive back Mike Bass for a Washington touchdown.

In 1973, Miami lost just two games, earning their second straight NFL championship with a 24-7 Super Bowl victory over the Minnesota Vikings. They seemed headed for a fourth straight Super Bowl appearance until a game-winning touchdown catch by Oakland running back Clarence Davis ended their streak in the 1974 playoffs. However, Shula went on the lead all NFL coaches with his six Super Bowl appearances, including two in the eighties. Only George Halas has won more NFL games.

Dallas Cowboys – America's Team

The Dolphins weren't the only team to grab center stage in the NFL's new world. The Dallas Cowboys, Pittsburgh Steelers – and, to a lesser degree, the Oakland Raiders, Washington Redskins, and Minnesota Vikings – formed a power elite during the first decade of reorganization.

Pittsburgh won four Super Bowls during the seventies, Dallas two, though the Cowboys made the playoffs in nine of the ten seasons. The Cowboys captured national attention and became known as "America's Team." Their interesting style of football and years of daredevil finishes were superb entertainment. Television loved it and constantly showcased them for a national audience.

The Cowboys' organization also became a trendsetter in pro football, the first to seek high-tech solutions for the drafting of players. The club chose Calvin Hill, a fullback from unbeaten Yale, in the first round of the 1969 draft. Suddenly the computer age had arrived in the NFL: the Cowboys said their computer had indicated Hill was the best choice at that time. Ivy League football players never had been considered first-round material, and few of them even were drafted by the NFL, but Hill broke that mold and became a star with some of Dallas's great teams. Although Hill's selection actually was dictated by human assessment, the Cowboys became "America's Computer Team." They freely advertised their reliance on such technology, applying it to everything from scouting to season tickets to formulating game plans. Before the decade ended, most NFL teams had adopted the same approach. The Cowboys' scouting was based on more than computers, though. They developed a network of scouts and tipsters that found players at schools seldom, if ever, visited by pro scouts. Several of their "discoveries" became stars.

Left: Opposing quarterbacks grew accustomed to taking punishing hits from Dallas defensive stalwarts Randy White (54) and Ed (Too Tall) Jones (72).

Below: Roger Staubach's desparation 50-yard touchdown pass to Drew Pearson in the 1975 NFC Divisional Playoff Game lifted the Cowboys to a 17-14 victory over the Minnesota Vikings.

The Cowboys' achievements on the field centered around head coach Tom Landry and quarterback Roger Staubach. Landry had coached the Cowboys since their formation as an expansion team in 1960, and had them in the playoffs within seven seasons. They came within a game of going to each of the first two Super Bowls.

Landry's genius as a defensive coach built his team. He also constructed an offense that featured the shifting of backs and receivers before they finally lined up in the designated formation, after which the ball was snapped quickly. Landry knew that a defense keyed its movements by the offensive formation, and the more it changed these formations before the play began, the better its chances of committing an error. Landry's defense became known as Doomsday. It was based on the same 4-3 concept that he had developed with the New York Giants. It ultimately became the Giants' equal. But Landry's success with his defenses was not built

solely on men nor formations. While still an assistant coach with the Giants, he had found from studying films that an offense usually called its plays in the same predictable manner – humans did the job, after all – so he built his defenses to cope with those tendencies. The Cowboys covered the eight slots along the line of scrimmage. The middle linebacker went to the expected point of attack and made most of the tackles. That had been why Sam Huff was a star in New York, and why Lee Roy Jordan, Landry's middle linebacker for many seasons in Dallas, became the Doomsday's delivery man.

But the featured performer in Landry's Doomsday Defense was tackle Bob Lilly, arguably the greatest defensive lineman in the game's history. Lilly, now in the Hall of Fame, was a 6-4, 260-pound player who inevitably found two or three men trying to block him, instead of one. He had tremendous strength and desire and, most important, great quickness. He often got into a play before blockers even touched him. One of his most memorable moments was a 29-yard sack of Miami quarterback Bob Griese in Super Bowl VI. No matter which way Griese zig-zagged backward, trying to escape, Lilly dogged him, finally cornering him for the huge loss.

Randy White, who succeeded Lilly at defensive tackle, was the key player in Doomsday II, helping Dallas reach three more Super Bowls. When the Cowboys won Super Bowl XII against Denver, White and defensive end Harvey Martin were named co-most valuable players.

Cowboys quarterback Roger Staubach first captured the nation's attention when he played for the United States Naval Academy and won the Heisman Trophy in 1963 as a junior. He was nicknamed "Roger the Dodger" then because of his scrambling ability. That, combined with his passing, helped the Middies turn in some dramatic finishes. After serving five years in the Navy, he joined the Cowboys in 1969 and became their starting quarterback midway through the 1971 season. Dallas was on the brink of being eliminated from the playoff race. The Cowboys were a troubled team. Their great running back, Duane Thomas, wouldn't talk to anyone, even his teammates. The Cowboys' reputation as the team that "couldn't win the big one," gnawed at their spirit.

Staubach helped change that. Dallas never lost another game that season and defeated Miami 24-3 in Super Bowl VI. Staubach was the game's MVP, passing for two touchdowns. In the next eight seasons until he retired, he took Dallas to the playoffs seven more times, the NFC Championship Game five times, and the Super Bowl three times.

During his 11 seasons with Dallas, Staubach specialized in hair-breadth finishes. He brought his team from behind 23 times in the fourth quarter for victories. He helped Dallas win 14 games in the final two minutes or in overtime. In the 1972 playoffs, Dallas trailed San Francisco 28-13 with about 16 minutes to play when Staubach, who had missed the regular season with an injury, replaced starter Craig Morton. The result was a 30-28 victory, as Staubach threw the winning touchdown pass to wide receiver Ron Sellers with 30 seconds to play.

Staubach directed the Cowboys' most famous comeback in the 1975 playoffs against Minnesota. The Cowboys trailed 14-10 with less than a minute to play. Staubach threw a 50-yard touchdown pass to Drew Pearson in the final seconds that won the game 17-14. (The pass later was tagged "Hail Mary"

because of the Cowboys' prayerful situation. The expression now is part of football jargon, used to describe any last-minute pass, successful or not.) He punctuated the legacy in the final regular season game of his career. With the 1979 NFC-East title at stake in a game against the Washington Redskins, he threw two touchdowns passes in the final 140 seconds, the last one on the Cowboys' final play to Tony Hill for the victory and the title.

At Last, the Steelers are Champions

Staubach waged some of his outstanding battles against the NFL's dynasty team of the decade, the Pittsburgh Steelers. Pittsburgh won four NFL titles in six years, after having been NFL doormats for nearly 40 years. The resurgence began when Art Rooney gave his two sons, Dan and Art Jr., active roles in the club's management.

The younger Rooney's first move was to hire Chuck Noll as head coach in 1969. Noll had played for several seasons with the great Cleveland Browns teams as a messenger guard and linebacker, and had learned about coaching from his association with Paul Brown. He later worked with Sid Gillman as an assistant coach for the San Diego Chargers of the American Football League, then coached Baltimore's great defenses of the late sixties before being hired by Pittsburgh.

Like all of pro football's great coaches, Noll was single-minded in his approach to the game and tolerated no individual deviation from his philosophy. He demanded perfection and never tolerated excuses for failure. There were times when he didn't think that his great quarterback, Terry Bradshaw, had his mind far enough into a game. He once clouted Bradshaw across the side of the helmet on the sideline to get his attention. Believing a team was built on good teaching, Noll hired coaches who were teachers as well as technicians. Off the field, he was considered a loner who relied on his family as his main non-football interest.

That image may have been too limited: he was a scuba diver, a devotee of the symphony, flew his own plane, and a regular at the best restaurants in Pittsburgh, where he knew his way around the best gourmet menu and the most select wine list. The way to success for Noll and the Steelers was painful. In his first season, they won only one game. The Noll-coached Steelers didn't have a winning season until 1972 when they won the first division title in the franchise's history. By that time, though, most elements of the Steelers dynasty already were in place.

The building had begun in 1969 with defensive lineman Joe Greene, a number-one draft pick from North Texas State. It continued with quarterback Terry Bradshaw of Louisiana Tech in 1970 and running back Franco Harris out of Penn State in 1972. In between came other future Hall of Fame players: defensive back Mel Blount, outside linebacker Jack Ham, and middle linebacker Jack Lambert. Other key players included defensive end L.C. Greenwood, running back Rocky Bleier, and the team's small, but very quick offensive line, anchored by Mike Webster. Later in the decade, the Steelers added two of the best wide receivers ever to play pro football, Lynn Swann and John Stallworth.

Players such as Greene, Blount, Ham, Greenwood, and Lambert were the keystones of Pittsburgh's famed Steel Curtain defense. The unit got as

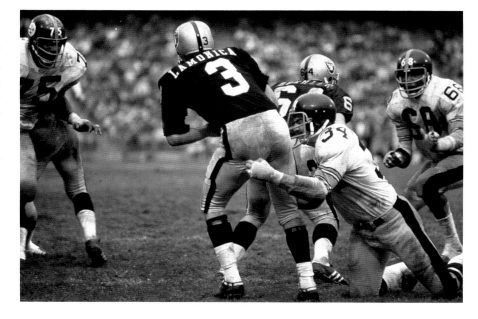

Inset below: *Art Rooney had to wait 42 years for his Steelers to win a world championship, then the team won four Super Bowls in six years.*

much recognition as Terry Bradshaw and the team's other offensive weapons. The defensive unit, more than any other, typified the style of the team and its surroundings, a steel town with few pretensions.

Ironically, the legacy of this team and its accomplishment had their genesis in a play that typified life's random nature: a 60-yard touchdown pass on Pittsburgh's final play of a 1972 playoff game against the Oakland Raiders that became the unforgettable "Immaculate Reception." The game appeared lost when Bradshaw faded back one last time, avoided an Oakland pass rusher, and, in one desperate heave threw a pass down the middle of the field to running back John (Frenchy) Fuqua. The ball bounced off Fuqua and Oakland defensive back Jack Tatum as they collided, then caromed backward toward Harris, who was running downfield. In full stride, Harris caught it at his ankles and ran for the winning touchdown.

The Steelers had played a strong game against the heavily-favored Raiders, and they were a sentimental choice. Everyone wanted Art Rooney to at last win something. In fact, Rooney didn't even see the Immaculate Reception. Before the play, certain that his team had no chance, he was en route to the locker room to offer consolation.

against Minnesota, he clinched the victory with a touchdown pass to Larry Brown. He threw the tying and winning scores on a pair of touchdown passes in Super Bowl X, the latter a 64-yarder punctuated by Swann's spectacular leaping catch. Bradshaw never saw it. He was knocked unconscious and had to be told about it after the game. In his team's 35-31 victory over Dallas in Super Bowl XIII – possibly the most competitive Super Bowl ever played – Bradshaw threw four touchdown passes. The following year against the Rams, when the Steelers won their fourth Super Bowl, he had two more, including a 73-yard go-ahead score to Stallworth.

Pride and Poise in Oakland

While Dallas and Pittsburgh lit up the NFL with their own particular fireworks, the Raiders also helped the Dolphins carry the torch for the old AFL. In pro football from 1963 to 1983, only the Cowboys won more games than the Raiders. The club's success is directly tied to Al Davis. In the early 1960s, Davis saved the Oakland organization from impending failure during his three successful seasons as general manager and head coach. It was during this period that he coined the team's motto, "Pride and Poise." Davis retired as coach in 1966 for his short term as commissioner of the American Football League. Following the AFL-NFL merger agreement, he returned to the Raiders where his hand again touched every aspect of the team, including weekly game plans for his coaches. He was a master trader and a clever manipulator. Davis also was a bit of a romantic: his long love affair with the great West Point football teams of the 1940s and early 1950s moved him to design similar uniforms for his own team.

The following week, the Steelers lost the AFC title game to Miami. Two years later, Rooney finally got a long-sought NFL championship when the Steelers beat the Minnesota Vikings 16-6 in Super Bowl IX. The Steel Curtain and Harris, who gained a record 158 rushing yards, made it happen.

Bradshaw flowered as a complete quarterback in 1975. Until then, he had been erratic, winning and losing the starting quarterback job to Terry Hanratty and Joe Gilliam and driving his coach to distraction with his inconsistency.

In postseason games during his 14-year career, Bradshaw compiled a record 30 touchdown passes and 3,833 yards. In six AFC title games, he threw 7 touchdown passes, including the go-ahead scoring passes when Pittsburgh twice beat Oakland in 1974 and 1975, plus a pair in each of two title games against Houston in 1978 and 1979. In Super Bowl IX

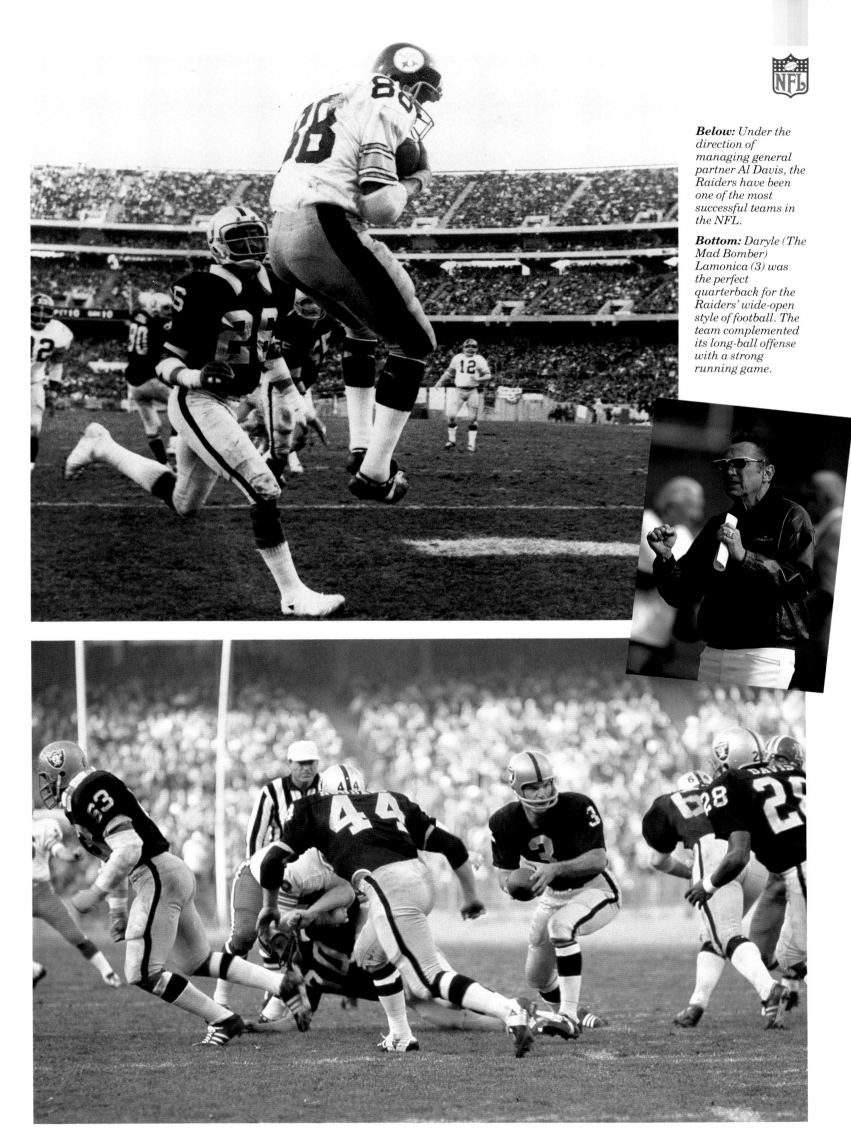

Below: Under the direction of managing general partner Al Davis, the Raiders have been one of the most successful teams in the NFL.

Bottom: Daryle (The Mad Bomber) Lamonica (3) was the perfect quarterback for the Raiders' wide-open style of football. The team complemented its long-ball offense with a strong running game.

Below: When visiting teams came to play in Minnesota during the winter, Vikings coach Bud Grant liked to use the sub-freezing temperatures as a psychological advantage.

Bottom: "The Purple People Eaters" from left to right: defensive ends Jim Marshall (70) and Carl Eller (81) and defensive tackles Alan Page (88) and Gary Larsen (77).

Regardless of who has coached his team, Davis always has insisted on his style of football: wide-open with plenty of long passes to swift receivers, complemented by a strong running game and an attacking, intimidating defense. Coaches who complied stayed and prospered as John Madden. He guided the club for 10 seasons, during which he won 112 games and Super Bowl XI, and reached the AFC championship game five other times. Madden, now a popular CBS television football commentator, always had talented teams. But he also was under Davis' direction which probably hurt him in the seven AFL/AFC title games that the Raiders lost against coaches who had total control over their teams. Tom Flores, a former Raiders quarterback who succeeded Madden in 1979, was more resourceful during his nine seasons as head coach, during which he produced two Super Bowl championships, XV and XVIII. In the late 1980s, the Raiders' great talent simply ran out and was not replaced. Davis was so engrossed in legal problems that he paid less attention to the football side of his franchise. Until then, the Raiders always had the kind of football talent they needed – quarterbacks with strong arms and receivers with fast legs. Davis traded Flores to Buffalo in the mid-sixties for Daryle Lamonica, known as "The Mad Bomber." (The term "bomb" became the synonym for a long pass just as the term "blitz" was an all-out rush by linebackers, all part of the post-1960 pro football vocabulary.) Lamonica

threw to receivers such as Warren Wells, Raymond Chester, and Fred Biletnikoff. In 1968 Davis drafted Ken Stabler, who pulled out several last-minute victories during his seasons as Oakland's number-one quarterback. These included the 1974 first-round playoff thriller with Miami, when Stabler, falling to his knees under a heavy rush, passed to Clarence Davis for the winning touchdown. Wide receiver Cliff Branch had world-class speed at college and rare catching ability for a track star. Branch became the Raiders' deep threat of the 1970s. Biletnikoff, now in the Hall of Fame, wasn't the fastest receiver, but he caught 589 passes for 8,974 yards and 76 touchdowns in 14 seasons with the Raiders. His big-play receptions in their 32-14 victory over Minnesota in Super Bowl XI earned him the game's most valuable player honors.

Davis also balanced his team with some shrewd trades. Beside Lamonica, he got Willie Brown, a defensive back from Denver, and Ted Hendricks, a fun-loving terror of an outside linebacker from Green Bay. Davis picked George Blanda off the waiver wire at age 39. All three are members of the Hall of Fame. Davis himself, as late as 1990, had yet to be so honored.

When Davis drafted, he sought players from winning programs. The University of Southern California, where he once coached, produced Heisman Trophy-winning tailback Marcus Allen. But Davis never was reluctant to look to smaller schools. His two best fullbacks, Marv Hubbard and Mark van Eeghen came from Colgate University. He drafted two Hall of Fame offensive linemen, tackle Art Shell from Maryland State University and guard Gene Upshaw from Texas A&I College. Shell and Upshaw played side-by-side on the left side of the offensive line, giving the team a "left-handed" attack. It was effective for two reasons: first, Stabler was a left-handed quarterback, so the handoffs to that side were more natural. Second, a defense's quickest, yet lightest, end, no match for Upshaw and the 290-pound Shell, usually played on that side. In Super Bowl XI against the Vikings, this pair dominated Jim Marshall and Alan Page, the right end and tackle of the Vikings' famed defense, who were outweighed more than 40 pounds per man.

Davis knew the difference between performance and patience. Stabler was a second-round draft pick from Alabama in 1968, but Davis knew he couldn't budge either Lamonica or Blanda. He sent Stabler to a minor league team for a year of seasoning, then placed him on the team's inactive list for another year. Stabler didn't become a starter for another three seasons, but in 1976, he helped produce the Raiders' first NFL championship. Jim Plunkett, battered and mentally worn from playing for poor teams in New England and San Francisco, was released by the 49ers in 1979. Davis believed Plunkett still had some football life. He signed the former Stanford Heisman Trophy winner as a free agent and allowed him to re-energize himself simply by taking the year off as an active player. When Stabler's career ended with Oakland in 1980, Plunkett became the starter and the Raiders became the first wild card team to win the NFL championship. Plunkett led them to another title in 1983.

Ice Cold Purple People Eaters

For the Raiders, the Super Bowl XV and XVIII titles helped wipe away some of the frustration of earlier seasons. But the Minnesota Vikings, their victims in Super Bowl XI, may be the most unfulfilled pro football team of all time. Under head coach Bud Grant, the Vikings were four-time losers in Super Bowl competition.

That negative statistic obscures their proudest long-term achievement: they vied with the Cowboys for dominance in the NFC during the late 1960s and for the first half of the 1970s. They always lived up to their nickname, playing outdoors at home during December and January when Minnesota was gripped by sub-freezing temperatures and snow. Grant, a steely eyed coach who had won five Grey Cup championships as head coach of Winnipeg in the Canadian Football League, was a no-frills leader who believed his team had to use its playing environment to its own advantage. So while opponents huddled around heaters by their bench, the Vikings had none and seemed to enjoy the Arctic-like conditions. This was a tremendous psychological advantage that in 1969, George Allen brought the Los Angeles Rams to Minnesota a week before they were scheduled to play a late-December playoff game against the Vikings – to get "used" to the weather. Instead, the frigid practice conditions made them more miserable and served only as a distraction. The Vikings came from behind and won the game, then went on to beat Cleveland for the last championship of the old National Football League.

Grant built his team on a great defense. Its front

Left: Quarterback Joe Kapp ignited the Minnesota offense with his wobbly passes and fiery demeanor. In 1969, Kapp tied an NFL record by throwing 7 touchdown passes in a 52-14 win over Baltimore.

Below: Vikings receiver Ahmad Rashad (28) had a penchant for making tough catches in the closing minutes of a game.

109

line, nicknamed "The Purple People Eaters," for its devastating pass rush, included Carl Eller and Gary Larsen with Page and Marshall. Marshall played 19 seasons with the Vikings and appeared in 282 consecutive games, both NFL records. He also is remembered for his "wrong way" run earlier in his NFL career. At San Francisco's Kezar Stadium, he scooped up a loose ball and got turned around. Believing he was running for a touchdown, he actually ended up in his own end zone and registered a two-point safety for the 49ers.

The Vikings' offense under Grant was run first by quarterback Joe Kapp, a fiery Californian who helped them win the 1969 NFL championship, then by Hall of Fame quarterback Fran Tarkenton, who holds the NFL records for most lifetime completions (3,686), passing yards (47,003), and touchdowns (342). Tarkenton spent the first six years of his NFL career (1961-66) with the Vikings, and the next five with the New York Giants before returning to Minnesota in 1972 to play out his career, which ended in 1978. Tarkenton probably was more renowned as the best "scrambling" quarterback in NFL history because he made it a personal art. The classic description came from one of his linemen who, standing in place during one of Tarkenton's scrambles, told a panting opponent, "I'm just going to stay here and wait because he's going to come this way again." But Tarkenton, rightly or wrongly, also became known as the quarterback "who couldn't win the big one" because he was the losing quarterback in three Super Bowls. The Vikings just became a different team once they left the frozen tundra of Metropolitan Stadium for milder Super Bowl sites, and found themselves physically outmanned by bigger teams like the Dolphins, Steelers, and Raiders.

The Juice Was Turned On

In Buffalo, O.J. Simpson revised the NFL's individual rushing statistics when he set a season record of 2,003 yards in 1973, the same year he gained a record 250 yards in a game against the New England Patriots. Simpson was identified – and recognized – by his nickname, "The Juice," a play on his initials, which stand for Orenthal James. He was a Heisman Trophy winner at the University of Southern California in 1968. The Bills made him their first choice in the 1969 NFL draft. Simpson was a slashing runner off the tackles. Around end, he was most effective because of his speed and his ability to change pace and direction in the open field. During his first few seasons in Buffalo, Simpson's main role was to draw the defense away from other players. When Lou Saban became the Bills' head coach in 1972, he saw the folly of that strategy and turned Simpson loose – to lead the NFL in rushing three times behind an offensive line that was nicknamed "The Electric Company"...because it turned on The Juice. He had five seasons in which he gained 1,000 or more yards. His single-game efforts included six games where he gained 200 or more yards, three of them in his record-setting 1973 season. He once had a streak of seven games in which he surpassed 100 yards, and he broke his 1973 single-game mark by gaining 273 yards against the Detroit Lions before a national television audience on Thanksgiving Day in 1976. Simpson was on a pace to break Jim Brown's career record of 12,312 yards when injuries cut him down with 11,236 in eleven seasons. The three "decoy" seasons in Buffalo ultimately cost him the record.

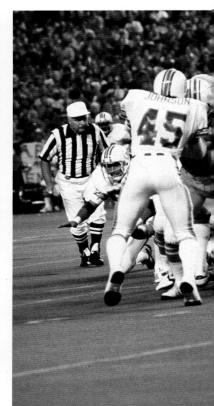

T.D. and the Earl of Campbell

Just as Simpson was finishing his career, two other Heisman Trophy winners, Tony Dorsett and Earl Campbell, were beginning theirs. Dorsett had led the University of Pittsburgh to the national collegiate championship before he joined the Dallas Cowboys in 1977. He immediately helped them to a victory over the Denver Broncos in Super Bowl XII. Dorsett was a well-muscled but small back who bridled under coach Tom Landry's reluctance to use him more. But Landry believed that Dorsett's career would be longer and more productive if he carried the ball 16 or 17 times a game, rather than 25 or 30 as he had done in college. Landry ultimately was proven correct because Dorsett became the second-leading ground gainer in NFL history with 12,739 yards in 12 seasons, 11 with the Cowboys. He had eight seasons in which he gained more than 1,000 yards, and five of them were consecutive. Like Simpson, Dorsett ran best off-tackle and to the outside, but Landry's system of misdirection plays also made him effective on traps and "comeback" plays into the middle, where he, too, had a marvelous change of pace. With his great acceleration, Dorsett often reached the line of scrimmage and was gone before a defense had much time to react.

He set an NFL record with a 99-yard run on a Monday night TV against the Minnesota Vikings, made all the more remarkable because the Cowboys had only ten men on the field. Dorsett broke off tackle, and his great acceleration carried him past a bunched-in Vikings' defense so quickly that he was in the clear in less than 20 yards and outran his pursuers.

Campbell, from the University of Texas, was just the opposite of Simpson and Dorsett. His 230 pounds of speed and power shattered defenses, whether there was much room to run or not. He was neither cute nor fancy during his seasons with the Houston Oilers and New Orleans Saints. He simply ran into people, over them, or through them. "I just tried to

Left: Tony Dorsett (33) explodes through the Minnesota defense en route to his record-setting 99-yard touchdown run. The Cowboys, who had only 10 players on the field on the play, lost the 1982 Monday night game, 31-27.

Below: Dorsett finished his brilliant college career at the University of Pittsburgh in 1976 by winning the Heisman Trophy and leading the Panthers to the national championship.

Above: Walter Payton (with ball) gains three yards against the New Orleans Saints and breaks Jim Brown's NFL career rushing mark of 12,312 yards.

Center: Payton (34) broke O.J. Simpson's single-game rushing record of 273 yards when he gained 275 yards in a 1977 game against the Minnesota Vikings.

Opposite top: William (The Refrigerator) Perry (72) dives for 1 of the 4 touchdowns that he scored in his memorable rookie season.

Opposite bottom: Gale Sayers (40) goes airborne to score 1 of his 6 touchdowns in the Bears' 61-20 win over San Francisco in 1965. Sayers, who was a rookie that season, set an NFL record with 22 touchdowns and led the league in scoring.

grab him and hold on for dear life until help arrived," Cowboys defensive end John Dutton said after playing against Campbell.

Campbell was as fast as he was strong, and could run around a defense, if necessary. One Monday night during his rookie season, 1978, he galloped 81 yards around right end for a touchdown, part of a 199-yard performance against the Miami Dolphins. That season, he carried the ball for 1,450 yards and became the first rookie since Jim Brown, in 1957, to lead the NFL in rushing.

Two years later, in 1980, he gained more than 200 yards in four different games, an NFL record, as part of a single-season record 11 games of more than 100 yards and won the third of his three consecutive NFL rushing titles with 1,934 yards. The following season, he won the AFC rushing title, but by then the pounding his legs had taken from his straight-on running style had begun to take its toll. Still, he finished his eight-season career with 9,407 yards.

In Chicago, All Was Sweetness

Walter Payton of the Chicago Bears came into the NFL as a top draft pick from Jackson State University in 1975, just ten years after Chicago had selected its last great running back, Kansas's Gale Sayers. A member of the Hall of Fame despite a career limited to seven years by knee injuries, Sayers was one of the most dynamic backs in league history. He led the NFL in rushing twice. He had a 203-yard day against Green Bay. He scored a record six touchdowns on a sloppy field against the San Francisco 49ers, part of a performance that yielded 113 yards on nine carries, 89 yards on two pass receptions (one an 80-yard touchdown), and 134 yards on six punt returns, the last one 85 yards for his final score.

Those are very special moments in contemporary Bears history, but they now stand in the shadow of Payton, who had eradicated the club rushing marks of Sayers and Bronco Nagurski before the end of his third season. Simpson once called Payton "an insane runner like me because there often is no rhyme or reason what we as runners do on a play. It's often all instinct." Many times, Payton started off in one direction, and those instincts told him to reverse his field and go the other way. It was not unusual to see him do that two or three times on the same play. "You

have to hold your blocks a long time for Walter," one of his head coaches, Jack Pardee, said, "because he's liable to sweep both ends on the same play."

Another of Payton's instincts told him that if he didn't want to change direction, or couldn't dodge defenders, he just lifted his legs, with their massive thighs, and tried to run through them. He often succeeded. His leg strength had a history: thousands of hours of running up and down a 60-foot-high levee and over a 65-yard sandbank near his Mississippi home when he was in college, and then months of daily, grueling workouts every off-season when he was with the Bears.

The man they called "Sweetness" was only in his third season in 1977 when he broke Simpson's single-game rushing record with a 275-yard day against the Minnesota Vikings. The Bears were trying to protect a 10-7 lead late in the game when Payton broke off a 58-yard run to Minnesota's nine-yard line, bringing him within five yards of Simpson's mark. Two plays and seven yards later, he had his record.

In 1984, Payton broke Jim Brown's NFL career rushing mark of 12,312 yards at Chicago's Soldier Field against the New Orleans Saints. Payton went into the game needing 67 yards and got 65 in the first

half. On his second carry of the third quarter, on a play called "Toss 28 weak," Payton swept toward the left side of his offensive formation. As Saints' defenders closed in, he leapt over a pile of players to gain three yards and break the record. The game was stopped as dozens of photographers and teammates rushed toward him, and again Payton's instinct took over. He turned and ran toward the Saints' bench to shake hands with them first.

Coincidentally, on the day Payton broke Brown's record, Eric Dickerson of the Los Angeles Rams gained 215 yards against the Houston Oilers, breaking Simpson's season record of 2,003 yards. Dickerson set a new season record of 2,105 yards the following week. A long way off were Payton's records of six consecutive seasons of 1,000 or more yards (he also had another four-year streak), 77 100-yard games, and a record-tying six NFL rushing titles.

While Payton was in the midst of establishing those memorable NFL rushing marks, he was complemented by the Bears' defense, which included a 330-pound defensive tackle named William Perry, more aptly nicknamed "The Refrigerator." The unit got its leadership from middle linebacker Mike Singletary, a throwback to Dick Butkus, Chicago's Hall of Fame linebacker of the 1960s and early 1970s.

game, had as much fun watching Perry's antics as did the rest of the country, with the possible exception of the New England Patriots, who lost to the Bears 46-10.

New Faces of the Eighties

Another team that revitalized its defensive heritage was the New York Giants. In 1981 they got another great linebacker, Lawrence Taylor of North Carolina, in the first round of the draft. Working from a 3-4 alignment, Taylor was most renowned as a pass rusher. Opponents were forced to use big offensive linemen to try to block him. The Giants, stymied during years of rebuilding, had been revitalized in the 1980s and finally won Super Bowl XXI after a 14-2 regular season record in 1986. Quarterback Phil Simms and running back Joe Morris turned in milestone performances. Morris established a club single-season rushing record, and Simms was named MVP of the Super Bowl, completing 22 of 25 passes, for a game-record 88 percent, for 265 yards and three touchdowns in New York's 39-20 victory over Denver. That was the first of three Super Bowl losses for the Broncos during the eighties, overshadowing the team's dominance of the AFC's Western Division. Quarterback John Elway was the catalyst for this success. A marvelously gifted quarterback, Elway used his athletic ability to bamboozle defenses. His hair-trigger pass release enabled him to wait until

Singletary epitomized Chicago Bears football with a rough-and-tumble style of play that helped the team win the 1985 NFC championship and Super Bowl XX. Coach Mike Ditka came up with a goal line offensive play putting "The Fridge" in the backfield either to block or carry the ball. He did both in one Monday night game against Green Bay. In another game, he caught a touchdown pass from this formation. He did it again in Super Bowl XX. Payton, who scored none of Chicago's five touchdowns in that

Above: Bears head coach Mike Dikta is given a victory ride by his players after their 46-10 rout of New England in Super Bowl XX.

Right: In this 1988 game against the New York Jets, Miami quarterback Dan Marino (13) passed for 521 yards, the second-highest single game passing yardage total in NFL history.

the last instant before throwing the ball. If he needed more time, his great mobility was another asset, helping him escape trouble, and he could throw almost as well on the run as he did standing still. Elway's shining moment came in the 1986 conference championship against the Cleveland Browns. With the Broncos trailing 20-13 and 5 minutes and 43 seconds to play, he drove his team 98 yards in 15 plays, finishing with a five-yard touchdown pass to Mark Jackson – and there still were 38 seconds on the clock. It became known as "The Drive," and the fact that the Broncos won the title on Rich Karlis's 33-yard field goal in overtime was almost an anti-climax to Elway's heroics.

Elway's Broncos also were victims of one of the greatest single-quarter performances in Super Bowl history. Quarterback Doug Williams of the Washington Redskins engineered a 35-point second quarter, throwing four touchdowns as the Redskins won Super Bowl XXII, their second NFL title of the 1980s. Coach Joe Gibbs had revitalized the team in the early eighties, putting together one of the most disparate groups of players in Redskins history – a massive offensive line called "The Hogs;" a group of tiny receivers known as "The Smurfs," and a frilly-haired fullback named John Riggins who always had marched to his own drummer. Running behind the Hogs, Riggins was a dominating force. Quarterback Joe Theismann, who during his early days with the Redskins had returned punts rather than sit and watch Kilmer and Jurgensen get all the playing time, was as gabby and animated as he was cocky and daring. Theismann led the team to an NFL title in Super Bowl XVII with a tie-breaking touchdown in the fourth quarter, and then helped them win another NFC title the following season. The Miami Dolphins were another revitalized team in the 1980s. In 1980, they played the San Diego Chargers in one of the most memorable playoff games ever, finally losing 41-38 in the second overtime period. The Chargers, behind another of the decade's great passers, Dan Fouts, had jumped to a 24-0 lead in the first quarter. But San Diego eventually had to battle back to tie the game and send it into overtime, as Fouts passed nine yards to James Brooks with 67 seconds to play. The two teams, playing to exhaustion, missed several opportunities to win the game on a field goal before the Chargers' Rolf Benirschke kicked a 29-yarder at 13:52 of the second overtime period for a 41-38 victory. The following week, the Chargers played Cincinnati for the AFC title. The wind-chill conditions were an almost life-threatening 59-degrees below zero. Wearing short-sleeved jerseys, as if to show it wasn't really too cold for them, the Bengals defeated the Chargers 27-7.

Miami made it to the Super Bowl the following season, losing to Riggins and the Redskins. A year later, Dolphins rookie quarterback Dan Marino set new standards for measuring pass production. After having been left available until the late stages of the

Far left: *Free-spirited running back John Riggins (44) churned out some big rushing games while leading the Washington Redskins to the 1982 NFL title.*

Above: *Steve Largent is tackled after making a reception in his 128th consecutive game, setting an NFL record in a 1986 game against San Diego.*

Left: *Largent (80), who holds the NFL career record with 100 receiving touchdowns, beats a San Diego defensive back to make a scoring catch.*

Right: *John Elway's passing and leadership propelled the Denver Broncos to three AFC championships in the 1980s.*

Below: *Much of John Elway's success was due to the Broncos' trio of excellent receivers known as "The Three Amigos." From left to right: Ricky Nattiel, Vance Johnson (82) and Mark Jackson (80). Jackson made the game-tying catch on "The Drive."*

Below right: *Mark Clayton (83) heads toward the end zone with his record-setting, eighteenth touchdown catch in the 1984 Monday night game against Dallas. Clayton and teammate Mark Duper are nicknamed the "Marks Brothers."*

Left: The San Francisco 49ers were a dynasty in the 1980s, as they totally dominated their competition and won a record-tying four Super Bowls.

Jerry Rice's ability to separate from defensive backs when catching the football makes him one of the most dangerous receivers in the NFL.

first round of the draft, Marino led the Dolphins to Super Bowl XIX. He had begun to rewrite the NFL record book thanks to the same kind of quick pass release that made Joe Namath and John Elway so productive. Marino threw mainly to two fine receivers, Mark Clayton and Mark Duper – nicknamed, of course, the "Marks Brothers."

Marino wasted no time making his mark, setting an NFL completion record for rookie quarterbacks. Going into the 1990s, he had completed more than 60 percent of his passes, second in NFL history, and had established some prodigious single season numbers – the only player to surpass 5,000 yards in a season (5,084 yards in 1984), during which he had four 400-yard games. In 1988, he gained 521 yards against the New York Jets, the second-highest single-game total in NFL history. Another great performer during the 1970s and 1980s, wide receiver Steve Largent of the Seattle Seahawks, was a member of the original Seahawks expansion team. Largent never had great speed but developed discipline in reading defenses and running precise pass routes. Late in 1989, his final season, he broke one of the NFL's most venerable records when he caught his 100th career touchdown pass. On a 10-yard pass from Dave Krieg against the Cincinnati Bengals Largent moved beyond Don Hutson's long-standing record of 99. He left pro football as the game's all-time pass-catcher with 819 catches for 13,089 yards.

In the Eighties, the 49ers Mined All the NFL's Gold

The San Francisco 49ers were to the 1980s what the Steelers were to the 1970s, the Packers to the 1960s, and the Browns to the 1950s. In an era when there were not supposed to be dynasties in the NFL, San Francisco fooled everyone, joining Pittsburgh as the

only team ever to win four Super Bowls. Part of the reason was the imaginative offense of coach Bill Walsh, who had benefited from his experience as an assistant coach at Cincinnati under Paul Brown and at San Diego under Don Coryell, both believers in the creative use of the forward pass. Walsh also enjoyed administrative support and deep pockets of the team's young owner, Edward DeBartolo, Jr. Whenever Walsh wanted anything, DeBartolo obliged, regardless of the cost. In 1984, he needed defensive line help and obtained three fine players –

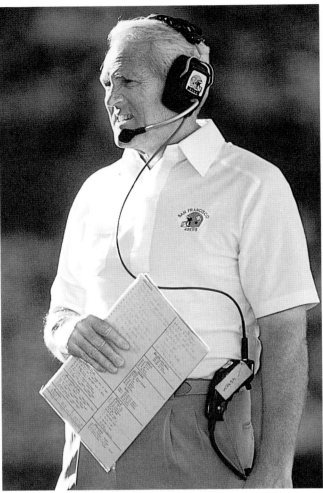

Right: Bill Walsh was an excellent coach with an imaginative, offensive mind. He usually had the 49ers' offensive plays written up on a script and his players would execute them to perfection.

Below: Joe Montana has been the constant factor in the 49ers' success during the 1980s. Former San Francisco head coach Bill Walsh built the 49ers' offense around Montana's abilities, and the ex-Notre Dame quarterback rewarded him with three NFL titles.

Fred Dean, Gary Johnson, and Louis Kelcher — all of whom were in salary disputes with the San Diego Chargers. The Chargers finally traded the trio to the 49ers for future draft picks, and San Francisco fulfilled their salary demands. It paid off for the 49ers in a second Super Bowl victory.

Walsh also was a superb teacher, having tutored Ken Anderson of the Bengals and Dan Fouts of the Chargers. The coach worked his magic on Joe Montana, whom he had picked in the third round of his first draft in 1979. Montana had been an off-and-on starter for Notre Dame, but always was a big-game, key-play performer. Walsh built the 49ers' offense around him. In the 1981 NFC Championship Game, the 49ers defeated the Dallas Cowboys on Montana's third-down touchdown pass to Dwight Clark with 51 seconds remaining. San Francisco then won its first NFL title ever, beating Cincinnati 26-21, thanks to a 20-0 first half and a goal-line stand that stopped the Bengals four times inside the 3-yard line. Three years later, Montana and Marino hooked up in what was billed as a classic duel in Super Bowl XIX. It was strictly no contest. The 49ers romped to

an easy victory 38-16. At the close of the decade, San Francisco turned in back-to-back Super Bowl victories, becoming the first team since the Steelers to do so. In Walsh's final game as head coach, Super Bowl XXIII, Montana led a 92-yard drive in the final three and a half minutes to beat the Bengals 20-16. He threw the winning touchdown pass 10 yards to John Taylor with 34 seconds remaining. Under new coach George Seifert, the 49ers blew out Denver 55-10 in Super Bowl XXIV.

The constant factor in the team's success during the eighties was Montana, supported by receiver Jerry Rice and running back Roger Craig, around whom all of the 49ers offensive schemes revolved. Walsh had schooled Craig and another former University of Nebraska player, Tom Rathman, who hardly had caught a pass during their college careers, giving his offense an added dimension. The 49ers' receivers played neat games with the defense, between a good mixture of runs, by moving quickly to areas where there were no defenders. It was up to Montana and his receivers to simultaneously "read" these areas, and they kept picking away until the defense became careless about its deep coverage. Montana then would unleash Rice, who in Super Bowl XXIV caught seven passes for 148 yards and three touchdowns. Rice had received the most valuable player award in Super Bowl XXIII for his 215 yards on 11 receptions, one of them for a touchdown.

There Was Plenty of Action Off the Field, As Well

It would be nice to say that all of the NFL's energies were restricted to its product on the field, but between 1970 and 1990, the league's continued

financial prosperity triggered a rash of problems that consumed more of Commissioner Pete Rozelle's time than any other area. Labor problems plagued the game, twice leading to player strikes. In 1982, when the game was at an all-time high in public acceptance, a players' strike cost 57 days of the season, reduced it by seven games, and forced a gerrymandered playoff schedule to preserve the Super Bowl's continuity. In 1987, there was a one-game hiatus, after which the owners turned to "replacement teams" to play three weeks of the schedule. This got the regular players back on the field for the final ten weeks.

There also were problems with franchises shifting cities. The Oakland Raiders moved to Los Angeles in 1982 over the objections of the other teams, who had previously voted on such matters. But Al Davis took the matter to court and it was ruled that clubs could move as they wished, thus providing the impetus for the Baltimore Colts' move to Indianapolis in 1984. When the Cardinals moved from St. Louis to Phoenix in 1988, it had the blessing of the NFL's owners.

As in the 1940s, and 1960s, the NFL found itself challenged by new leagues. The World Football League started in 1974 and lasted a year and a half before drowning in red ink. Nonetheless, it stripped the NFL champion Miami Dolphins of three stars – Larry Csonka, Jim Kiick, and Paul Warfield – and touched off another upward spiral in player salaries. The Florida Blazers won the WFL's only title, but their players weren't paid for the final 15 weeks of the season. In 1983, the United States Football League, playing from March through July and fortified by network and cable television contracts, began a four-season run before folding in 1986. The USFL had a much more dramatic effect on life in the

NFL. It attracted many players, most of them near the ends of their careers but recognizable names just the same. It also signed a number of college stars, many of them now playing in the NFL.

Money was the real lure, enough to attract three consecutive Heisman Trophy winners – Herschel Walker, Mike Rozier, and Doug Flutie – over the NFL. Current NFL stars such as Anthony Carter (a wide receiver for Minnesota who played on the USFL's first championship team, the Michigan Panthers), defensive end Reggie White of the Philadelphia Eagles, and quarterback Jim Kelly of the Buffalo Bills–also began their pro careers in the rival league. Quarterback Steve Young, a sure top draft pick in the NFL after an excellent career at Brigham Young and later a member of Tampa Bay and the 49ers – was the USFL's marquee acquisition. Young, signed a contract full of annuities, with the USFL's Los Angeles Express that would have netted him an estimated $40 million Young got very little of the money because the team folded and the deal soon proved worthless.

The league also attracted veteran NFL coaches such as George Allen, who led the Phoenix team to a conference title, Chuck Fairbanks, and Jack Pardee. It also developed future NFL coaches, such as Jim Mora and Lindy Infante. Mora's Philadelphia and Baltimore Stars played in all four of the USFL's title games, winning the last three.

The league's undoing came when new owners, such as developer Donald Trump, deviated from the original springtime format and decided to challenge the NFL at the gate. This was aggravated by poor attendance and financial problems of many teams whose fans simply would not support another professional football league, and that turned away the television networks. In a last gasp to recoup some of its losses, and perhaps force a merger involving some of its teams, the USFL filed a $1.7 billion anti-trust suit against the NFL. A jury concurred with some of the anti-trust allegations, but rejected all of the USFL's television-related charges and awarded the renegade league three dollars in damages.

Opposite:
Philadelphia Eagles defensive end Reggie White began his professional career with the USFL's Memphis Showboats. White was named all-USFL in his second year in the league.

Above: The San Francisco 49ers stand during the playing of the National Anthem before they battled the Los Angeles Rams in the 1989 American Bowl in Tokyo, Japan.

Right: An English 'bobby' oversees a 49ers practice at Crystal Palace. The team was preparing for its game against the Miami Dolphins in the 1988 American Bowl.

The NFL changed its rules to reflect the creative talents of its coaches, who constantly found ways to combat imbalances that grew from ever-changing offensive or defensive strategies. In the early 1970s, defenses had begun to smother the game. The NFL's Competition Committee, its rules-makers, spent almost the entire decade making it easier to produce more offense. The new rules included moving hashmarks in from the sidelines. They now would be the width of the goal posts, thus giving teams more room between the ball and the near sideline on every play; moving the goal posts to the end lines of the end zones, cutting down on a proliferation of field goals and forcing teams either to try to score a touchdown or keep the ball in play with a punt; moving all kickoffs to a team's 35-yard line instead of its 40; returning missed field-goal attempts from outside an opponent's 20-yard line to the previous line of scrimmage, instead of the 20-yard line as before, inviting teams to consider going for more than a field goal; and gradually restricting defenders' contact with wide receivers coming off the line of scrimmage to the first five yards, allowing them to get into the pattern more quickly and open up the passing game. The passing game was advanced further when offensive linemen were allowed to fully extend their arms in blocking. In the past, the rules required that they keep their arms flat against their chests.

In 1986, NFL owners voted to use "instant replay" to review officials' decisions touching on the disposition of the ball — out of bounds, fumbles, possession on pass completions. The results were a mixed bag, finding some public favor but scorned by most coaches. The method did decide one game, in 1989. The final play in a game between Green Bay and Chicago at first was ruled "no catch," but later was reversed, giving Green Bay a victory.

In 1974, the NFL instituted sudden death overtime for all its games, not just the championship contests. In 1977, the league expanded its schedule to 16 games. In an effort to cut down on injuries and needless incidents of violence, the rules-makers restricted the areas of the body where a block could be made; and developed an "in the grasp" rule to protect quarterbacks from late hits.

The league also began its annual visits overseas for preseason games, beginning in 1986 when Dallas and the Chicago Bears played at Wembley Stadium in London before nearly 83,000 fans in the first American Bowl. The NFL began the 1990s with a new Commissioner, Paul Tagliabue, and with the prospect that pro football would take on a global look. Hope abounded, and with good reason. Since the turn of the century, pro football has proved itself truly a game for all ages.

Philadelphia Stars coach Jim Mora (left) talks with Arizona Wranglers coach George Allen after the 1984 USFL Championship Game. The Stars won 23-3.

THE SUPER BOWLS

 GREEN BAY PACKERS 35

KANSAS CITY CHIEFS 10

Green Bay fullback Jim Taylor (31), who rushed for 56 yards and scored a touchdown in Super Bowl I, gained 1,000 yards rushing in five consecutive NFL seasons.

There was no shortage of talk before the first AFL-NFL Championship Game. But when January 15 of 1967 finally came, the talk ceased; it was time for football's biggest showdown.

The Green Bay Packers would carry the 47-year-old shield of the established, entrenched National Football League against the Kansas City Chiefs, champions of the 7-year-old American Football League.

Tom Catlin, defensive coach for the Los Angeles Rams, was in a position to know about this first matchup. The previous season he had been defensive coach for the Chiefs.

"I don't expect Kansas City to win," he said, "but it's not at all impossible that they might. They would have to play an almost perfect game and the Green Bay defense creates situations in which you make mistakes."

In the first half, the Packers, playing without injured running back Paul Hornung and receiver Boyd Dowler, sparred and probed. Their probing brought them 14 points, but their defense seemed confused on how to contain Kansas City's moving pocket.

Members of the NFL establishment wore looks of worry at the halftime break. But, in the Green Bay locker room, coach Vince Lombardi was about to activate the Packers' warhead.

The explosion was set off by a defensive tactic that

Participants
KANSAS CITY CHIEFS, champions of the American Football League, and
GREEN BAY PACKERS, champions of the National Football League
Date – January 15, 1967
Site – Los Angeles Memorial Coliseum
Time – 1:05 P.M. PST
Condition – 72 degrees, sunny
Playing Surface – Grass
Television and Radio
National Broadcasting Company (NBC) and
Columbia Broadcasting System (CBS)
Regular Season Records
KANSAS CITY, 11-2-1
GREEN BAY, 12-2
League Championships
Kansas City defeated the Buffalo Bills 31-7 for the AFL title
Green Bay defeated the Dallas Cowboys 34-27 for the NFL title
Players' Shares
$15,000 to each member of the winning team;
$7,500 to each member of the losing team
Attendance – 61,946
Gross Receipts – $2,768,211.64
Officials
Referee, Norm Schachter, NFL
umpire, George Young, AFL
line judge, Al Sabato, AFL
head linesman, Bernie Ulman, NFL
back judge, Jack Reader, AFL
field judge, Mike Lisetski, NFL
Coaches
Hank Stram, Kansas City
Vince Lombardi, Green Bay

KANSAS CITY	Starters, Offense	GREEN BAY
Chris Burford	WR	Carroll Dale
Jim Tyrer	LT	Bob Skoronski
Ed Budde	LG	Fred (Fuzzy) Thurston
Wayne Frazier	C	Bill Curry
Curt Merz	RG	Jerry Kramer
Dave Hill	RT	Forrest Gregg
Fred Arbanas	TE	Marv Fleming
Otis Taylor	WR	Boyd Dowler
Len Dawson	QB	Bart Starr
Mike Garrett	RB	Elijah Pitts
Curtis McClinton	RB	Jim Taylor
	Starters, Defense	
Jerry Mays	LE	Willie Davis
Andy Rice	LT	Ron Kostelnik
Buck Buchanan	RT	Henry Jordan
Chuck Hurston	RE	Lionel Aldridge
Bobby Bell	LLB	Dave Robinson
Sherrill Headrick	MLB	Ray Nitschke
E. J. Holub	RLB	Lee Roy Caffey
Fred Williamson	LCB	Herb Adderley
Willie Mitchell	RCB	Bob Jeter
Bobby Hunt	LS	Tom Brown
Johnny Robinson	RS	Willie Wood

Lombardi had always scorned: the blitz. In this case it was a two-man attack that rattled Len Dawson, the Chiefs' quarterback.

Dawson, hurried and bumped on a third-quarter pass, failed to see Packers safety Willie Wood hovering near tight end Fred Arbanas, the intended receiver. Wood intercepted the pass and returned it 50 yards to set up a touchdown by Elijah Pitts.

Minutes later, Green Bay had the ball again. Bart Starr passed three times to veteran Max McGee and the Packers had their fourth touchdown – and, later, another score for Pitts to take the game 35-10. Starr was named most valuable player, but McGee was most valuable receiver with seven catches for 138 yards.

Left: Bart Starr completed 16 of 23 passes for 250 yards and two touchdowns and was voted the most valuable player of Super Bowl I.

Below: Packers running back Elijah Pitts (22) scores the final touchdown of Super Bowl I on a 1 yard run. Pitts rushed for 45 yards on 11 carries and scored twice.

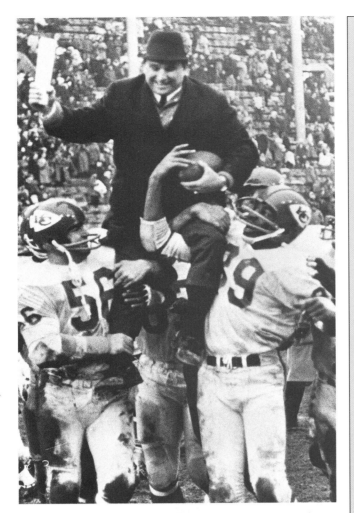

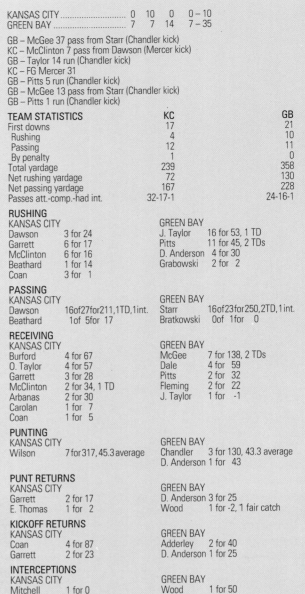

Right: *Kansas city linebacker Walt Corey (56) and wide receiver Otis Taylor (89) carry head coach Hank Stram off the field after the Chiefs defeated Buffalo 31-7 in the 1966 AFL Championship Game.*

Below: *Green Bay receiver Boyd Dowler (86) is flipped by Dallas defensive back Mike Gaechter (27) after scoring on a 16-yard pass in the 1966 NFL Championship Game.*

KANSAS CITY	0	10	0	0 – 10	
GREEN BAY	7	7	14	7 – 35	

GB – McGee 37 pass from Starr (Chandler kick)
KC – McClinton 7 pass from Dawson (Mercer kick)
GB – Taylor 14 run (Chandler kick)
KC – FG Mercer 31
GB – Pitts 5 run (Chandler kick)
GB – McGee 13 pass from Starr (Chandler kick)
GB – Pitts 1 run (Chandler kick)

TEAM STATISTICS	KC	GB
First downs	17	21
Rushing	4	10
Passing	12	11
By penalty	1	0
Total yardage	239	358
Net rushing yardage	72	130
Net passing yardage	167	228
Passes att.-comp.-had int.	32-17-1	24-16-1

RUSHING

KANSAS CITY		GREEN BAY	
Dawson	3 for 24	J. Taylor	16 for 53, 1 TD
Garrett	6 for 17	Pitts	11 for 45, 2 TDs
McClinton	6 for 16	D. Anderson	4 for 30
Beathard	1 for 14	Grabowski	2 for 2
Coan	3 for 1		

PASSING

KANSAS CITY		GREEN BAY	
Dawson	16of27for211,1TD,1int.	Starr	16of23for250,2TD,1int.
Beathard	1of 5for 17	Bratkowski	0of 1for 0

RECEIVING

KANSAS CITY		GREEN BAY	
Burford	4 for 67	McGee	7 for 138, 2 TDs
O. Taylor	4 for 57	Dale	4 for 59
Garrett	3 for 28	Pitts	2 for 32
McClinton	2 for 34, 1 TD	Fleming	2 for 22
Arbanas	2 for 30	J. Taylor	1 for -1
Carolan	1 for 7		
Coan	1 for 5		

PUNTING

KANSAS CITY		GREEN BAY	
Wilson	7 for 317, 45.3 average	Chandler	3 for 130, 43.3 average
		D. Anderson	1 for 43

PUNT RETURNS

KANSAS CITY		GREEN BAY	
Garrett	2 for 17	D. Anderson	3 for 25
E. Thomas	1 for 2	Wood	1 for -2, 1 fair catch

KICKOFF RETURNS

KANSAS CITY		GREEN BAY	
Coan	4 for 87	Adderley	2 for 40
Garrett	2 for 23	D. Anderson	1 for 25

INTERCEPTIONS

KANSAS CITY		GREEN BAY	
Mitchell	1 for 0	Wood	1 for 50

GREEN BAY PACKERS 33

OAKLAND RAIDERS 14

The rumors had circulated around the NFL for weeks: Vince Lombardi was returning to his native New York to coach the Jets. Or, he was accepting the challenge of rebuilding the Chicago Bears. Or, he was easing off, moving full time to the front office.

One thing seemed certain, though. The second Super Bowl would be his last game as head coach of the Packers. An era—in Green Bay and the NFL—was drawing to a close.

Lombardi made it semi-official to his players two days before their game with the Oakland Raiders, telling them during a meeting, "It may be the last time we are all together."

If the Raiders were mismatched against the Packers, as some contended, their handicap would be enormous now that the Green Bay veterans, the men who had been with Lombardi from the start, saw the game as one giant goingaway party for Lombardi.

What a celebration they made it!

Green Bay scored on its first three possessions. Don Chandler kicked a 39-yard field goal, and then a 20-yarder after an eight-minute drive that began at the Packers' 3-yard line.

The third score was a thunderbolt. After punting the ball away, Oakland decided to blitz on first down. Starr's primary target, Carroll Dale, was covered closely by Willie Brown, but safety Howie Williams

Above: *Bart Starr*

Left: *In the 1961 AFL Championship Game, Houston running back Charley Tolar (44) rushed for 52 yards on 16 carries in the Oilers' 10-3 win over the San Diego Chargers. Both teams were slowed by their own mistakes, as Houston turned the ball over seven times and San Diego six.*

failed to pick up Boyd Dowler from cornerback Kent McCloughan; Starr lofted a pass to Dowler for a 62-yard touchdown.

"Bart Starr," Raiders defensive tackle Tom Keating was to marvel later, "reads a 'dog' better than any man I've ever seen."

The Raiders came back to score a touchdown on Daryle Lamonica's 23-yard pass to Bill Miller. But Starr's bomb had shaken the young AFL team. Linebacker Dan Conners stopped Travis Williams of the Packers on third down at the Green Bay 16, but Oakland's Rodger Bird muffed the punt return and Dick Capp recovered for the Packers.

Chandler's subsequent 43-yard field goal and Herb Adderley's fourth-quarter 60-yard interception return for a score assured the success of the farewell party.

Right and below:
Bart Starr was chosen the most valuable player of Super Bowl II after completing 13 of 24 passes for 202 yards and 1 touchdown.

Participants
OAKLAND RAIDERS, champions of the American Football League, and GREEN BAY PACKERS, champions of the National Football League

Date – January 14, 1968
Site – Orange Bowl, Miami
Time – 3:05 P.M. EST
Conditions – 86 degrees, partly cloudy
Playing Surface – Grass
Television and Radio – Columbia Broadcasting System (CBS)
Regular Season Records
OAKLAND, 13-1
GREEN BAY, 9-4-1
League Championships
Oakland defeated the Houston Oilers 40-7 for the AFL title
Green Bay defeated the Dallas Cowboys 21-17 for the NFL title
Players' Shares
$15,000 to each member of the winning team
$7,500 to each member of the losing team
Attendance – 75,546
Gross Receipts –$3,349,106.89
Officials
Referee, Jack Vest, AFL
umpire, Ralph Morcroft, NFL
line judge, Bruce Alford, NFL
head linesman, Tony Veteri, AFL
back judge, Stan Javie, NFL
field judge, Bob Bauer, AFL
Coaches
John Rauch, Oakland
Vince Lombardi, Green Bay

GREEN BAY	Starters, Offense	OAKLAND
Boyd Dowler	WR	Bill Miller
Bob Skoronski	LT	Bob Svihus
Gale Gillingham	LG	Gene Upshaw
Ken Bowman	C	Jim Otto
Jerry Kramer	RG	Wayne Hawkins
Forrest Gregg	RT	Harry Schuh
Marv Fleming	TE	Billy Cannon
Carroll Dale	WR	Fred Biletnikoff
Bart Starr	QB	Daryle Lamonica
Donny Anderson	RB	Pete Banaszak
Ben Wilson	RB	Hewritt Dixon
	Starters, Defense	
Willie Davis	LE	Isaac Lassiter
Ron Kostelnik	LT	Dan Birdwell
Henry Jordan	RT	Tom Keating
Lionel Aldridge	RE	Ben Davidson
Dave Robinson	LLB	Bill Laskey
Ray Nitschke	MLB	Dan Conners
Lee Roy Caffey	RLB	Gus Otto
Herb Adderley	LCB	Kent McCloughan
Bob Jeter	RCB	Willie Brown
Tom Brown	LS	Warren Powers
Willie Wood	RS	Howie Williams

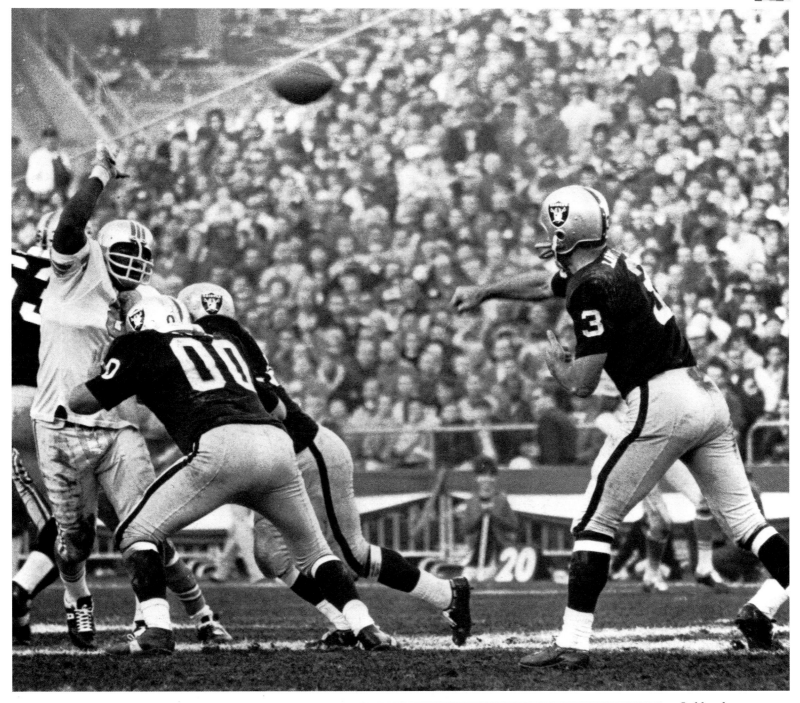

| GREEN BAY | | 3 | 13 | 10 | 7 – 33 |
| OAKLAND | | 0 | 7 | 0 | 7 – 14 |

GB – FG Chandler 39
GB – FG Chandler 20
GB – Dowler 62 pass from Starr (Chandler kick)
Oak – Miller 23 pass from Lamonica (Blanda kick)
GB – FG Chandler 43
GB – Anderson 2 run (Chandler kick)
GB – FG Chandler 31
GB – Adderley 60 interception return (Chandler kick)
Oak – Miller 23 pass from Lamonica (Blanda kick)

TEAM STATISTICS

	GB	Oak
First downs	19	16
Rushing	11	5
Passing	7	10
By penalty	1	1
Total yardage	322	293
Net rushing yardage	160	107
Net passing yardage	162	186
Passes att.-comp.-had int.	24-13-0	34-15-1

RUSHING

GREEN BAY		OAKLAND	
Wilson	17 for 62	Dixon	12 for 54
Anderson	14 for 48, 1 TD	Todd	2 for 37
Williams	8 for 36	Banaszak	6 for 16
Starr	1 for 14		
Mercein	1 for 0		

PASSING

GREEN BAY		OAKLAND	
Starr	13 of 24 for 202, 1 TD	Lamonica	15 for 34 for 208, 2 TDs, 1 int.

RECEIVING

GREEN BAY		OAKLAND	
Dale	4 for 43	Miller	5 for 84, 2 TDs
Fleming	4 for 35	Banaszak	4 for 69
Dowler	2 for 71, 1 TD	Cannon	2 for 25
Anderson	2 for 18	Biletnikoff	2 for 10
McGee	1 for 35	Wells	1 for 17
		Dixon	1 for 3

PUNTING

GREEN BAY		OAKLAND	
Anderson	6 for 234, 39.0 average	Eischeid	6 for 264, 44.0 average

PUNT RETURNS

GREEN BAY		OAKLAND	
Wood	5 for 35	Bird	2 for 12, 1 fair catch

KICKOFF RETURNS

GREEN BAY		OAKLAND	
Adderley	1 for 24	Todd	3 for 63
Williams	1 for 18	Grayson	2 for 61
Crutcher	1 for 7	Hawkins	1 for 3
		Kocourek	1 for 0
		(Kocourek lateraled to Grayson, who returned 11 yards)	

INTERCEPTIONS

GREEN BAY		OAKLAND	
Adderley	1 for 60, 1 TD	None	

Oakland quarterback Daryle Lamonica (3) completed 10 of 24 passes for 111 yards and 2 touchdowns in the Raiders' 40-7 win over Houston in the 1967 AFL Championship Game.

SUPER BOWL III

NEW YORK JETS 16

BALTIMORE COLTS 7

Baltimore shut out Cleveland 34-0 in the 1968 NFL Championship Game, limiting the Browns to only 56 yards rushing.

ou Michaels, the pugnacious Baltimore defensive end and kicker, was relaxing in a Ft. Lauderdale bar several nights before Game III. His eyes scanned the room and found a dark-haired, sleepy-eyed man he knew only by reputation.

"Namath," said Michaels, approaching the table of the young Jets quarterback. "You been doing a lot of talking."

"Lot to talk about," answered Joe Namath. "We're going to kick the hell out of your team."

Michaels was nonplussed. Here was this wise guy

Namath, not only saying that his Jets would beat the Colts, not only disparaging Baltimore quarterbacks Earl Morrall and Johnny Unitas, but, later (at a sports dinner the Thursday night before the game), actually guaranteeing victory in public.

The game started as if the guarantee could never be redeemed. The Colts drove deep into New York territory on their first possession, but came up short; Michaels missed a 27-yard field goal. The third time the Colts had the ball, Al Atkinson deflected Morrall's pass from the Jets' 6. It was intercepted by Randy Beverly.

Participants
NEW YORK JETS, champions of the American Football League, and
BALTIMORE COLTS, champions of the National Football League
Date – January 12,1969
Site – Orange Bowl, Miami
Time – 3:05 P.M. EST
Conditions – 73 degrees, overcast, threat of rain
Playing Surface – Grass
Television and Radio – National Broadcasting Company (NBC)
Regular Season Records
NEW YORK, 11-3
BALTIMORE, 13-1
League Championships
New York defeated the Oakland Raiders 27-23 for the AFL title
Baltimore defeated the Cleveland Browns 34-0 for the NFL title
Players' Shares
$15,000 to each member of the winning team
$7,500 to each member of the losing team
Attendance – 75,377
Gross Receipts – $3,374,985.64
Officials
Referee, Tommy Bell, NFL
umpire, Walt Parker, AFL
line judge, Cal LePore, AFL
head linesman, George Murphy, NFL
back judge, Jack Reader, AFL
field judge, Joe Gonzales, NFL
Coaches
Weeb Ewbank, New York
Don Shula, Baltimore

N.Y. JETS	Starters, Offense	BALTIMORE
George Sauer	WR	Jimmy Orr
Winston Hill	LT	Bob Vogel
Bob Talamini	LG	Glenn Ressler
John Schmitt	C	Bill Curry
Randy Rasmussen	RG	Dan Sullivan
Dave Herman	RT	Sam Ball
Pete Lammons	TE	John Mackey
Don Maynard	WR	Willie Richardson
Joe Namath	QB	Earl Morrall
Emerson Boozer	RB	Tom Matte
Matt Snell	RB	Jerry Hill

	Starters, Defense	
Gerry Philbin	LE	Charles (Bubba) Smith
Paul Rochester	LT	Billy Ray Smith
John Elliott	RT	Fred Miller
Verlon Biggs	RE	Ordell Braase
Ralph Baker	LLB	Mike Curtis
Al Atkinson	MLB	Dennis Gaubatz
Larry Grantham	RLB	Don Shinnick
Johnny Sample	LCB	Bobby Boyd
Randy Beverly	RCB	Lenny Lyles
Jim Hudson	LS	Jerry Logan
Bill Baird	RS	Rick Volk

Left: *Joe Namath completed 17 of 28 passes for 206 yards in Super Bowl III and was chosen as the game's most valuable player.*

Below: *In the 1968 AFL Championship Game, Namath (12) ignored the icy winds in New York's Shea Stadium and passed for 266 yards and 3 touchdowns to lead the Jets to a 27-23 victory over Oakland.*

The Jets suddenly were aroused, as was the crowd in the Orange Bowl. Namath confidently moved his team downfield. When Namath's pass to wide receiver George Sauer gave New York a first down on the Colts' 23, the Baltimore defenders cursed themselves in frustration.

A played called "19 Option," with Matt Snell carrying four yards into the end zone, gave the AFL its first lead in Super Bowl history.

The Colts' poise deteriorated just before the half when Morrall failed to see an open Jimmy Orr in the end zone on a flea-flicker play and was intercepted by Jim Hudson.

The Colts fumbled on their first play of the second half. Nine downs later the Jets had a 10-0 lead on Jim Turner's 32-yard field goal. Turner kicked two more before Baltimore scored.

The game ended with the Jets 16-7 victors. Namath trotted off the field, forefinger raised signifying that, for the moment, he, the Jets, head coach Weeb Ewbank, and the AFL were all number one in professional football.

Top: After guaranteeing the Jets a victory in Super Bowl III, Namath (12) and his teammates picked the Baltimore defense apart and gave the AFL its first world championship.
Above: Former Jets head coach Weeb Ewbank is the only head coach to win world championships in both the AFL and the NFL. Besides leading the Jets to victory in Super Bowl III, Ewbank also coached the 1958 and 1959 Baltimore Colts to NFL titles.

NEW YORK JETS	0	7	6	3 – 16
BALTIMORE	0	0	0	7 – 7

NYJ – Snell 4 run (Turner kick)
NYJ – FG Turner 32
NYJ – FG Turner 30
NYJ – FG Turner 9
Balt – Hill 1 run (Michaels kick)

TEAM STATISTICS

	NYJ	Balt
First downs	21	18
Rushing	10	7
Passing	10	9
By penalty	1	2
Total yardage	337	324
Net rushing yardage	142	143
Net passing yardage	195	181
Passes att.-comp.-had int.	29-17-0	41-17-4

RUSHING

NEW YORK JETS		BALTIMORE	
Snell	30 for 121, 1 TD	Matte	11 for 116
Boozer	19 for 19	Hill	9 for 29, 1 TD
Mathis	3 for 2	Unitas	1 for 0
		Morrall	2 for -2

PASSING

NEW YORK JETS		BALTIMORE	
Namath	17 of 28 for 206	Morrall	6 of 17 for 71, 3 int.
Parilli	0 of 1 for 0	Unitas	11 of 24 for 110, 1 int.

RECEIVING

NEW YORK JETS		BALTIMORE	
Sauer	8 for 133	Richardson	6 for 58
Snell	4 for 40	Orr	3 for 42
Mathis	3 for 20	Mackey	3 for 35
Lammons	2 for 13	Matte	2 for 30
		Hill	2 for 1
		Mitchell	1 for 15

PUNTING

NEW YORK JETS		BALTIMORE	
Johnson	4 for 155, 38.8 average	Lee	3 for 144, 44.3 average

PUNT RETURNS

NEW YORK JETS		BALTIMORE	
Baird	1 for 0, 1 fair catch	Brown	4 for 34

KICKOFF RETURNS

NEW YORK JETS		BALTIMORE	
Christy	1 for 25	Pearson	2 for 59
		Brown	2 for 46

INTERCEPTIONS

NEW YORK JETS		BALTIMORE	
Beverly	2 for 0	None	
Hudson	1 for 9		
Sample	1 for 0		

KANSAS CITY CHIEFS 23
MINNESOTA VIKINGS 7

Kansas City – with head coach Hank Stram's crazy-quilt offense – did its homework before Super Bowl IV. The book on Minnesota was that the Vikings liked to score quickly, take control, then tee off on the opposing quarterback with their Purple People Eaters defensive line.

But taking control against the Chiefs would not be easy. In 16 regular-season and playoff games, they had allowed only seven touchdowns in the first half.

On this day it would allow none, which was remarkable because it was a stormy afternoon and the field was wet. Also remarkable was the fact that quarterback Len Dawson showed up as ready to play as he did. Prior to the game he had to deal with allegations that he had underworld associations.

The story was reported on the Huntley-Brinkley NBC newscast, January 6, 1970. It said a special Justice Department Task Force was about to call seven professional football players to testify about their relationship with known gamblers. Among the

Despite allegations that he was linked to a federal gambling investigation, Chiefs quarterback Len Dawson remained poised and led his team to victory in Super Bowl IV by completing 12 of 17 passes for 142 yards and 1 touchdown. Dawson was voted as the game's MVP.

Kansas City wide receiver Otis Taylor (89) makes a key 35-yard catch to keep alive a 94-yard scoring drive in the 1969 AFL Championship Game. The Chiefs defeated Oakland 17-7 in the AFL's last game.

players scheduled to testify, it reported, was Dawson (who eventually was cleared on all charges).

Despite this added pressure, Dawson completed his first two passes for 37 yards and Jan Stenerud kicked a 48-yard field goal. He completed three more and Stenerud kicked a 32-yarder.

The Chiefs made the Vikings' heavy rush work against them with Frank Pitts's 19-yard reverse. Then Stenerud came on again and kicked a 25-yarder for a 9-0 lead. The Vikings fumbled the ensuing kickoff, and Dawson supervised a six-play drive, climaxed by Mike Garrett's five-yard touchdown run.

Joe Kapp, Minnesota's charismatic quarterback, rallied for a third-quarter touchdown drive, but the Chiefs countered with one of their own, capped by a 46-yard pass to Otis Taylor.

Defense is what failed Kansas City in Super Bowl I. This time around, it was the key to the Chiefs' success. Minnesota's last three possessions ended with interceptions, and all day was denied a ground game.

And as for Dawson, he was again in the headlines – as Game IV's MVP.

Chiefs linebacker Bobby Bell (78) and defensive tackle Buck Buchanan (86) combine to stop Oakland's Charlie Smith (23) in the 1968 AFL Championship Game. The Kansas City defense intercepted 4 passes and completely shut down the Raiders' running game.

Participants
KANSAS CITY CHIEFS, champions of the American Football League, and
MINNESOTA VIKINGS, champions of the National Football League

Date – January 11, 1970
Site – Tulane Stadium, New Orleans
Time – 2:35 P.M. CST
Conditions – 61 degrees, heavy overcast, wet field
Playing Surface – Grass
Television and Radio – Columbia Broadcasting System (CBS)
Regular Season Records
KANSAS CITY, 11-3
MINNESOTA, 12-2
League Championships
Kansas City defeated the Oakland Raiders 17-7 for the AFL title
Minnesota defeated the Cleveland Browns 27-7 for the NFL title
Players' Shares
$15,000 to each member of the winning team
$7,500 to each member of the losing team
Attendance – 80,562
Gross Receipts – $3,817,872.69
Officials
Referee, John McDonough, NFL
umpire, Lou Palazzi, AFL
line judge, Bill Schleibaum, NFL
head linesman, Harry Kessel, NFL
back judge, Tom Kelleher, NFL
field judge, Charley Musser, AFL

Coaches
Hank Stram, Kansas City
Bud Grant, Minnesota

MINNESOTA	Starters, Offense	KANSAS CITY
Gene Washington	WR	Frank Pitts
Grady Alderman	LT	Jim Tyrer
Jim Vellone	LG	Ed Budde
Mick Tingelhoff	C	E. J. Holub
Milt Sunde	RG	Mo Moorman
Ron Yary	RT	Dave Hill
John Beasley	TE	Fred Arbanas
John Henderson	WR	Otis Taylor
Joe Kapp	QB	Len Dawson
Dave Osborn	RB	Mike Garrett
Bill Brown	RB	Robert Holmes
	Starters, Defense	
Carl Eller	LE	Jerry Mays
Gary Larsen	LT	Curley Culp
Alan Page	RT	Buck Buchanan
Jim Marshall	RE	Aaron Brown
Roy Winston	LLB	Bobby Bell
Lonnie Warwick	MLB	Willie Lanier
Wally Hilgenberg	RLB	Jim Lynch
Earsell Mackbee	LCB	Jim Marsalis
Ed Sharockman	RCB	Emmitt Thomas
Karl Kassulke	LS	Jim Kearney
Paul Krause	RS	Johnny Robinson

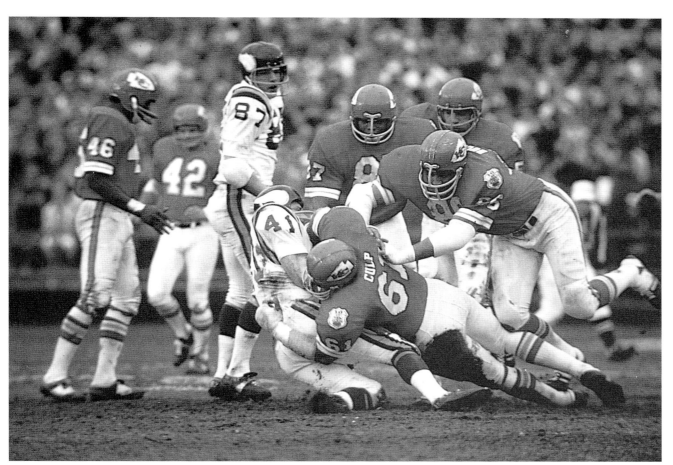

Left: *Kansas City defensive tackle Curley Culp (61) wraps up Minnesota's Dave Osborn (41) in Super Bowl IV. The Chiefs limited the Vikings to 67 rushing yards.*

Below: *Minnesota running back Dave Osborn (41) exploded for 108 yards and a touchdown on 18 carries in the Vikings' 27-7 win over Cleveland in the 1969 NFL title game.*

MINNESOTA	0	0	7	0 – 7	
KANSAS CITY	3	13	7	0 – 23	

KC – FG Stenerud 48
KC – FG Stenerud 32
KC – FG Stenerud 25
KC – Garrett 5 run (Stenerud kick)
Minn-Osborn 4 run (Cox kick)
KC – Taylor 46 pass from Dawson (Stenerud kick)

TEAM STATISTICS	Minn	KC
First downs	13	18
Rushing	2	8
Passing	10	7
By penalty	1	3
Total yardage	239	273
Net rushing yardage	67	151
Net passing yardage	172	122
Passes att.-comp.-had int.	8-17-3	17-12-1

RUSHING

MINNESOTA		KANSAS CITY	
Osborn	7 for 15, 1 TD	McVea	12 for 26
Brown	6 for 26	Garrett	11 for 39, 1 TD
Reed	4 for 17, 1 TD	Hayes	8 for 31
Kapp	2 for 9	Holmes	5 for 7
		Pitts	3 for 37
		Dawson	3 for 11

PASSING

MINNESOTA		KANSAS CITY	
Kapp	16 of 25 for 183, 2 int.	Dawson	12 of 17
Cuozzo	1 of 3 for 16, 1 int.		for 142, 1 TD, 1 int.

RECEIVING

MINNESOTA		KANSAS CITY	
Henderson	7 for 111	Taylor	6 for 81, 1 TD
Brown	3 for 11	Pitts	3 for 33
Beasley	2 for 41	Garrett	2 for 25
Reed	2 for 16	Hayes	1 for 3
Osborn	2 for 11		
Washington	1 for 9		

PUNTING

MINNESOTA		KANSAS CITY	
Lee	3 for 111, 37.0 average	Wilson	4 for 194, 48.5 average

PUNT RETURNS

MINNESOTA		KANSAS CITY	
West	2 for 18	Garrett	1 for 0

KICKOFF RETURNS

MINNESOTA		KANSAS CITY	
West	3 for 46	Hayes	2 for 36
Jones	1 for 33		

INTERCEPTIONS

MINNESOTA		KANSAS CITY	
Krause	1 for 0	Lanier	1 for 9
		Robinson	1 for 9

SUPER BOWL V

BALTIMORE COLTS 16

DALLAS COWBOYS 13

Baltimore receiver Eddie Hinton (33) repeatedly got open against the Oakland secondary in the 1970 AFC Championship Game. The former number one draft choice from Oklahoma caught 5 passes for 115 yards in the Colts' 27-17 victory.

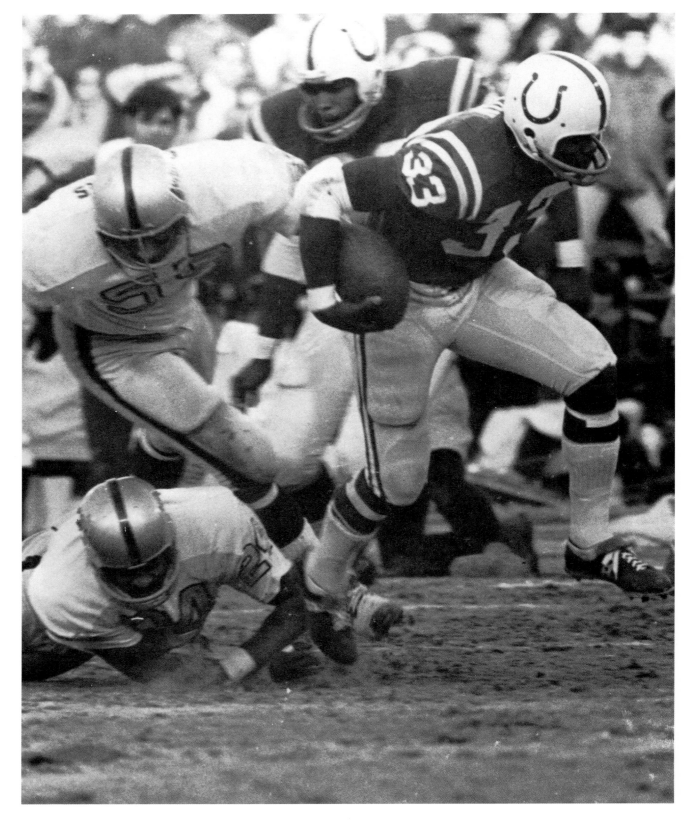

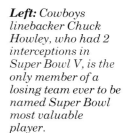

T his was the first Super Bowl (the four previous games had been known as the 'AFL-NFL World Championship Game'). All 79,204 seats in the Orange Bowl had been sold and 20,000 more ticket seekers were turned down.

The game was not one for football purists, who counted 16 major mistakes. The Cowboys alone had 10 penalties. There were interceptions, dropped and bad passes, and fumbles.

The day was typified by the first touchdown. Johnny Unitas of the Colts aimed a pass at Eddie Hinton. It caromed off him, ricocheted off Dallas cornerback Mel Renfro, and settled into the hands of Colts' tight end John Mackey, who rumbled untouched to complete a record 75-yard play. The extra point was blocked, tying the score 6-6. Later in the quarter, Unitas was injured and Earl Morrall came in.

By the third quarter, the Cowboys led 13-6, but Baltimore pushed to midfield, close enough for Jim O'Brien to try a 52-yard field goal. O'Brien, a rookie, never had kicked a field goal longer than 48 yards, but the Colts were willing to let him try. The kid they called "Lassie" because of his long hair was loose enough to do anything, they figured.

O'Brien's attempt was short, but in keeping with the zaniness of the game, the kick was allowed to roll and died inside the 1-yard line.

Everything seemed to go wrong for the Colts in the

Left: Cowboys linebacker Chuck Howley, who had 2 interceptions in Super Bowl V, is the only member of a losing team ever to be named Super Bowl most valuable player.

Below: Earl Morrall replaced an injured John Unitas at quarterback in Super Bowl V and completed 7 of 15 passes for 147 yards.

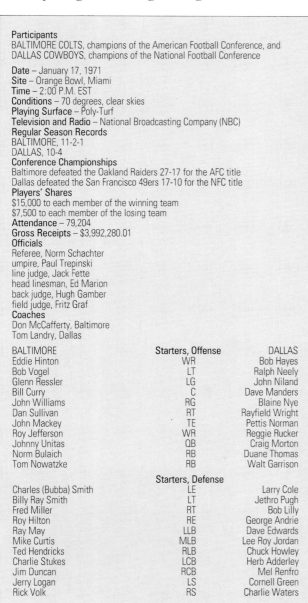

Participants
BALTIMORE COLTS, champions of the American Football Conference, and
DALLAS COWBOYS, champions of the National Football Conference

Date – January 17, 1971
Site – Orange Bowl, Miami
Time – 2:00 P.M. EST
Conditions – 70 degrees, clear skies
Playing Surface – Poly-Turf
Television and Radio – National Broadcasting Company (NBC)
Regular Season Records
BALTIMORE, 11-2-1
DALLAS, 10-4
Conference Championships
Baltimore defeated the Oakland Raiders 27-17 for the AFC title
Dallas defeated the San Francisco 49ers 17-10 for the NFC title
Players' Shares
$15,000 to each member of the winning team
$7,500 to each member of the losing team
Attendance – 79,204
Gross Receipts – $3,992,280.01
Officials
Referee, Norm Schachter
umpire, Paul Trepinski
line judge, Jack Fette
head linesman, Ed Marion
back judge, Hugh Gamber
field judge, Fritz Graf
Coaches
Don McCafferty, Baltimore
Tom Landry, Dallas

BALTIMORE	Starters, Offense	DALLAS
Eddie Hinton	WR	Bob Hayes
Bob Vogel	LT	Ralph Neely
Glenn Ressler	LG	John Niland
Bill Curry	C	Dave Manders
John Williams	RG	Blaine Nye
Dan Sullivan	RT	Rayfield Wright
John Mackey	TE	Pettis Norman
Roy Jefferson	WR	Reggie Rucker
Johnny Unitas	QB	Craig Morton
Norm Bulaich	RB	Duane Thomas
Tom Nowatzke	RB	Walt Garrison
	Starters, Defense	
Charles (Bubba) Smith	LE	Larry Cole
Billy Ray Smith	LT	Jethro Pugh
Fred Miller	RT	Bob Lilly
Roy Hilton	RE	George Andrie
Ray May	LLB	Dave Edwards
Mike Curtis	MLB	Lee Roy Jordan
Ted Hendricks	RLB	Chuck Howley
Charlie Stukes	LCB	Herb Adderley
Jim Duncan	RCB	Mel Renfro
Jerry Logan	LS	Cornell Green
Rick Volk	RS	Charlie Waters

second half. They drove to the Dallas 11, but Morrall's pass was intercepted by Chuck Howley in the end zone. They tried a flea-flicker from the Cowboys' 30. It short-circuited; running back Sam Havrilak threw to Hinton, and it might have turned into a touchdown except that Hinton fumbled at the 5 and lost possession.

Still, with a minute to play, Mike Curtis, Baltimore's middle linebacker, intercepted Craig Morton's pass, which had deflected off a leaping Dan Reeves, and returned it 13 yards to Dallas's 28.

With five seconds left, O'Brien lined up to kick a 32-yard field goal. Dallas called time out, but the stalling tactic didn't work. O'Brien's kick sailed true. The Colts were winners and the Super Bowl III loss had been avenged.

Top: In 1969, Baltimore's Gino Marchetti (89) was selected as the best defensive end in the NFL's first 50 years.

Above: Jim O'Brien's (80) 32-yard field goal with five seconds remaining in Super Bowl V gave the Colts a 16-13 win over Dallas.

BALTIMORE	0	6	0	10 – 16
DALLAS	3	10	0	0 – 13

Dall – FG Clark 14
Dall – FG Clark 30
Balt – Mackey 75 pass from Unitas (kick blocked)
Dall – Thomas 7 pass from Morton (Clark kick)
Balt – Nowatzke 2 run (O'Brien kick)
Balt – FG O'Brien 32

TEAM STATISTICS	Balt	Dall
First downs	14	10
Rushing	4	4
Passing	6	5
By penalty	4	1
Total yardage	329	215
Net rushing yardage	69	102
Net passing yardage	260	113
Passes att.-comp.-had int.	25-11-3	26-12-3

RUSHING

BALTIMORE		DALLAS	
Bulaich	18 for 28	Thomas	18 for 35
Nowatzke	10 for 33, 1 TD	Garrison	12 for 65
Unitas	1 for 4	Morton	1 for 2
Havrilak	1 for 3		
Morrall	1 for 1		

PASSING

BALTIMORE		DALLAS	
Morrall	7 of 15 for 147, 1 int	Morton	12 of 26 for 127, 1 TD, 3 int.
Unitas	3 of 9 for 88, 1 TD, 2 int.		
Havrilak	1 of 1 for 25		

RECEIVING

BALTIMORE		DALLAS	
Jefferson	3 for 52	Reeves	5 for 46
Mackey	2 for 80, 1 TD	Thomas	4 for 21, 1 TD
Hinton	2 for 51	Garrison	2 for 19
Havrilak	2 for 27	Hayes	1 for 41
Nowatzke	1 for 45		
Bulaich	1 for 5		

PUNTING

BALTIMORE		DALLAS	
Lee	4 for 168, 41.5 average	Widby	9 for 377, 41.9 average

PUNT RETURNS

BALTIMORE		DALLAS	
Logan	1 for 8	Hayes	3 for 9
Gardin	4 for 4, 3 fair catches		

KICKOFF RETURNS

BALTIMORE		DALLAS	
Duncan	4 for 90	Harris	1 for 18
		Hill	1 for 14
		Kiner	1 for 2

INTERCEPTIONS

BALTIMORE		DALLAS	
Volk	1 for 30	Howley	2 for 22
Logan	1 for 14	Renfro	1 for 0
Curtis	1 for 13		

DALLAS COWBOYS 24
MIAMI DOLPHINS 3

Dallas' enigmatic rookie running back Duane Thomas (33) rushed for 143 yards and a touchdown in leading the Cowboys past San Francisco 17-10 in the 1970 NFC Championship Game.

The story of Super Bowl VI began at the end of Super Bowl V, with the helmet of Bob Lilly bouncing to midfield after he had slammed it to the turf following the Colts' last-second victory.

Lilly's disgust was a capsule of the Cowboys' past. "Next Year's Champions" they were called, more in jest than prophecy. "They can't win the big one," was their universal indictment.

Not only had the Cowboys lost the last Super Bowl, but they had failed in four divisional or league championship games in the previous four seasons.

Game VI gave them their retribution.

In Dallas's first series of plays on this very cold January day, they ran only once and ended up punting. But by the time the afternoon ended, the Cowboys, with Duane Thomas, Calvin Hill, and Walt Garrison, had run for 252 yards, 92 yards more than

Left: Roger Staubach was voted the most valuable player of Super Bowl VI after completing 12 of 19 passes for 119 yards and 2 touchdowns.

Miami used its consistent running game to easily defeat the defending world champion Baltimore Colts 21-0 in the 1971 AFC Championship Game. Running back Jim Kiick (21) and Larry Csonka combined for 126 yards rushing.

Green Bay had piled up in beating Oakland in Super Bowl II.

Dallas ran so successfully because the hub of the Miami defense, middle linebacker Nick Buoniconti, was controlled on virtually every play.

Meanwhile, the vaunted Dolphins' offense was stymied. Larry Csonka, who had not fumbled all season, lost the ball on his second carry of the game. And dangerous Dolphins wide receiver Paul Warfield was shut down by cornerback Mel Renfro and safety Cornell Green.

The Dolphins began wearing down late in the first half. The Cowboys ran seven times on a 76-yard drive and only one rush gained less than five yards. The touchdown came when Roger Staubach, who led Dallas to 10 straight victories after taking over the quarterback job from Craig Morton, passed seven yards to Lance Alworth.

The game was all but over after Dallas took the second-half kickoff. The Cowboys bulled 71 yards for the touchdown, with the enigmatic Thomas accounting for half of them. "They're too young to win the Super Bowl," said Dallas linebacker Dave Edwards about the Dolphins. However, Miami, which had its first winning season just the year before, would be back.

DALLAS		3 7 7 7 – 24
MIAMI		0 3 0 0 – 3

Dall – FG Clark 9
Dall – Alworth 7 pass from Staubach (Clark kick)
Mia – FG Yepremian 31
Dall – D Thomas 3 run (Clark kick)
Dall – Ditka 7 pass from Staubach (Clark kick)

TEAM STATISTICS	Dallas	Miami
First downs	15	7
Rushing	8	3
Passing	7	4
By penalty	0	0
Total yardage	352	185
Net rushing yardage	252	80
Net passing yardage	100	105
Passes att.-comp.-had int.	19-12-0	23-12-1

RUSHING

DALLAS		MIAMI	
D. Thomas	19 for 95, 1 TD	Kiick	10 for 40
Garrison	14 for 74	Csonka	9 for 40
Hill	7 for 25	Griese	1 for 0
Staubach	5 for 18		
Ditka	1 for 17		
Hayes	1 for 16		
Reeves	1 for 7		

PASSING

DALLAS		MIAMI	
Staubach	12 of 19 for 119, 2 TDs	Griese	12 of 23 for 134, 1 int.

RECEIVING

DALLAS		MIAMI	
D. Thomas	3 for 17	Warfield	4 for 39
Alworth	2 for 28, 1 TD	Kiick	3 for 21
Ditka	2 for 28, 1 TD	Csonka	2 for 18
Hayes	2 for 23	Fleming	1 for 27
Garrison	2 for 11	Twilley	1 for 20
Hill	1 for 12	Mandich	1 for 9

PUNTING

DALLAS		MIAMI	
Widby	5 for 166, 33.2 average	Seiple	5 for 200, 40 average

PUNT RETURNS

DALLAS		MIAMI	
Hayes	1 for -1, 1 fair catch	Scott	1 for 21
Harris	2 fair catches.		

KICKOFF RETURNS

DALLAS		MIAMI	
I. Thomas	1 for 23	Morris	4 for 90
Waters	1 for 11	Ginn	1 for 32

INTERCEPTIONS

DALLAS		MIAMI	
Howley	1 for 41	None	

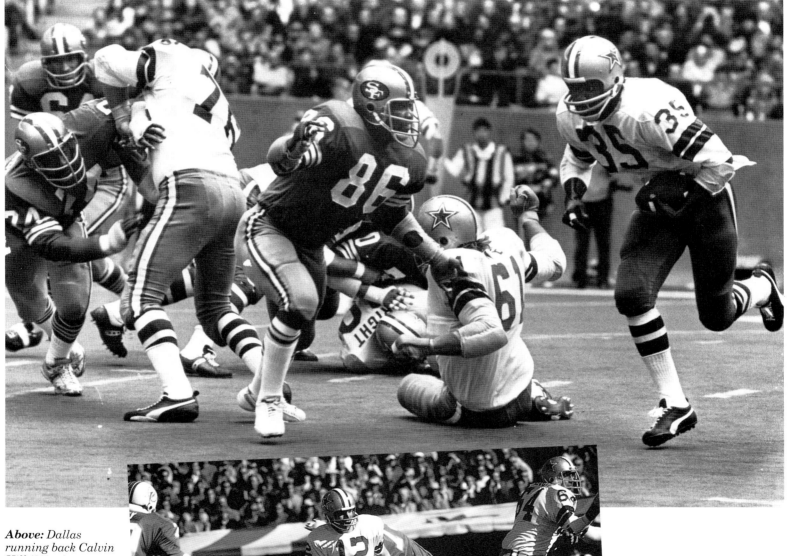

Above: Dallas running back Calvin Hill (35) tries to elude San Francisco's Cedrick Hardman (86) in the Cowboys' 14-3 win in the 1971 NFC Championship Game. Hill's one-yard touchdown run broke a scoreless tie in the second quarter.

Left: Roger Staubach's scrambling contributed to the Cowboys' rushing record of 252 yards in Super Bowl VI.

SUPER BOWL VII

MIAMI DOLPHINS 14

WASHINGTON REDSKINS 7

The "Over-the-Hill Gang's" defensive unit huddle before doing battle.

It was the No Names versus the Over-the-Hill Gang, a western-style gunfight in the Los Angeles Memorial Coliseum with 90,182 in the stands and 75 million watching on television. Washington got its nickname the season before, when George Allen became the head coach and traded for veteran talent others felt was "over the hill."

It was Tom Landry's unwitting comment before Super Bowl VI that gave Miami's defense its name: "I can't recall their names, but they are a matter of great concern to us."

History weighed heavily on the Dolphins. They were unbeaten in 16 games. No previous NFL team ever played an entire season without losing. The

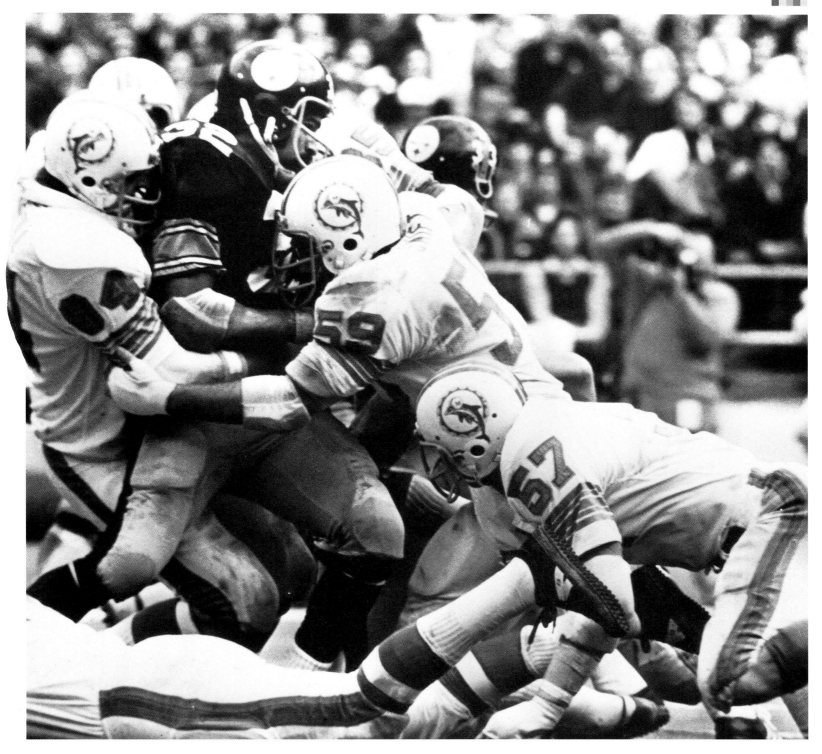

Participants
MIAMI DOLPHINS, champions of the American Football Conference, and
WASHINGTON REDSKINS, champions of the National Football Conference

Date – January 14, 1973
Site – Los Angeles Memorial Coliseum
Time – 12:30 P.M. PST
Conditions – 84 degrees, sunny, hazy
Playing Surface – Grass
Television and Radio – National Broadcasting Company (NBC)
Regular Season Records
MIAMI, 14-0
WASHINGTON, 11-3
Conference Championships
Miami defeated the Pittsburgh Steelers 21-17 for the AFC title
Washington defeated the Dallas Cowboys 26-3 for the NFC title
Players' Shares
$15,000 to each member of the winning team
$7,500 to each member of the losing team
Attendance – 90,182
Gross Receipts – $4,180,086.53
Officials
Referee, Tommy Bell
umpire, Lou Palazzi
line judge, Bruce Alford
head linesman, Tony Veteri
back judge, Tom Kelleher
field judge, Tony Skover

Coaches
Don Shula, Miami
George Allen, Washington

MIAMI	Starters, Offense	WASHINGTON
Paul Warfield	WR	Charley Taylor
Wayne Moore	LT	Terry Hermeling
Bob Kuechenberg	LG	Paul Laaveg
Jim Langer	C	Len Hauss
Larry Little	RG	John Wilbur
Norm Evans	RT	Walter Rock
Marv Fleming	TE	Jerry Smith
Howard Twilley	WR	Roy Jefferson
Bob Griese	QB	Billy Kilmer
Jim Kiick	RB	Larry Brown
Larry Csonka	RB	Charley Harraway
	Starters, Defense	
Vern Den Herder	LE	Ron McDole
Manny Fernandez	LT	Bill Brundige
Bob Heinz	RT	Diron Talbert
Bill Stanfill	RE	Verlon Biggs
Doug Swift	LLB	Jack Pardee
Nick Buoniconti	MLB	Myron Pottios
Mike Kolen	RLB	Chris Hanburger
Lloyd Mumphord	LCB	Pat Fischer
Curtis Johnson	RCB	Mike Bass
Dick Anderson	LS	Brig Owens
Jake Scott	RS	Roosevelt Taylor

Dolphins defensive end Bill Stanfill (84) and linebacker Doug Swift (59) trap Pittsburgh's Franco Harris (32) in the 1972 AFC title game. Miami won 21-17.

cynics doubted that Miami could keep the streak alive. That doubt began to erode in the first quarter when Bob Griese, out most of the season with a broken ankle, completed a 28-yard pass for a touchdown to Howard Twilley. Twilley carried defender Pat Fischer five yards into the end zone. Griese passed only 11 times all day, completing 8.

Another Miami touchdown was nullified by a penalty, but middle linebacker Nick Buoniconti intercepted a pass and returned it 32 yards to the Redskins' 27. Jim Kiick eventually plunged a yard for the second touchdown.

The No-Names made big play after big play to frustrate Washington. Safety Jake Scott stopped two Redskins drives with interceptions, and the line shut down Larry Brown, the NFC's leading rusher. It wasn't until the final two minutes that the Redskins scored on the game's most memorable – and most unusual – play. Bill Brundige blocked a field goal. Miami kicker Garo Yepremian picked it up and fumbled attempting to pass. Mike Bass of the Redskins recovered and ran 49 yards to score.

"This team has gone into an area that no other team has gone before," said Dolphins coach Don Shula, for whom the victory was personal redemption after two previous Super Bowl losses (one with Baltimore).

"In the past, there was always the feeling of not having achieved the ultimate. This is the ultimate."

Above: *Miami safety Jake Scott stopped two Redskins drives with interceptions in Super Bowl VII and was selected as the game's most valuable player.*

Right: *In the 1972 NFC Championship Game, Washington receiver Charley Taylor caught 7 passes for 146 yards and 2 touchdowns to lead the Redskins to a 26-3 victory over Dallas.*

Opposite: *With less than five minutes to play in Super Bowl VII, Dolphins safety Jake Scott returned his second interception of the game from three yards deep into the end zone to the Redskins' 48-yard line.*

MIAMI	7 7 0 0 – 14		
WASHINGTON	0 0 0 7 – 7		

Mia – Twilley 28 pass from Griese (Yepremian kick)
Mia – Kiick 1 run (Yepremian kick)
Wash – Bass 49 fumble recovery return (Knight kick)

TEAM STATISTICS		Mia	Wash
First downs		12	16
Rushing		7	9
Passing		5	7
By penalty		0	0
Total yardage		253	228
Net rushing yardage		184	141
Net passing yardage		69	87
Passes att.-comp.-had int.		11-8-1	28-14-3

RUSHING

MIAMI		WASHINGTON	
Csonka	15 for 112	Brown	22 for 72
Kiick	12 for 38, 1 TD	Harraway	10 for 37
Morris	10 for 34	Kilmer	2 for 18
		C. Taylor	1 for 8
		Smith	1 for 6

PASSING

MIAMI		WASHINGTON	
Griese	8 of 11 for 88, 1 TD, 1 int.	Kilmer	14 of 28 for 104, 3 int.

RECEIVING

MIAMI		WASHINGTON	
Warfield	3 for 36	Jefferson	5 for 50
Kiick	2 for 6	Brown	5 for 26
Twilley	1 for 28, 1 TD	C. Taylor	2 for 20
Mandich	1 for 19	Smith	1 for 11
Csonka	1 for -1	Harraway	1 for -3

PUNTING

MIAMI		WASHINGTON	
Seiple	7 for 301, 43.0 average	Bragg	5 for 156, 31.2 average

PUNT RETURNS

MIAMI		WASHINGTON	
Scott	2 for 4, 2 fair catches	Haymond	4 for 9
Anderson	2 fair catches	Vactor	2 fair catches

KICKOFF RETURNS

MIAMI		WASHINGTON	
Morris	2 for 33	Haymond	2 for 30
		Mul-Key	1 for 15

INTERCEPTIONS

MIAMI		WASHINGTON	
Scott	2 for 63	Owens	1 for 0
Buoniconti	1 for 32		

 MIAMI DOLPHINS 24

MINNESOTA VIKINGS 7

Right: Miami running back Larry Csonka was selected as the most valuable player of Super Bowl VIII.

Below: Csonka trots untouched into the end zone on an 11-yard run in the Dolphins's 27-10 win over Oakland in the 1973 AFC Championship Game.

Opposite: Csonka (39) rushed 33 times for a record 145 yards in the Dolphins' 24-7 victory over the Vikings in Super Bowl VIII.

It is the third quarter. The score is Miami 17, Minnesota 0. The Dolphins have the ball on the Vikings' 2-yard line. Suddenly, Bob Griese, about to take the snap from center, whirls and asks: "What the hell is the snap count?"

"One," says running back Jim Kiick.

"Two," says fullback Larry Csonka.

Griese takes Csonka's word. It is an error. When Griese gets the ball, Kiick and Csonka are still in their stances. Nevertheless, Csonka roars ahead, takes the handoff, and plunges into the end zone.

Super Bowl VIII was virtually over before it began. Minnesota had won 14 games, but the Vikings were ranked twenty-third among the 26 NFL teams in stopping the run. Miami, which had emerged as one of the most relentless running teams of all time, took advantage of Minnesota's weakness with well-conceived misdirection plays. It also threw its "53" defense, one of the earliest of the 3-4s, at the Vikings.

Griese, who threw only 11 passes in the previous

Participants
MIAMI DOLPHINS, champions of the American Football Conference, and
MINNESOTA VIKINGS, champions of the National Football Conference

Date – January 13, 1974
Site – Rice Stadium, Houston
Time – 2:30 P.M. CST
Conditions – 50 degrees, overcast
Playing Surface – AstroTurf
Television and Radio – Columbia Broadcasting System (CBS)
Regular Season Records
MIAMI, 12-2
MINNESOTA, 12-2
Conference Championships
Miami defeated the Oakland Raiders 27-10 for the AFC title
Minnesota defeated the Dallas Cowboys 27-10 for the NFC title
Players' Shares
$15,000 to each member of the winning team
$7,500 to each member of the losing team
Attendance – 68,142
Gross Receipts – $3,953,641.22
Officials
Referee, Ben Dreith
umpire, Ralph Morcroft
line judge, Jack Fette
head linesman, Leo Miles
back judge, Stan Javie
field judge, Fritz Graf

Coaches
Don Shula, Miami
Bud Grant, Minnesota

MINNESOTA	Starters, Offense	MIAMI
Carroll Dale	WR	Paul Warfield
Grady Alderman	LT	Wayne Moore
Ed White	LG	Bob Kuechenberg
Mick Tingelhoff	C	Jim Langer
Frank Gallagher	RG	Larry Little
Ron Yary	RT	Norm Evans
Stu Voigt	TE	Jim Mandich
John Gilliam	WR	Marlin Briscoe
Fran Tarkenton	QB	Bob Griese
Chuck Foreman	RB	Eugene (Mercury) Morris
Oscar Reed	RB	Larry Csonka
	Starters, Defense	
Carl Eller	LE	Vern Den Herder
Gary Larsen	LT	Manny Fernandez
Alan Page	RT	Bob Heinz
Jim Marshall	RE	Bill Stanfill
Roy Winston	LLB	Doug Swift
Jeff Siemon	MLB	Nick Buoniconti
Wally Hilgenberg	RLB	Mike Kolen
Nate Wright	LCB	Lloyd Mumphord
Bobby Bryant	RCB	Curtis Johnson
Jeff Wright	LS	Dick Anderson
Paul Krause	RS	Jake Scott

The Minnesota rushing attack kept Dallas off-balance in the 1973 NFC title game, as the Vikings accumulated 203 rushing yards. Running back Chuck Foreman (44) led the way with 76 yards and a touchdown on 19 carries.

Super Bowl, passed only seven times this day, completing six.

But the game belonged more to players such as Csonka, a massive rusher; Jim Langer, a pit bull of a center; and Bob Kuechenberg, a tenacious guard. Csonka gained a record 145 yards on 33 carries and scored two touchdowns.

But his path was cleared, sometimes yards beyond the line of scrimmage, by Langer and Kuechenberg, who took turns controlling Alan Page, the quick Vikings defensive tackle. Page was asked when Miami began to look invincible. "After the first couple

of plays," he admitted.

Csonka, an old-fashioned type of player, gave his blockers full credit. "I never got touched until I got to the secondary," he said. "They just did everything to us on the running game," said Vikings defensive end Carl Eller. "Sweeps, traps, whatever."

There was a certain sadness, though, pervading the Dolphins' victory. There was a feeling, which proved accurate, that this was a last hurrah for the team, that it would be breaking up. "The only adjective that fits this team is 'great'," said jubilant coach Don Shula.

| MINNESOTA | 0 | 0 | 0 | 7 – 7 |
| MIAMI | 14 | 3 | 7 | 0 – 24 |

Mia – Csonka 5 run (Yepremian kick)
Mia – Kiick 1 run (Yepremian kick)
Mia – FG Yepremian 28
Mia – Csonka 2 run (Yepremian kick)
Minn – Tarkenton 4 run (Cox kick)

TEAM STATISTICS

	Minn	Mia
First downs	14	21
Rushing	5	13
Passing	8	4
By penalty	1	4
Total yardage	238	259
Net rushing yardage	72	196
Net passing yardage	166	63
Passes att.-comp.-had int.	28-18-1	7-6-0

RUSHING

MINNESOTA		MIAMI	
Reed	11 for 32	Csonka	33 for 145, 2TDs
Foreman	7 for 18	Morris	11 for 34
Tarkenton	4 for 17, 1 TD	Kiick	7 for 10, 1 TD
Marinaro	1 for 3	Griese	2 for 7
B. Brown	1 for 2		

PASSING

MINNESOTA		MIAMI	
Tarkenton	18 of 28 for 182, 1int.	Griese	6 of 7 for 73

RECEIVING

MINNESOTA		MIAMI	
Foreman	5 for 27	Warfield	2 for 33
Gilliam	4 for 44	Mandich	2 for 21
Voigt	3 for 46	Briscoe	2 for 19
Marinaro	2 for 39		
B. Brown	1 for 9		
Kingsriter	1 for 9		
Lash	1 for 9		
Reed	1 for -1		

PUNTING

MINNESOTA		MIAMI	
Eischeid	5 for 211, 42.2 ave.	Seiple	3 for 119, 39.7 ave.

PUNT RETURNS

MINNESOTA		MIAMI	
Bryant	1 fair catch	Scott	3 for 20, 1 fair catch

KICKOFF RETURNS

MINNESOTA		MIAMI	
Gilliam	2 for 41	Scott	2 for 47
West	2 for 28		

INTERCEPTIONS

MINNESOTA		MIAMI	
None		Johnson	1 for 10

PITTSBURGH STEELERS 16
MINNESOTA VIKINGS 6

It had taken the Pittsburgh Steelers 42 years to get to the championship game of the NFL and now it looked as if they were sleep-walking through it. They led at halftime, but the score was a mere 2-0 against a Minnesota team that could generate almost no offense. Something happened, though, in the last two minutes of the second quarter that seemed to jar the Steelers awake. Vikings receiver John Gilliam cut across the middle, deep in Pittsburgh territory. Fran Tarkenton hit him on the numbers, but Steelers safety Glen Edwards hit him even harder. Gilliam fumbled and Mel Blount recovered for Pittsburgh. Instead of having a first down on the Steelers' 5, the Vikings had seen their best scoring chance dissipate. In fact, their only score would come in the fourth quarter on a blocked punt recovered for a touchdown.

The Pittsburgh defense, called the Steel Curtain, had been built painstakingly by Chuck Noll, who became head coach of the team in 1969.

After winning their first game under Noll, the Steelers lost their next 13. The fans were clamoring

Left: Pittsburgh's Franco Harris ran for a record 158 yards on 34 carries in Super Bowl IX.

Below: Pittsburgh's offense proved to be unstoppable in the Steelers' drive to the NFL title in 1974.

for offensive stars, but in his first draft Noll took Joe Greene, a defensive tackle from North Texas State. A Pittsburgh newspaper asked "Joe Who?" in its headline.

In time they found out about Greene, and also about Blount, L.C. Greenwood, Jack Ham, Jack Lambert, Andy Russell, and Dwight White, the steel of the Steel Curtain.

Noll's hand-picked defense arrived earlier than the offense. In that first championship season the quarterback job floated among Terry Bradshaw, Joe Gilliam, and Terry Hanratty. Bradshaw finally got it back late in the year. Franco Harris, the main ball carrier, gained only 125 yards in his first three games, then gained 881 in his last nine, when he was fully healthy. By the end of Game IX, Harris had a Super Bowl-record 158 yards and a 12-yard touchdown run.

But it was the Steelers' defense that reigned, allowing the Vikings just 17 rushing yards and only 102 yards passing.

Fran Tarkenton's passing (10 of 20 for 123 yards and 1 touchdown) led the Vikings to a 14-10 win over the Los Angeles Rams in the 1974 NFC title game.

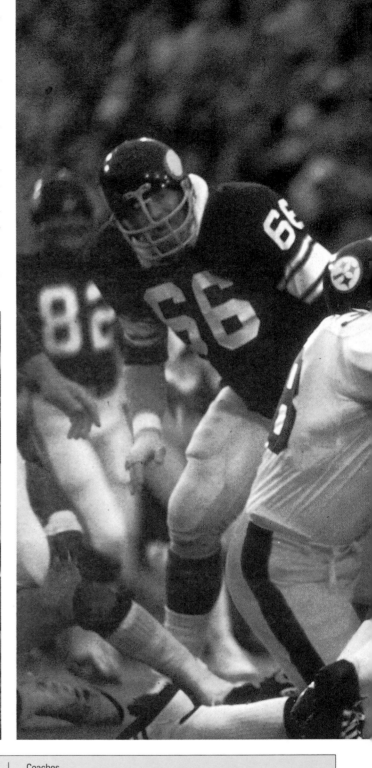

Participants
PITTSBURGH STEELERS, champions of the American Football Conference, and MINNESOTA VIKINGS, champions of the National Football Conference

Date – January 12,1975
Site – Tulane Stadium, New Orleans
Time – 2:00 PM CST
Conditions – 46 degrees, cloudy
Playing Surface – Poly-Turf
Television and Radio – National Broadcasting Company (NBC)
Regular Season Records
PITTSBURGH, 10-3-1
MINNESOTA, 10-4
Conference Championships
Pittsburgh defeated the Oakland Raiders 24-13 for the AFC title
Minnesota defeated the Los Angeles Rams 14-10 for the NFC title
Players' Shares
$15,000 to each member of the winning team
$7,500 to each member of the losing team
Attendance – 80,997
Gross Receipts – $5,259,766.90
Officials
Referee, Bernie Ulman
umpire, Al Conway
line judge, Bruce Alford
head linesman, Ed Marion
back judge, Ray Douglas
field judge, Dick Dolack

Coaches
Chuck Noll, Pittsburgh
Bud Grant, Minnesota

PITTSBURGH	Starters, Offense	MINNESOTA
Frank Lewis	WR	Jim Lash
Jon Kolb	LT	Charles Goodrum
Jim Clack	LG	Andy Maurer
Ray Mansfield	C	Mick Tingelhoff
Gerry Mullins	RG	Ed White
Gordon Gravelle	RT	Ron Yary
Larry Brown	TE	Stu Voigt
Ron Shanklin	WR	John Gilliam
Terry Bradshaw	QB	Fran Tarkenton
Rocky Bleier	RB	Chuck Foreman
Franco Harris	RB	Dave Osborn
	Starters, Defense	
L. C. Greenwood	LE	Carl Eller
Joe Greene	LT	Doug Sutherland
Ernie Holmes	RT	Alan Page
Dwight White	RE	Jim Marshall
Jack Ham	LLB	Roy Winston
Jack Lambert	MLB	Jeff Siemon
Andy Russell	RLB	Wally Hilgenberg
J. T. Thomas	LCB	Nate Wright
Mel Blount	RCB	Jackie Wallace
Mike Wagner	LS	Jeff Wright
Glen Edwards	RS	Paul Krause

The Steelers' defense limited Minnesota to only 119 yards total offense in Super Bowl IX, including a record low of 17 yards rushing.

PITTSBURGH............................ 0   2   7   7 – 16
MINNESOTA............................. 0   0   0   6 – 6

Pitt – Safety, White tackled Tarkenton in end zone
Pitt – Harris 12 run (Gerela kick)
Minn – T. Brown recovered blocked punt in end zone (kick failed)
Pitt – L. Brown 4 pass from Bradshaw (Gerela kick)

TEAM STATISTICS

	Pitt	Minn
First downs	17	9
Rushing	11	2
Passing	5	5
By penalty	1	2
Total yardage	333	119
Net rushing yardage	249	17
Net passing yardage	84	102
Passes att.-comp.-had int.	14-9-0	26-11-3

RUSHING

PITTSBURGH
Harris   34 for 158, 1 TD
Bleier   17 for 65
Bradshaw   5 for 33
Swann   1 for -7

MINNESOTA
Foreman   12 for 18
Osborn   8 for -1
Tarkenton   1 for 0

PASSING

PITTSBURGH
Bradshaw   9 of 14 for 97, 1 TD.

MINNESOTA
Tarkenton   11 of 26 for 102, 3 int.

RECEIVING

PITTSBURGH
Brown   3 for 49, 1 TD
Stallworth 3 for 24
Bleier   2 for 11
Lewis   1 for 12

MINNESOTA
Foreman   5 for 50
Voigt   2 for 31
Osborn   2 for 7
Gilliam   1 for 16
Reed   1 for -2

PUNTING

PITTSBURGH
Walden   7 for 243, 34.7 average

MINNESOTA
Eischeid   6 for 223, 37.2 average

PUNT RETURNS

PITTSBURGH
Swann   3 for 34
Edwards   2 for 2

MINNESOTA
McCullum   3 for 11
N. Wright   1 for 1
Wallace   1 fair catch.

KICKOFF RETURNS

PITTSBURGH
Harrison   2 for 17
Pearson   1 for 15

MINNESOTA
McCullum   1 for 26
McClanahan 1 for 22
B. Brown   1 for 2

INTERCEPTIONS

PITTSBURGH
Wagner   1 for 26
Blount   1 for 10
Greene   1 for 10

MINNESOTA
None

SUPER BOWL X

PITTSBURGH STEELERS 21
DALLAS COWBOYS 17

Super Bowl X most valuable player Lynn Swann set a Super Bowl record with 161 yards on 4 receptions.
Opposite: *He outleaps Dallas cornerback Mark Washington in Super Bowl X for a remarkable 53-yard reception.*

This was the Bicentennial Super Bowl. It also was the Hollywood Super Bowl; scenes for the film Black Sunday were being shot during the game, which had enough action, excitement, and drama to be a feature film itself.

Dallas, the first wild card team ever to reach the Super Bowl, scored first when the Steelers' punter Bobby Walden took his eyes off the snap and the ball got away from him. Billy Joe DuPree tackled him on the Pittsburgh 29. On the next play, Roger Staubach, playing with injured ribs, passed down the middle to Drew Pearson, who split the defense at the 14 and raced into the end zone.

It was the first time all season the Steelers had yielded a point in the first quarter. Pittsburgh stormed back. Terry Bradshaw passed 32 yards to Lynn Swann, who made a leaping catch at the sideline, then 7 yards to tight end Randy Grossman for a touchdown. Swann had made only a cameo appearance in the previous Super Bowl and for a while it seemed he wouldn't play at all in this one. He had been knocked out of the AFC Championship Game by Oakland and spent the next three days in a hospital recovering from a concussion. The Steelers' defense was savage, sacking Roger Staubach seven times, three each by L.C. Greenwood and Dwight White, and intercepting him three times.

The defensive pressure – and Jack Lambert's fierce play – produced eight unanswered points (two field goals and a safety), which gave Pittsburgh a 15-10 lead. Then, late in the fourth quarter, Brad-

shaw went for the jugular. It was third and four from the Pittsburgh 36. Dallas blitzed.

Linebacker D.D. Lewis was just a trifle off course. Cliff Harris arrived a split second too late from his safety spot. Bradshaw's pass went far downfield to Swann, covered by just one man, Mark Washington.

Washington tried valiantly, but Swann made another spectacular, leaping reception and the Steelers had a 64-yard touchdown.

Staubach came up with some last-second heroics of his own, but Dallas fell short. The Steelers prevailed 21-17.

Participants
PITTSBURGH STEELERS, champions of the American Football Conference, and DALLAS COWBOYS, champions of the National Football Conference

Date – January 18, 1976
Site – Orange Bowl, Miami
Time – 2:00 P.M. EST
Conditions – 57 degrees, clear
Playing Surface – Poly-Turf
Television and Radio – Columbia Broadcasting System (CBS)
Regular Season Records
PITTSBURGH, 12-2
DALLAS, 10-4
Conference Championships
Pittsburgh defeated the Oakland Raiders 16-10 for the AFC title
Dallas defeated the Los Angeles Rams 37-7 for the NFC title
Players' Shares
$15,000 to each member of the winning team
$7,500 to each member of the losing team
Attendance – 80,187
Gross Receipts – $5,242,641.25
Officials
Referee, Norm Schachter
umpire, Joe Connell
line judge, Jack Fette
head linesman, Leo Miles
back judge, Stan Javie
field judge, Bill O'Brien
Coaches
Chuck Noll, Pittsburgh
Tom Landry, Dallas

DALLAS	Starters, Offense	PITTSBURGH
Golden Richards	WR	John Stallworth
Ralph Neely	LT	Jon Kolb
Burton Lawless	LG	Jim Clack
John Fitzgerald	C	Ray Mansfield
Blaine Nye	RG	Gerry Mullins
Rayfield Wright	RT	Gordon Gravelle
Jean Fugett	TE	Larry Brown
Drew Pearson	WR	Lynn Swann
Roger Staubach	QB	Terry Bradshaw
Preston Pearson	RB	Rocky Bleier
Robert Newhouse	RB	Franco Harris
	Starters, Defense	
Ed Jones	LE	L. C. Greenwood
Jethro Pugh	LT	Joe Greene
Larry Cole	RT	Ernie Holmes
Harvey Martin	RE	Dwight White
Dave Edwards	LLB	Jack Ham
Lee Roy Jordan	MLB	Jack Lambert
D. D. Lewis	RLB	Andy Russell
Mark Washington	LCB	J. T. Thomas
Mel Renfro	RCB	Mel Blount
Charlie Waters	LS	Mike Wagner
Cliff Harris	RS	Glen Edwards

DALLAS	7	3	0	7 – 17	
PITTSBURGH	7	0	0	14 – 21	

Dall – D. Pearson 29 pass from Staubach (Fritsch kick)
Pitt – Grossman 7 pass from Bradshaw (Gerela kick)
Dall – FG Fritsch 36
Pitt – Safety, Harrison blocked Hoopes' punt through end zone
Pitt – FG Gerela 36
Pitt – FG Gerela 18
Pitt – Swann 64 pass from Bradshaw (kick failed)
Dall – P. Howard 34 pass from Staubach (Fritsch kick)

TEAM STATISTICS	Dall	Pitt
First downs	14	13
Rushing	6	7
Passing	8	6
By penalty	0	0
Total yardage	270	339
Net rushing yardage	108	149
Net passing yardage	162	190
Passes att.-comp.-had int.	24-15-3	19-9-0

RUSHING
DALLAS		PITTSBURGH	
Newhouse	16 for 56	Harris	27 for 82
Staubach	5 for 22	Bleier	15 for 51
Dennison	5 for 16	Bradshaw	4 for 16
P. Pearson	5 for 14		

PASSING
DALLAS		PITTSBURGH	
Staubach	15of24for204,2TDs,3int.	Bradshaw	9 of 19 for 209, 2 TDs

RECEIVING
DALLAS		PITTSBURGH	
P. Pearson	5 for 53	Swann	4 for 161, 1 TD
Young	3 for 31	Stallworth	2 for 8
D. Pearson	2 for 59, 1 TD	Harris	1 for 26
Newhouse	2 for 12	Grossman	1 for 7
P. Howard	1 for 34, 1 TD	L. Brown	1 for 7
Fugett	1 for 9		
Dennison	1 for 6		

PUNTING
DALLAS		PITTSBURGH	
Hoopes,	7 for 245, 35.0 average	Walden,	4 for 159, 39.8 average

PUNT RETURNS
DALLAS		PITTSBURGH	
Richards,	1 for 5, 3 fair catches	D. Brown	3 for 14
		Edwards	2 for 17

KICKOFF RETURNS
DALLAS		PITTSBURGH	
T. Henderson	48 after a lateral	Blount	3 for 64
P. Pearson	4 for 48.	Collier	1 for 25

INTERCEPTIONS
DALLAS	PITTSBURGH	
None	Edwards	1 for 35
	Thomas	1 for 35
	Wagner	1 for 19

OAKLAND RAIDERS 32
MINNESOTA VIKINGS 14

Right: Sticky-fingered receiver Fred Biletnikoff made four key receptions for the Raiders in Super Bowl XI, which earned him most valuable player honors.

Opposite top: The Raiders' defense led by linebackers Ted Hendricks (83) and Willie Hall (39) and defensive end Otis Sistrunk, smother Baltimore's Roosevelt Leaks (48). The Raiders defeated the Colts 37-31 in a high-scoring, double-overtime AFC divisional playoff game in 1977.

Three times the Minnesota Vikings had gone to a Super Bowl and each time they had lost. This time, against Oakland, they swore it would be different. "This team has a new dimension," said Bud Grant. "Emotion."

Grant seemed like a prophet when, late in the opening quarter, Minnesota did what no other team had done before – block one of Ray Guy's punts. Fred McNeill, who had knifed in to make the block, recovered on the Oakland 3.

The Vikings desperately needed a touchdown. Not only would it put them ahead for the first time in a Super Bowl game, it would give them precious momentum. But on their second play, they fumbled. Phil Villapiano smashed into running back Brent McClanahan, and Willie Hall recovered for Oakland.

Oakland then drove 90 yards, and Errol Mann kicked a 24-yard field goal.

The matchup between Jim Marshall and Art Shell became a microcosm of the game itself; Marshall, the savvy, determined, 240-pound Vikings defensive end, versus Shell, the savvy, massive 285-pound Raiders offensive tackle. Shell, and with him the Raiders, won.

With Ken Stabler passing to Fred Biletnikoff and Dave Casper, with Oakland's runners churning behind Shell and guard Gene Upshaw, Oakland rolled up a 19-0 lead before Minnesota scored.

"We have a bunch of renegades who play well together," explained Stabler.

Four of those renegades, Upshaw, Biletnikoff, Pete Banaszak, and Willie Brown, had played on the Oakland team beaten by Green Bay in Super Bowl II.

Their moment of fulfillment was assured when Brown streaked 75 yards with a fourth quarter interception for a touchdown and a 32-7 lead.

The Raiders, who gained a record-breaking 429 yards, won their first National Football League title before a record Super Bowl crowd (103,438) plus 81 million television viewers, the largest audience ever to watch a sporting event.

Participants
OAKLAND RAIDERS, champions of the American Football Conference, and
MINNESOTA VIKINGS, champions of the National Football Conference

Date – January 9, 1977
Site – Rose Bowl, Pasadena
Time – 12:30 P.M. PST
Conditions – 58 degrees, clear and sunny
Playing Surface – Grass
Television and Radio – National Broadcasting Company (NBC)
Regular Season Records
OAKLAND, 13-1
MINNESOTA, 11-2-1
Conference Championships
Oakland defeated the Pittsburgh Steelers 24-7 for the AFC title
Minnesota defeated the Los Angeles Rams 24-13 for the NFC title
Players' Shares
$15,000 to each member of the winning team
$7,500 to each member of the losing team
Attendance – 103,438
Gross Receipts – $5,768,772.73
Officials
Referee, Jim Tunney
umpire, Lou Palazzi
line judge, Bill Swanson
head linesman, Ed Marion
back judge, Tom Kelleher
field judge, Armen Terzian

Coaches
John Madden, Oakland
Bud Grant, Minnesota

OAKLAND	Starters, Offense	MINNESOTA
Cliff Branch	WR	Ahmad Rashad
Art Shell	LT	Steve Riley
Gene Upshaw	LG	Charles Goodrum
Dave Dalby	C	Mick Tingelhoff
George Buehler	RG	Ed White
John Vella	RT	Ron Yary
Dave Casper	TE	Stu Voigt
Fred Biletnikoff	WR	Sammy White
Ken Stabler	QB	Fran Tarkenton
Mark van Eeghen	RB	Chuck Foreman
Clarence Davis	RB	Brent McClanahan
	Starters, Defense	
John Matuszak	LE	Carl Eller
Dave Rowe	NT-LT	Doug Sutherland
Otis Sistrunk	RE-RT	Alan Page
Phil Villapiano	LOLB-RE	Jim Marshall
Monte Johnson	LILB-LLB	Matt Blair
Willie Hall	RILB-MLB	Jeff Siemon
Ted Hendricks	ROLB-RLB	Wally Hilgenberg
Alonzo (Skip) Thomas	LCB	Nate Wright
Willie Brown	RCB	Bobby Bryant
George Atkinson	LS	Jeff Wright
Jack Tatum	RS	Paul Krause

| OAKLAND | | 0 | 16 | 3 | 13 – 32 |
| MINNESOTA | | 0 | 0 | 7 | 7 – 14 |

Oak – FG Mann 24
Oak – Casper 1 pass from Stabler (Mann kick)
Oak – Banaszak 1 run (kick failed)
Oak – FG Mann 40
Minn – S White 8 pass from Tarkenton (Cox kick)
Oak – Banaszak 2 run (Mann kick)
Oak – Brown 75 interception return (kick failed)
Minn – Voigt 13 pass from Lee (Cox kick)

TEAM STATISTICS

	Oak	Minn
First downs	21	20
Rushing	13	2
Passing	8	15
By penalty	0	3
Total yardage	429	353
Net rushing yardage	266	71
Net passing yardage	163	282
Passes att.-comp.-had int.	19-12-0	44-24-2

RUSHING

OAKLAND		MINNESOTA	
van Eeghen	18 for 73	Foreman	17 for 44
Davis	16 for 137	McClanahan	3 for 3
Banaszak	10 for 19, 2 TDs	Johnson	2 for 9
Garrett	4 for 19	Miller	2 for 4
Ginn	2 for 9	S White	1 for 7
Rae	2 for 9	Lee	1 for 4

PASSING

OAKLAND		MINNESOTA	
Stabler	12 of 19 for 180, 1 TD	Tarkenton	17 of 35 for 205, 1 TD, 2 int.
		Lee	7 of 9 for 81, 1 TD.

RECEIVING

OAKLAND		MINNESOTA	
Biletnikoff	4 for 79	S. White	5 for 77, 1 TD
Casper	4 for 70, 1 TD	Foreman	5 for 62
Branch	3 for 20	Voigt	4 for 49, 1 TD
Garrett	1 for 11	Miller	4 for 19
		Rashad	3 for 53
		Johnson	3 for 26

PUNTING

OAKLAND		MINNESOTA	
Guy	4 for 162, 40.5 average	Clabo,	7 for 265, 37.9 average

PUNT RETURNS

OAKLAND		MINNESOTA	
Colzie	4 for 43	Willis	3 for 57

KICKOFF RETURNS

OAKLAND		MINNESOTA	
Garrett	2 for 47	S. White	4 for 79
Siani	1 for 0	Willis	3 for 57

INTERCEPTIONS

OAKLAND		MINNESOTA	
Brown	1 for 75, 1 TD	None	
Hall	1 for 16		

Right: Los Angeles Raiders coach Art Shell, whose blocking played a prominent role in the Raiders' win in Super Bowl XI, became the first black head coach in the modern history of the NFL in 1989.

Below: Clarence Davis (28) ignited the Raiders' running game in Super Bowl XI by rushing for 137 yards on 16 carries.

SUPER BOWL XII

DALLAS COWBOYS 27
DENVER BRONCOS 10

Harvey Martin applied a heavy pass rush and recovered a fumble in Super Bowl XII. He was named co-most valuable player with Randy White.

D allas's opening play was a fumble, but it also was a message. Tom Landry's call was for a double reverse. Butch Johnson fumbled the last exchange of the ball, but recovered for a nine-yard loss.

"Landry was warning them [the Denver Broncos] to look for anything," said Cliff Harris, the Cowboys' safety. "Landry was letting them know they had to stay at home."

Immobilizing the Denver defense, the intense play of which had made the Broncos the surprise team of

The Cowboys' defense, led by co-most valuable player Randy White, made 4 interceptions and 4 fumble recoveries in Super Bowl XII.

the season, was sound practice. The Broncos would manage to sack Roger Staubach five times. They would force six fumbles.

But Denver still had to worry about Dallas's unpredictability. It was such that Landry was ready to use a special play in which Staubach was to end up the receiver, but it was never needed.

Nevertheless, this was to be a defensive game, a clash of nicknamed units – Denver's Orange Crush against Dallas's Doomsday II – that was dominated by the Cowboys.

That was evident in Denver's first three possessions: Craig Morton was sacked by Randy White for

Participants
DENVER BRONCOS, champions of the American Football Conference, and DALLAS COWBOYS, champions of the National Football Conference
Date – January 15, 1978
Site – Louisiana Superdome, New Orleans
Time – 5:15 PM CST
Conditions – 70 degrees, indoors
Playing Surface – Astro-Turf
Television and Radio – Columbia Broadcasting System (CBS)
Regular Season Records
DENVER, 12-2
DALLAS, 12-2
Conference Championships
Denver defeated the Oakland Raiders 20-17 for the AFC title
Dallas defeated the Minnesota Vikings 23-6 for the NFC title
Players' Shares
$18,000 to each member of the winning team
$9,000 to each member of the losing team
Attendance – 75,583
Gross Receipts – $6,923,141.50
Officials
Referee, Jim Tunney
umpire, Joe Connell
line judge, Art Holst
head linesman, Tony Veteri
back judge, Ray Douglas
field judge, Bob Wortman
Coaches
Red Miller, Denver
Tom Landry, Dallas

DALLAS	Starters, Offense	DENVER
Butch Johnson	WR	Jack Dolbin
Ralph Neely	LT	Andy Maurer
Herbert Scott	LG	Tom Glassic
John Fitzgerald	C	Mike Montler
Tom Rafferty	RG	Paul Howard
Pat Donovan	RT	Claudie Minor
Billy Joe DuPree	TE	Riley Odoms
Drew Pearson	WR	Haven Moses
Roger Staubach	QB	Craig Morton
Robert Newhouse	RB	Jon Keyworth
Tony Dorsett	RB	Otis Armstrong
	Starters, Defense	
Ed Jones	LE	Barney Chavous
Jethro Pugh	LT-NT	Rubin Carter
Randy White	RT-RE	Lyle Alzado
Harvey Martin	RE-LOLB	Bob Swenson
Thomas Henderson	LLB-LILB	Joe Rizzo
Bob Breunig	MLB-RILB	Randy Gradishar
D. D. Lewis	RLB-ROLB	Tom Jackson
Benny Barnes	LCB	Louis Wright
Aaron Kyle	RCB	Steve Foley
Charlie Waters	LS	Billy Thompson
Cliff Harris	RS	Bernard Jackson

an 11-yard loss to end the first; Randy Hughes intercepted Morton to end the second; and Aaron Kyle intercepted Morton to finish the third.

Denver had the ball eight times in the first half and turned it over six times, either by interception or fumble. Yet the Cowboys' lead was just 13-0.

It took one of the great catches in Super Bowl history, Johnson's reception of Staubach's 45-yard pass in the end zone, to break open the game in the third quarter.

The finishing touch came midway through the fourth quarter when fullback Robert Newhouse pulled up short on a sweep to the left and fired a 29-yard pass to Golden Richards for a touchdown.

Just how much the Dallas defense controlled the game was recognized when White and Harvey Martin were named co-winners of the MVP award.

Martin put the honour in perspective when he said: "We feel we are representing our entire line."

Top: *Butch Johnson (86) gets behind Denver defensive backs Bernard Jackson (29) and Steve Foley (43) to make a diving 45-yard touchdown catch in the third quarter of Super Bowl XII.*

Above: *Denver defensive end Lyle Alzado (77) meets Oakland's Mark van Eeghen head-on in the Broncos' 20-17 win in the 1977 AFC Championship Game.*

DALLAS	10	3	7	7 – 27
DENVER	0	0	10	0 – 10

Dall – Dorsett 3 run (Herrera kick)
Dall – FG Herrera 35
Dall – FG Herrera 43
Den – FG Turner 47
Dall – Johnson 45 pass from Staubach (Herrera kick)
Den – Lytle 1 run (Turner kick)
Dall – Richards 29 pass from Newhouse (Herrera kick)

TEAM STATISTICS

	Dall	Den
First downs	17	11
Rushing	8	8
Passing	8	1
By penalty	1	2
Total yardage	325	156
Net rushing yardage	143	121
Net passing yardage	182	35
Passes att.-comp.-had int.	28-19-0	25-8-4

RUSHING

DALLAS		DENVER	
Dorsett	15 for 66, 1 TD	Lytle	10 for 35, 1 TD
Newhouse	14 for 55	Armstrong	7 for 27
P. Pearson	3 for 11	Keyworth	5 for 9
Staubach	3 for 6	Weese	3 for 26
D. White	1 for 13	Perrin	3 for 8
Laidlaw	1 for 1	Jensen	1 for 16
Johnson	1 for -9		

PASSING

DALLAS		DENVER	
Staubach	17 of 30 for 228, 1 TD	Morton	4 of 15 for 39, 4 int.
Newhouse	1 of 1 for 29, 1 TD	Weese	4 of 10 for 22
D. White	1 of 2 for 5		

RECEIVING

DALLAS		DENVER	
P. Pearson	5 for 37	Dolbin	2 for 24
DuPree	4 for 66	Odoms	2 for 9
Newhouse	3 for -1	Moses	1 for 21
Johnson	2 for 53, 1 TD	Upchurch	1 for 9
Richards	2 for 38, 1 TD	Jensen	1 for 5
Dorsett	2 for 11	Perrin	1 for -7
D. Pearson	1 for 13		

PUNTING

DALLAS		DENVER	
D. White	5 for 208, 41.6 average	Dilts	4 for 153, 38.3 average

PUNT RETURNS

DALLAS		DENVER	
Hill	1 for 1	Upchurch	3 for 22
		Schultz	1 for 0

KICKOFF RETURNS

DALLAS		DENVER	
Johnson	2 for 29	Upchurch	3 for 94
Brinson	1 for 22	Schultz	2 for 62
		Jensen	1 for 17

INTERCEPTIONS

DALLAS		DENVER	
Washington	1 for 27	None	
Kyle	1 for 19		
Barnes	1 for 0		
Hughes	1 for 0		

PITTSBURGH STEELERS 35

DALLAS COWBOYS 31

In the highest-scoring Super Bowl of all, Terry Bradshaw (12) set records by passing for 318 yards and 4 touchdowns in the Steelers' 35-31 win over Dallas in Super Bowl XIII.

Participants
PITTSBURGH STEELERS, champions of the American Football Conference, and DALLAS COWBOYS, champions of the National Football Conference.

Date – January 21, 1979
Site – Orange Bowl, Miami
Time – 4:15 P.M. EST
Conditions – 71 degrees, cloudy
Playing surface – Grass
Television – National Broadcast Company (NBC)
Radio – Columbia Broadcasting System (CBS)
Regular Season Records
PITTSBURGH, 14-2
DALLAS, 12-4
Conference Championships
Pittsburgh defeated the Houston Oilers 34-5 for the AFC title
Dallas defeated the Los Angeles Rams 28-0 for the NFC title
Players' Shares
$18,000 to each member of the winning team
$9,000 to each member of the losing team
Attendance – 79,484
Gross Receipts – $8,833,185.26
Officials
Referee, Pat Haggerty
umpire, Art Demmas
line judge, Jack Fette
head linesman, Jerry Bergman
back judge, Pat Knight
side judge, Dean Look
field judge, Fred Swearingen

Coaches
Chuck Noll, Pittsburgh
Tom Landry, Dallas

PITTSBURGH	Starters, Offense	DALLAS
John Stallworth	WR	Tony Hill
Jon Kolb	LT	Pat Donovan
Sam Davis	LG	Herbert Scott
Mike Webster	C	John Fitzgerald
Gerry Mullins	RG	Tom Rafferty
Ray Pinney	RT	Rayfield Wright
Randy Grossman	TE	Billy Joe DuPree
Lynn Swann	WR	Drew Pearson
Terry Bradshaw	QB	Roger Staubach
Rocky Bleier	RB	Robert Newhouse
Franco Harris	RB	Tony Dorsett
	Starters, Defense	
L. C. Greenwood	LE	Ed Jones
Joe Greene	LT	Larry Cole
Steve Furness	RT	Randy White
John Banaszak	RE	Harvey Martin
Jack Ham	LLB	Thomas Henderson
Jack Lambert	MLB	Bob Breunig
Loren Toews	RLB	D. D. Lewis
Ron Johnson	LCB	Benny Barnes
Mel Blount	RCB	Aaron Kyle
Donnie Shell	LS	Charlie Waters
Mike Wagner	RS	Cliff Harris

The NFL owners had changed the rules of pro football, making it easier to protect the passer and allowing receivers to move into the secondary without being bounced around like bumper pool balls. Most teams had approached the changes gingerly. In this rematch of Game X, Pittsburgh would exploit them fully.

Pittsburgh quarterback Terry Bradshaw started by connecting with John Stallworth for a 28-yard touchdown. Before he was finished he threw three more scoring aerials, including a record-tying 75-yarder, and had amassed 318 yards passing.

When linebacker Thomas (Hollywood) Henderson roughed Bradshaw after a whistle blew, Franco Harris become enraged. Bradshaw immediately sent Harris up the middle against a blitz for a 22-yard scoring run. "Franco ran as hard as I've ever seen him run," said Bradshaw.

But the Cowboys were not exactly wallflowers. They answered the Steelers' first score with one of their own – a 39-yard pass to Tony Hill. Dallas went ahead in the second quarter when blitzing linebacker Mike Hegman stripped the ball from Bradshaw's hands and bolted 37 yards for a touchdown. But on a pivotal play in the third quarter, with Pittsburgh leading 21-14, Dallas tight end Jackie Smith dropped a sure touchdown pass in the end zone, and the Cowboys had to settle for a field goal.

It was close right to the end, with Dallas scoring on Roger Staubach's second and third touchdown passes within a little more than two minutes as the fourth quarter wound down.

Both touchdown drives were sandwiched around a successful onside kick.

The first drive ended with an eight-yard scoring pass to tight end Billy Joe DuPree. The second drive followed the onside kick. With 26 seconds left in the game, wide receiver Butch Johnson caught a four-yard touchdown pass.

Dallas tried another onside kick, but it was recovered by Rocky Bleier to end the game.

"Bradshaw was the difference," said Dallas safety Charlie Waters.

"He can throw a ball twenty yards," added Cliff Harris, "like I can throw a dart twenty feet."

Bradshaw's phenomenal passing day earned him Super Bowl XIII's most valuable player award.

PITTSBURGH	7	14	0	14 – 35
DALLAS	7	7	3	14 – 31

Pitt – Stallworth 28 pass from Bradshaw (Gerela kick)
Dall – Hill 39 pass from Staubach (Septien kick)
Dall – Hegman 37 fumble recovery return (Septien kick)
Pitt – Stallworth 75 pass from Bradshaw (Gerela kick)
Pitt – Bleier 7 pass from Bradshaw (Gerela kick)
Dall – FG Septien 27
Pitt – Harris 22 run (Gerela kick)
Pitt – Swann 18 pass from Bradshaw (Gerela kick)
Dall – DuPree 7 pass from Staubach (Septien kick)
Dall – Johnson 4 pass from Staubach (Septien kick)

TEAM STATISTICS	Pitt	Dall
First downs	19	21
Rushing	2	6
Passing	15	13
By penalty	2	2
Total yardage	357	330
Net rushing yardage	66	154
Net passing yardage	291	176
Passes att.-comp.-had int.	30-17-1	30-17-1

RUSHING

PITTSBURGH		DALLAS	
Harris	20 for 68, 1 TD	Dorsett	16 for 96, 1 TD
Bleier	2 for 3	Newhouse	8 for 3
Bradshaw	2 for -5	Staubach	4 for 37
		Laidlaw	3 for 12
		P. Pearson	1 for 6

PASSING

PITTSBURGH		DALLAS	
Bradshaw	17 of 30 for 318 yards, 4TDs, 1 int.	Staubach	17 of 30 for 228, 3TDs, 1 int.

RECEIVING

PITTSBURGH		DALLAS	
Swann	7 for 124, 1 TD	Dorsett	5 for 44
Stallworth	3 for 115, 2 TDs	Pearson	4 for 73
Grossman	3 for 29	Hill	2 for 49, 1 TD
Bell	2 for 21	Johnson	2 for 30, 1 TD
Harris	1 for 22	DuPree	2 for 17, 1 TD
Bleier	1 for 7, 1 TD	P. Pearson	2 for 15

PUNTING

PITTSBURGH		DALLAS	
Colquitt	3 for 129, 43.0 average	D. White	5 for 198, 39.6 average

PUNT RETURNS

PITTSBURGH		DALLAS	
Bell	4 for 27	Johnson	2 for 33

KICKOFF RETURNS

PITTSBURGH		DALLAS	
Anderson	2 for 29	Johnson	3 for 63
		Brinson	2 for 41
		R. White	1 for 0

INTERCEPTIONS

PITTSBURGH		DALLAS	
Blount	1 for 13	Lewis	1 for 21

 PITTSBURGH STEELERS 31

LOS ANGELES RAMS 19

Above: Terry Bradshaw earned his second most valuable player trophy in Super Bowl XIV, after setting career Super Bowl records for most touchdown passes (9) and most passing yards (932).

The Los Angeles Rams had come into the game with the poorest record ever for a Super Bowl participant: 9-7. Cynics had a field day.

The oddsmakers made them 11-point underdogs to the mighty Steelers, who had made the Super Bowl their personal festival. Not since Game IV, when Kansas City was considered 13 points inferior to Minnesota, had there been such a disparity.

But the Steelers – along with everyone else – got more than they expected.

At the end of the third quarter, the Rams led 19-17. Their defense had done something only Dallas (in Game XIII) had been able to do to the Steelers'

running game: stop it. Unfortunately for Los Angeles, it couldn't shut off the passing game as well.

Early in the fourth quarter, Pittsburgh was confronted with a third and eight on its 27. Two receivers, the gifted Lynn Swann and Theo Bell, already had been forced out of the game.

Terry Bradshaw sent wide receiver John Stallworth deep downfield. Rod Perry had inside coverage on him. Dave Elmendorf had outside coverage.

The pass was perfect. The play covered 73 yards for a touchdown to put the Stellers ahead 24-19.

The Rams came right back, driving to the Steelers' 32. Quarterback Vince Ferragamo went back to pass on first down, but didn't see middle linebacker Jack

Participants
PITTSBURGH STEELERS, champions of the American Football Conference, and LOS ANGELES RAMS, champions of the National Football Conference

Date – January 20, 1980
Site – Rose Bowl, Pasadena
Time – 3:15 P.M. PST
Conditions – 67 degrees, sunny
Playing Surface – Grass
Television and Radio – Columbia Broadcasting System (CBS)
Regular Season Records
PITTSBURGH, 12-4
LOS ANGELES, 9-7
Conference Championships
Pittsburgh defeated the Houston Oilers 27-13 for the AFC title
Los Angeles defeated the Tampa Bay Buccaneers 9-0 for the NFC title
Players' Shares
$18,000 to each member of the winning team
$9,000 to each member of the losing team
Attendance – 103,985
Gross Receipts – $9,489,274.00
Officials
Referee, Fred Silva
umpire, Al Conway
line judge, Bob Beeks
head linesman, Burl Toler
back judge, Stan Javie
side judge, Ben Tompkins
field judge, Charley Musser

Coaches
Chuck Noll, Pittsburgh
Ray Malavasi, Los Angeles

Starters, Offense

LOS ANGELES		PITTSBURGH
Billy Waddy	WR	John Stallworth
Doug France	LT	Jon Kolb
Kent Hill	LG	Sam Davis
Rich Saul	C	Mike Webster
Dennis Harrah	RG	Gerry Mullins
Jackie Slater	RT	Larry Brown
Terry Nelson	TE	Bennie Cunningham
Preston Dennard	WR	Lynn Swann
Vince Ferragamo	QB	Terry Bradshaw
Cullen Bryant	RB	Rocky Bleier
Wendell Tyler	RB	Franco Harris

Starters, Defense

LOS ANGELES		PITTSBURGH
Jack Youngblood	LE	L. C. Greenwood
Mike Fanning	LT	Joe Greene
Larry Brooks	RT	Gary Dunn
Fred Dryer	RE	John Banaszak
Jim Youngblood	LLB	Dennis Winston
Jack Reynolds	MLB	Jack Lambert
Bob Brudzinski	RLB	Robin Cole
Pat Thomas	LCB	Ron Johnson
Rod Perry	RCB	Mel Blount
Dave Elmendorf	LS	Donnie Shell
Nolan Cromwell	RS	J. T. Thomas

Left: *John Stallworth (82) catches a 73-yard scoring pass behind Los Angeles Rams cornerback Rod Perry in Super Bowl XIV. Stallworth caught 3 Bradshaw passes for 121 yards.*

LOS ANGELES	7	6	6	0 – 19
PITTSBURGH	3	7	7	14 – 31

Pitt – FG Bahr 41
LA – Bryant 1 run (Corral kick)
Pitt – Harris 1 run (Bahr kick)
LA – FG Corral 31
LA – FG Corral 45
Pitt – Swann 47 pass from Bradshaw (Bahr kick)
LA – R. Smith 24 pass from McCutcheon (kick failed)
Pitt – Stallworth 73 pass from Bradshaw (Bahr kick)
Pitt – Harris 1 run (Bahr kick)

TEAM STATISTICS	LA	Pitt
First downs	16	19
Rushing	6	8
Passing	9	10
By penalty	1	1
Total yardage	301	393
Net rushing yardage	107	84
Net passing yardage	194	309
Passes att.-comp.-had int.	26-16-1	21-14-3

RUSHING

LOS ANGELES		PITTSBURGH	
Tyler	17 for 60	Harris	20 for 46, 2 TDs
Bryant	6 for 30, 1 TD	Bleier	10 for 25
McCutcheon	5 for 10	Thornton	4 for 4
Ferragamo	1 for 7	Bradshaw	3 for 9

PASSING

LOS ANGELES		PITTSBURGH	
Ferragamo	15 of 25 for 212, 1 int.	Bradshaw	14 of 21 for 309, 2 TDs, 3 int.
McCutcheon	1 of 1 for 24, 1 TD		

RECEIVING

LOS ANGELES		PITTSBURGH	
Waddy	3 for 75	Swann	5 for 79, 1 TD
Bryant	3 for 21	Stallworth	3 for 121, 1 TD
Tyler	3 for 20	Harris	3 for 66
Dennard	2 for 32	Cunningham	2 for 21
Nelson	2 for 20	Thornton	1 for 22
D. Hill	1 for 28		
Smith	1 for 24, 1 TD		
McCutcheon	1 for 16		

PUNTING

LOS ANGELES		PITTSBURGH	
Clark	5 for 220, 44.0 average	Colquitt	2 for 85, 42.5 average

PUNT RETURNS

LOS ANGELES		PITTSBURGH	
Brown	1 for 4	Bell	2 for 17
		Smith	2 for 14

KICKOFF RETURNS

LOS ANGELES		PITTSBURGH	
E. Hill	3 for 47	L. Anderson	5 for 162
Jodat	2 for 32		
Andrews	1 for 0		

INTERCEPTIONS

LOS ANGELES		PITTSBURGH	
Elmendorf	1 for 10	Lambert	1 for 16
Brown	1 for 6		
Perry	1 for -1		

Lambert, who had dropped deep. Lambert sprang in front of intended receiver Ron Smith and intercepted on the 14 to shut off the Rams' threat.

Bradshaw then completed another pass, for 45 yards, to Stallworth. Five plays later, Franco Harris cracked over from the 1 for the deciding points.

The final score, 31-19, was deceiving, though. The Rams had made it one of the most exciting Super Bowl games of all; the lead changed hands six times.

But in the end, it was the Steelers celebrating yet another great moment, a fourth Super Bowl victory. "This was an invitation engraved in gold," said defensive great Joe Green. "An invitation to immortality."

SUPER BOWL XV

OAKLAND RAIDERS 27
PHILADELPHIA EAGLES 10

Jim Plunkett, who became a starter after the sixth game of the 1980 season, was named the most valuable player of Super Bowl XV after completing 13 of 21 passes for 261 yards and three touchdowns.

The matchup between Oakland and Philadelphia could have been an anti-climax. The teams had met earlier in the regular season and the Eagles won 10-7 in a primitive, hard-hitting game.

The score was less important than what the Eagles' defense had done to Oakland's passing game. The aging Raiders' offensive linemen could not protect Cinderella quarterback Jim Plunkett. The Eagles sacked him eight times, three by Claude Humphrey.

Evidence that the Super Bowl game would be different came when Ron Jaworski threw his first pass of the game and linebacker Rod Martin intercepted it.

Oakland moved to the Eagles' 2-yard line. The Philadelphia pass rushers went after Plunkett, but he scrambled deftly out of trouble, passing to Cliff Branch in the end zone for the Raiders' first touchdown.

In the final minute of the first quarter, the Eagles forced Plunkett from the pocket again. On the run, he spotted Kenny King at the Raiders' 39 and passed to him. King ran the rest of the way to the end zone

untouched for the longest touchdown play in Super Bowl history, 80 yards.

Philadelphia kicker Tony Franklin came through on a 30-yard field goal in the second quarter, but the quarter ended on a block of his 28-yard attempt by freelancing Raiders linebacker Ted Hendricks. The score was 14-3; the Raiders were rolling.

By the third quarter, the Raiders' linemen were totally dominating the Eagles' pass rushers, giving Plunkett ease and comfort. He threw 32 yards to wide receiver Bob Chandler and then 29 yards to Branch,

---

Participants
OAKLAND RAIDERS, champions of the American Football Conference, and PHILADELPHIA EAGLES, champions of the National Football Conference

Date – January 25, 1981
Site – Louisiana Superdome, New Orleans
Time – 5:15 P.M. CST
Conditions – 72 degrees, indoors
Playing Surface – AstroTurf
Television – National Broadcasting Company (NBC)
Radio – Columbia Broadcasting System (CBS)
Regular Season Records
OAKLAND, 11-5
PHILADELPHIA, 12-4
Conference Championships
Oakland defeated the San Diego Chargers 34-27 for the AFC title
Philadelphia defeated the Dallas Cowboys 20-7 for the NFC title
Players' Shares
$18,000 to each member of the winning team
$9,000 to each member of the losing team
Attendance – 76,135
Gross Receipts – $10,328,664.57
Officials
Referee, Ben Dreith
umpire, Frank Sinkovitz
line judge, Tom Dooley
head linesman, Tony Veteri
back judge, Tom Kelleher
side judge, Dean Look
field judge, Fritz Graf
Coaches
Tom Flores, Oakland
Dick Vermeil, Philadelphia

OAKLAND	Starters, Offense	PHILADELPHIA
Clif Branch	WR	Harold Carmichael
Art Shell	LT	Stan Walters
Gene Upshaw	LG	Petey Perot
Dave Dalby	C	Guy Morriss
Mickey Marvin	RG	Woody Peoples
Henry Lawrence	RT	Jerry Sisemore
Raymond Chester	TE	Keith Krepfle
Bob Chandler	WR-TE	John Spagnola
Jim Plunkett	QB	Ron Jaworski
Mark van Eeghen	RB	Leroy Harris
Kenny King	RB	Wilbert Montgomery
	Starters, Defense	
John Matuszak	LE	Dennis Harrison
Reggie Kinlaw	NT	Charlie Johnson
Dave Browning	RE	Carl Hairston
Ted Hendricks	LOLB	John Bunting
Matt Millen	LILB	Bill Bergey
Bob Nelson	RILB	Frank LeMaster
Rod Martin	ROLB	Jerry Robinson
Lester Hayes	LCB	Roynell Young
Dwayne O'Steen	RCB	Herman Edwards
Mike Davis	LS	Randy Logan
Burgess Owens	RS	Brenard Wilson

```
OAKLAND .................................14   0   10   3 – 27
PHILADELPHIA .........................  0   3    0   7 – 10
```

Oak – Branch 2 pass from Plunkett (Bahr kick)
Oak – King 80 pass from Plunkett (Bahr kick)
Phil – FG Franklin 30
Oak – Branch 29 pass from Plunkett (Bahr kick)
Oak – FG Bahr 46
Phil – Krepfle 8 pass from Jaworski (Franklin kick)
Oak – FG Bahr 35

TEAM STATISTICS

	Oak	Phil
First downs	17	19
Rushing	6	3
Passing	10	14
By penalty	1	2
Total yardage	377	360
Net rushing yardage	117	69
Net passing yardage	260	291
Passes att.-comp.-had int.	21-13-0	38-18-3

RUSHING

OAKLAND		PHILADELPHIA	
van Eeghen	19 for 80	Montgomery	16 for 44
King	6 for 18	Harris	7 for 14
Jensen	3 for 12	Giammona	1 for 7
Plunkett	3 for 9	Harrington	1 for 4
Whittington	3 for -2	Jaworski	1 for 0

PASSING

OAKLAND		PHILADELPHIA	
Plunkett	13 of 21 for 261, 3 TDs	Jaworski	18 of 38 for 291, 1 TD, 3 int.

RECEIVING

OAKLAND		PHILADELPHIA	
Branch	5 for 67, 2 TDs	Montgomery	6 for 91
Chandler	4 for 77	Carmichael	5 for 83
King	2 for 93, 1 TD	Smith	2 for 59
Chester	2 for 24	Krepfle	2 for 16, 1 TD
		Spagnola	1 for 22
		Parker	1 for 19
		Harris	1 for 1

PUNTING

OAKLAND		PHILADELPHIA	
Guy	3 for 126, 42.0 average.	Runager	3 for 110, 36.7 average

PUNT RETURNS

OAKLAND		PHILADELPHIA	
Matthews	2 for 1	Sciarra	2 for 18
		Henry	1 for 2

KICKOFF RETURNS

OAKLAND		PHILADELPHIA	
Matthews	2 for 29	Campfield	5 for 87
Moody	1 for 19	Harrington	1 for 0

INTERCEPTIONS

OAKLAND		PHILADELPHIA	
Martin	3 for 44	None	

who seemed covered perfectly by rookie Roynell Young, but then took position and made a leaping reception for a touchdown.

Philadelphia gamely pushed to the Raiders' 34, then Martin made the second of his record three interceptions. Chris Bahr's subsequent field goal made it 24-3 and the Raiders were on their way to becoming the first wild card team to win the Super Bowl in a game played at the Louisiana Superdome in New Orleans.

The Raiders became the first wild-card team to win the NFL championship after their decisive 27-10 victory over Philadelphia in Super Bowl XV.

SAN FRANCISCO 49ers 26
CINCINNATI BENGALS 21

The Bengals relied upon the tough running of fullback Pete Johnson (46) and Cincinnati's sub-zero temperature to shut down the high-powered San Diego Chargers 27-7 in the 1981 AFC Championship Game.

Game XVI was the first northern Super Bowl, played in the Pontiac Silverdome, some 40 miles north of frigid, snow-covered Detroit in the midst of the worst winter in memory. The action inside the dome, though, was hot right from the start. San Francisco 49ers rookie Amos Lawrence fumbled the opening kickoff and the Cincinnati Bengals recovered at the 49ers' 26. But, six plays later, the momentum reversed as 49ers safety Dwight Hicks intercepted Ken Anderson's pass at the San Francisco 5 and returned it 27 yards.

From there, quarterback Joe Montana drove the 49ers to the Bengals' 1, where he took the ball in himself on a sneak.

Another turnover cued the 49ers' second touchdown. Eric Wright, one of three rookies starting in the 49ers' secondary, stripped the ball from Cris Collinsworth after the Bengals' rookie wide receiver had made a 19-yard reception. Then another rookie, cornerback Lynn Thomas, recovered at the 49ers' 8.

Montana, the game's most valuable player, made the most of the turnover with the longest touchdown

Participants
CINCINNATI BENGALS, champions of the American Football Conference, and
SAN FRANCISCO 49ers, champions of the National Football Conference

Date – January 24, 1982
Site – Pontiac Silverdome, Pontiac
Time – 4:00 P.M. EST
Conditions – 70 degrees, indoors
Playing Surface – AstroTurf
Television and Radio – Columbia Broadcasting System (CBS)
Regular Season Records
CINCINNATI, 12-4
SAN FRANCISCO, 13-3
Conference Championships
Cincinnati defeated the San Diego Chargers 27-7 for the AFC title
San Francisco defeated the Dallas Cowboys 28-27 for the NFC title

Players' Shares
$18,000 to each member of the winning team
$9,000 to each member of the losing team
Attendance – 81,270
Gross Receipts – $10,641,034.83
Officials
Referee, Pat Haggerty
umpire, Al Conway
line judge, Bob Beeks
head linesman, Jerry Bergman
back judge Bill Swanson
side judge, Bob Rice
field judge, Don Hakes
Coaches
Forrest Gregg, Cincinnati
Bill Walsh, San Francisco

SAN FRANCISCO	Starters, Offense	CINCINNATI
Dwight Clark	WR	Cris Collinsworth
Dan Audick	LT	Anthony Munoz
John Ayers	LG	Dave Lapham
Fred Quillan	C	Blair Bush
Randy Cross	RG	Max Montoya
Keith Farnhorst	RT	Mike Wilson
Charle Young	TE	Dan Ross
Freddie Solomon	WR	Isaac Curtis
Joe Montana	QB	Ken Anderson
Ricky Patton	RB	Pete Johnson
Earl Cooper	RB	Charles Alexander

	Starters, Defense	
Jim Stuckey	LE	Eddie Edwards
Archie Reese	NT	Wilson Whitley
Dwaine Board	RE	Ross Browner
Willie Harper	LOLB	Bo Harris
Jack Reynolds	LILB	Jim LeClair
Craig Puki	RILB	Glenn Cameron
Keena Turner	ROLB	Reggie Williams
Ronnie Lott	LCB	Louis Breeden
Eric Wright	RCB	Ken Riley
Carlton Williamson	LS	Bobby Kemp
Dwight Hicks	RS	Bryan Hicks

SAN FRANCISCO	7	13	0	6 – 26
CINCINNATI	0	0	7	14 – 21

SF – Montana 1 run (Wersching kick)
SF – Cooper 11 pass from Montana (Wersching kick)
SF – FG Wersching 22
SF – FG Wersching 26
Cin – Anderson 5 run (Breech kick)
Cin – Ross 4 pass from Anderson (Breech kick)
SF – FG Wersching 40
SF – FG Wersching 23
Cin – Ross 3 pass from Anderson (Breech kick)

TEAM STATISTICS	SF	Cin
First downs	20	24
Rushing	9	7
Passing	9	13
By penalty	2	4
Total yardage	275	356
Net rushing yardage	127	72
Net passing yardage	148	284
Passes att.-comp.-had int.	22-14-0	34-25-2

RUSHING

SAN FRANCISCO		CINCINNATI	
Patton	17 for 55	Johnson	14 for 36
Cooper	9 for 34	Alexander	5 for 17
Montana	6 for 18, 1 TD	Anderson	4 for 15
Ring	5 for 17	A. Griffin	1 for 4
J. Davis	2 for 5		
Clark	1 for -2		

PASSING

SAN FRANCISCO		CINCINNATI	
Montana	14 of 22 for 157, 1 TD	Anderson	25of34for300,2TDs,2int.

RECEIVING

SAN FRANCISCO		CINCINNATI	
Solomon	4 for 52, 2 TDs	Ross	11 for 104, 2 TD
Clark	4 for 45	Collinsworth	5 for 107
Cooper	2 for 15, 1 TD	Curtis	3 for 42
Wilson	1 for 22	Kreider	2 for 36
Young	1 for 14	Johnson	2 for 8
Patton	1 for 8	Alexander	2 for 3
Ring	1 for 3		

PUNTING

SAN FRANCISCO		CINCINNATI	
Miller	4for185,46.3average.	McInally	3 for 131, 43.7 average

PUNT RETURNS

SAN FRANCISCO		CINCINNATI	
Hicks	1 for 6	Fuller	4 for 35
Solomon	1 fair catch		

KICKOFF RETURNS

SAN FRANCISCO		CINCINNATI	
Hicks	1 for 23	Verser	4 for 52
Lawrence	1 for 17	Frazier	1 for 0
		A. Griffin	1 for 0

INTERCEPTIONS

SAN FRANCISCO		CINCINNATI	
Hicks	1 for 27	None	
Wright	1 for 25		

Jubilant 49ers receiver Dwight Clark spikes the football after catching a 6-yard scoring pass with 51 seconds remaining in the 1981 NFC title game. San Francisco defeated Dallas 28-27.

Right: *Joe Montana's controlled passing (14 of 22 passes for 157 yards, 1 touchdown) earned him most valuable player honours in Super Bowl XVI.*

Below: *San Francisco defensive tackle Archie Reese (78) celebrates after the 49ers stopped Cincinnati's offense on fourth and goal in Super Bowl XVI.*

drive in Super Bowl history, 92 yards.

The 49ers padded their lead with 15 seconds remaining in the first half with a 22-yard field goal by Ray Wersching. Wersching's ensuing kickoff, a bounding squibber (the kind that gave the Bengals fits all day), was fumbled by Archie Griffin and the 49ers recovered at the 4 with five seconds left. A 26-yard field goal made the halftime score 20-0, the largest Super Bowl halftime deficit ever.

Anderson came out firing in the second half, engineering an 83-yard scoring drive capped by his own five-yard run. Later in the third period, after a 49-yard reception by Collinsworth, the Bengals had a first-and-goal at the 3.

With one of the great Super Bowl defensive efforts (including a third-down, one-on-one goal-line tackle of running back Charles Alexander by linebacker Dan Bunz), the 49ers held.

The Bengals drew within six points (20-14) early in the fourth quarter, but Wersching's third and fourth field goals of the game (tying a Super Bowl record) put it out of reach. A final score for Cincinnati only made the score closer.

SUPER BOWL XVII

WASHINGTON REDSKINS 27

MIAMI DOLPHINS 17

Below: Led by Bob Baumhower (73), Bob Brudzinski (59), and Doug Betters (75), the Dolphins' Killer Bees defense bring down New York Jets running back Freeman McNeil (24).

Bottom: Dolphins linebacker A.J. Duhe (77) holds aloft the football after 1 of his 2 interceptions in the 1982 AFC Championship Game. Miami shut out the New York Jets 14-0.

S uper Bowl XVII was the Hogs (the Washington Redskins' huge offensive line plus the man they opened holes for, honorary hog John Riggins) versus the Killer Bees (the Miami Dolphins' swarming defense, so named because so many of the starters' last names began with "B") in a 10-year anniversary rematch of Super Bowl Vll.

Miami got an early score on a 76-yard pass from David Woodley to wide-open Jimmy Cefalo. Then, after trading second-quarter field goals, the Redskins tied the game on Joe Theismann's four-yard lob to Alvin Garrett.

Fulton Walker took the ensuing kickoff and did what he threatened to do on his previous 42-yard return—he took it all the way, 98 yards for the longest

Washington fullback John Riggins, Super Bowl XVII's most valuable player, rushed for a record 166 yards on 38 carries.

Theismann threw for one more fourth-quarter touchdown – six yards to Charlie Brown – to earn the team a 27-17 victory and a postgame congratulatory call phone from President Ronald Reagan. Still, Riggins had the last word. "At least for tonight," he said, "Ron may be the President, but I'm the king."

MIAMI	7	10	0	0 – 17
WASHINGTON	0	10	3	14 – 27

Mia – Cefalo 76 pass from Woodley (von Schamann kick)
Wash – FG Moseley 31
Mia – FG von Schamann 20
Wash – Garrett 4 pass from Theismann (Moseley kick)
Mia – Walker 98 kickoff return (von Schamann kick)
Wash – FG Moseley 20
Wash – Riggins 43 run (Moseley kick)
Wash – Brown 6 pass from Theismann (Moseley kick)

TEAM STATISTICS	Mia	Wash
First downs	9	24
Rushing	7	14
Passing	2	9
By penalty	0	1
Total yardage	176	400
Net rushing yardage	96	276
Net passing yardage	80	124
Passes att.-comp.-had int.	17-4-1	23-15-2

RUSHING

MIAMI		WASHINGTON	
Franklin	16 for 49	Riggins	38 for 166, 1 TD
Nathan	7 for 26	Harmon	9 for 40
Woodley	4 for 16	Theismann	3 for 20
Vigorito	1 for 4	Garrett	1 for 44
Harris	1 for 1	Walker	1 for 6

PASSING

MIAMI		WASHINGTON	
Woodley	4 of 14 for 97, 1 TD, 1 int	Theismann,	15 of 23 for 143, 2 TD, 2 int.
Strock	0 of 3 for 0		

RECEIVING

MIAMI		WASHINGTON	
Cefalo	2 for 82, 1 TD	Brown	6 for 60, 1 TD
Harris	2 for 15	Warren	5 for 28
		Garrett	2 for 13, 1 TD
		Walker	1 for 27
		Riggins	1 for 15

PUNTING

MIAMI		WASHINGTON	
Orosz	6 for 227, 37.8 average.	Hayes	4 for 168, 42.0 average

PUNT RETURNS

MIAMI		WASHINGTON	
Vigorito	2 for 22	Nelms	6 for 52

KICKOFF RETURNS

MIAMI		WASHINGTON	
Walker	4 for 190, 1 TD	Nelms	2 for 44
L. Blackwood	2 for 32	Wonsley	1 for 13

INTERCEPTIONS

MIAMI		WASHINGTON	
Duhe	1 for 0	Murphy	1 for 0
L. Blackwood	1 for 0		

kickoff return in Super Bowl history and the first one for a score (1 of 11 individual and 13 team records set in the game).

Despite being on the wrong end of the 17-10 halftime score, Washington head coach Joe Gibbs had "a good feeling" about the second half that proved precognizant. The Redskins' defense came out and totally shut down Miami; neither Woodley nor backup Don Strock completed a pass in the second half.

Even the Redskins offense contributed defensively. Shortly before the end of the third quarter, with Miami leading 17-13, Theismann went back to pass from his own 18. The pass he threw was tipped back at him by defensive end Kim Bokamper. As the pass hung in the air, Bokamper, on the dead run toward the Washington goal line, reached for it, but Theismann lunged and knocked the ball away.

The Dolphins weakened; Riggins (who gained a record 166 yards on 38 carries) seemed to get stronger. His 43-yard early fourth-quarter touchdown run, the longest scoring run from scrimmage in a Super Bowl, cemented the game's most valuable player award for him.

Opposite top:
"The Hogs" fire out to block the Dallas Cowboys in the 1982 NFC title game. Riggins (44) rushed for 140 yards and 2 touchdowns in the Redskins' 31-17 victory.

Opposite bottom:
Riggins breaks away from Miami cornerback Don McNeal (28) on his 43-yard scoring run in the fourth quarter of Super Bowl XVII. The play occurred on fourth-and-one and it gave Washington its first lead of the game.

Participants
MIAMI DOLPHINS, champions of the American Football Conference, and
WASHINGTON REDSKINS, champions of the National Football Conference

Date – January 30, 1983
Site – Rose Bowl, Pasadena
Time – 3:00 P.M. PST
Conditions – 61 degrees, clear
Playing Surface – Grass
Television – National Broadcasting Company (NBC)
Radio – Columbia Broadcasting System (CBS)
Regular Season Records
MIAMI, 7-2
WASHINGTON, 8-1
Conference Championships
Miami defeated the New York Jets 14-0 for the AFC title
Washington defeated the Dallas Cowboys 31-17 for the NFC title
Players' Shares
$36,000 to each member of the winning team
$18,000 to each member of the losing team
Attendance – 103,667
Gross Receipts – $19,997,330.86
Officials
Referee, Jerry Markbreit
umpire, Art Demmas
line judge, Bill Reynolds
head linesman, Dale Hamer
back judge, Dick Hantak
field judge, Don Orr
side judge, Dave Parry

Coaches
Don Shula, Miami
Joe Gibbs, Washington

MIAMI	Starters, Offense	WASHINGTON
Duriel Harris	WR	Alvin Garrett
Jon Glesler	LT	Joe Jacoby
Bob Kuechenberg	LG	Russ Grimm
Dwight Stephenson	C	Jeff Bostic
Jeff Toews	RG	Fred Dean
Eric Laakso	RT	George Starke
Bruce Hardy	TE	Don Warren
Jimmy Cefalo	WR	Charlie Brown
Davld Woodley	QB	Joe Theismann
Tony Nathan	RB	John Riggins
Andra Franklin	RB-TE	Rick Walker
	Starters, Defense	
Doug Betters	LE	Mat Mendenhall
Bob Baumhower	NT-LT	Dave Butz
Kim Bokamper	RE-RT	Darryl Grant
Bob Brudzinski	LOLB-RE	Dexter Manley
A. J. Duhe	LILB-LLB	Mel Kaufman
Earnie Rhone	RILB-MLB	Neal Olkewicz
Larry Gordon	ROLB-RLB	Rich Milot
Gerald Small	LCB	Jeris White
Don McNeal	RCB	Vernon Dean
Glenn Blackwood	LS	Tony Peters
Lyle Blackwood	RS	Mark Murphy

SUPER BOWL
★ XVIII ★

LOS ANGELES RAIDERS 38
WASHINGTON REDSKINS 9

Below: The Redskins's "Fun Bunch" celebrates (89) Alvin Garrett's 4-yard touchdown catch in Super Bowl XVII.

Right: Super Bowl XVIII most valuable player Marcus Allen.

The Los Angeles Raiders' defense shut down the most prolific offense in NFL history, and Marcus Allen rushed for a Super Bowl-record 191 yards, as the Raiders defeated the Washington Redskins 38-9, then the biggest margin of victory in a Super Bowl.

In completing one of the most impressive runs through the playoffs ever, all three of the Raiders' platoons – offense, defense, and special teams – scored touchdowns at Tampa Stadium in Florida.

Early in the first quarter, after Washington's first possession, the Raiders' Derrick Jensen broke through the Redskins' line, blocked Jeff Hayes's punt, and recovered it in the end zone to give Los Angeles a 7-0 advantage.

The Redskins' special teams had a chance to return the favor on the third play of the second quarter, but couldn't. A high snap sent punter Ray Guy leaping for the ball. Guy pulled it in with one hand, landed on his feet, and, unhurried by any rush, boomed a punt through Washington's end zone.

After holding the Redskins, the Raiders came out throwing. On first down, Jim Plunkett passed 50 yards down the middle to Cliff Branch. Two plays later, he found Branch again, for a 12-yard touchdown and a 14-0 lead.

The Redskins responded with a 13-play, 73-yard drive, but it netted only a field goal by Mark Moseley. Washington regained the ball on its own 12-yard line, with 12 seconds left in the half. Joe Theismann called a swing pass to halfback Joe Washington, a play that had gained 67 yards when the two clubs met earlier in the season. This time, linebacker Jack Squirek stepped in front of the intended receiver at the Washington 5 and dashed into the end zone for a touchdown and a 21-3 halftime lead.

After the intermission, the Redskins looked as if they were going to make a game of it. After receiving the second-half kickoff, Washington went 70 yards on three passes by Theismann and six runs by John Riggins, who scored on a one-yard plunge behind tackle George Starke. The momentum didn't remain long, however; reserve tight end Don Hasselbeck blocked Moseley's extra-point attempt.

Then the Raiders put the game away. Helped by a 38-yard pass interference penalty against Washington cornerback Darrell Green, Plunkett engineered an eight-play, 70-yard drive, which was capped by a five-yard touchdown run by Marcus Allen.

On the last play of the quarter, Allen struck again. On first and 10 at the Raiders' 26, he took a pitch, swept left, reversed his direction when he spotted safety Ken Coffey closing in, circled back to the middle, and cut upfield. Suddenly, he was in the open and on his way to a 74-yard touchdown run, the longest of his career and the longest in Super Bowl history. He was also on his way to the game's most valuable player honors.

The Raiders added a 21-yard field goal by Chris Bahr in the fourth quarter to break Green Bay's and Pittsburgh's Super Bowl record for points in a game. Meanwhile, the defense finished its day having held Riggins to a 2.5-yard-per-carry rushing average while intercepting Theismann twice and sacking him six times. Nose tackle Reggie Kinlaw was the main force in stopping Riggins, while cornerbacks Mike Haynes and Lester Hayes held Washington wide receivers Charlie Brown and Art Monk to only four receptions, none in the decisive first half.

"I don't want to sound conceited, but . . . I knew we'd beat 'em today," Allen said after the game. "I think anybody who knew about football knew that."

	1	2	3	4	
WASHINGTON	0	3	6	0	– 9
LA RAIDERS	7	14	14	3	– 38

LA – Jensen recovered blocked punt in end zone (Bahr kick)
LA – Branch 12 pass from Plunkett (Bahr kick)
Wash – FG Moseley 24
LA – Squirek 5 interception return (Bahr kick)
Wash – Riggins 1 run (kick blocked)
LA – Allen 5 run (Bahr kick)
LA – Allen 74 run (Bahr kick)
LA – FG Bahr 21

TEAM STATISTICS

	Wash	LA
First downs	19	18
Rushing	7	8
Passing	10	9
By penalty	2	1
Total yardage	283	385
Net rushing yardage	90	231
Net passing yardage	193	154
Passes att.-comp.-had int.	35-16-2	25-16-0

RUSHING

WASHINGTON		LA RAIDERS	
Riggins	26 for 64, 1 TD	Allen	20 for 191, 2TDs
Theismann	3 for 18	Pruitt	5 for 17
J. Washington	3 for 8	King	3 for 12
		Hawkins	3 for 6
		Willis	1 for 7
		Plunkett	1 for 2

PASSING

WASHINGTON		LA RAIDERS	
Theismann	16 of 35 for 243, 2 int.	Plunkett	16 of 25 for 172, 1 TD

RECEIVING

WASHINGTON		LA RAIDERS	
Didier	5 for 65	Branch	6 for 94, 1 TD
Brown	3 for 93	Christensen	4 for 32
J. Washington	3 for 20	Hawkins	2 for 20
Giaquinto	2 for 21	Allen	2 for 18
Monk	1 for 26	King	2 for 8
Garrett	1 for 17		
Riggins	1 for 1		

PUNTING

WASHINGTON		LA RAIDERS	
Hayes,	7 for 259, 37.0 average	Guy,	7 for 299, 42.7 average

PUNT RETURNS

WASHINGTON		LA RAIDERS	
Green	1 for 34	Pruitt	1 for 3, 3 fair catches
Giaquinto	1 for 1, 2 fair catches	Wans	1 for 0

KICKOFF RETURNS

WASHINGTON		LA RAIDERS	
Garrett	5 for 100	Pruitt	1 for 17
Grant	1 for 32		
Kimball	1 for 0		

INTERCEPTIONS

WASHINGTON		LA RAIDERS	
None		Squirek	1 for 5, 1 TD
		Haynes	1 for 0

Participants
WASHINGTON REDSKINS, champions of the National Football Conference, and LOS ANGELES RAIDERS, champions of the American Football Conference

Date – January 22, 1984
Site – Tampa Stadium, Tampa
Time – 4:30 P.M. EST
Conditions – 68 degrees, partly cloudy
Playing Surface – Grass
Television and Radio – Columbia Broadcasting Company (CBS)
Regular Season Records
LOS ANGELES, 12-4
WASHINGTON 14-2
Conference Championships
Washington defeated the San Francisco 49ers 24-21 for the NFC title
Los Angeles defeated the Seattle Seahawks 30-14 for the AFC title
Players' Shares
$36,000 to each member of the winning team
$18,000 to each member of the losing team
Attendance – 72,920
Gross Receipts – $20,002,390.28
Officials
Referee, Gene Barth
umpire, Gordon Weils
line judge, Bob Beeks
head linesman, Jerry Bergman
back judge, Ben Tompkins
side judge, Gil Mace
field judge, Fritz Graf
Coaches
Joe Gibbs, Washington
Tom Flores, LA Raiders

WASHINGTON	Starters, Offense	L.A. RAIDERS
Charlie Brown	WR	Cliff Branch
Joe Jacoby	LT	Bruce Davis
Russ Grimm	LG	Charley Hannah
Jeff Bostic	C	Dave Dalby
Mark May	RG	Mickey Marvin
George Starke	RT	Henry Lawrence
Don Warren	TE	Todd Christensen
Art Monk	WR	Malcolm Barnwell
Joe Theismann	QB	Jim Plunkett
Rick Walker	TE-RB	Kenny King
John Riggins	RB	Marcus Allen

WASHINGTON	Starters, Defense	
Todd Liebenstein	LE	Howie Long
Dave Butz	LT-NT	Reggie Kinlaw
Darryl Grant	RT-RE	Lyle Alzado
Dexter Manley	RE-LOLB	Ted Hendricks
Mel Kaufman	LLB-LILB	Matt Miilen
Neal Olkewicz	MLB-RILB	Bob Nelson
Rich Milot	RLB-ROLB	Rod Martin
Darrell Green	LCB	Lester Hayes
Anthony Washington	RCB	Mike Haynes
Ken Coffey	SS	Mike Davis
Mark Murphy	FS	Vann McElroy

Allen (32) rushed for a Super Bowl record 191 yards and scored 2 touchdowns, including a spectacular 74-yard run in the third quarter.

SUPER BOWL
★★★ XIX ★★★

Joe Montana joined Green Bay's Bart Starr and Pittsburgh's Terry Bradshaw as the Super Bowl's only two-time most valuable players. He completed 24 of 35 passes for a record 331 yards and 3 touchdowns in Super Bowl XIX.

SAN FRANCISCO 49ers 38

MIAMI DOLPHINS 16

Joe Montana outdueled his more heralded quarterback counterpart, Dan Marino, and the San Francisco defense dominated a one-dimensional Miami offense, as the 49ers overran the Dolphins 38-16 to win their second Super Bowl in four years.

Going into the game, Miami's offense looked unstoppable behind the record-setting Marino, and the early stages of the contest gave no indication otherwise. After holding the 49ers on the game's initial possession, the Dolphins took over at the Miami 36. Marino completed four of five passes to set up a 37-yard field goal by Uwe von Schamann.

The 49ers counterpunched immediately. Montana nickeled-and-dimed his way to third and seven at the Miami 48. He then flashed the major difference between him and Marino when he ran 15 yards for a first down. On the next play, Montana hit Carl Monroe for a touchdown, giving the 49ers a 7-3 lead.

Miami quickly engineered its most effective drive of the day. Going without a huddle, Marino drove his team 70 yards in six plays, including five completions

in a row, the last a two-yard touchdown to tight end Dan Johnson.

Yet, in a sense, Marino's lightning-quick strike helped undermine Miami's offense. It forced San Francisco head coach Bill Walsh to put in his elephant defense, a 4-2-5, in which Tom Holmoe became the nickel back and rookie Jeff Fuller, in reality a defensive back, lined up at linebacker with Keena Turner to concentrate on short passes. It worked so well that Marino, who had completed 9 of 10 passes at the time, didn't complete another until after the two-minute warning, while the Dolphins' running game was totally shut down.

Early in the second quarter, the 49ers held Miami without a first down, and then, after a short punt by Reggie Roby, started a drive from Miami's 47. On first down, Montana ran 18 yards. He then passed 16 yards to Dwight Clark, and, two plays later, eight yards for a touchdown to Roger Craig.

The next four series were virtual replays. The Dolphins ran six plays netting only five yards. Meanwhile, the 49ers scored twice, on a six-yard run by Montana and a two-yard run by Craig, the latter giving them a 28-10 lead. Facing a rout, the Dolphins scored two field goals in the last 12 seconds of the half, the second after San Francisco lineman Guy McIntyre fumbled a kickoff and Jim Jensen of Miami recovered.

But that was all for Miami. With Marino passing on almost every down in the second half, the 49ers turned loose their defensive line, which sacked him four times, pressured him constantly, and helped force two interceptions.

The 49ers, on the other hand, kept moving the ball relentlessly. Their first drive of the second half resulted in a 27-yard field goal by Ray Wersching. The second possession ended when Montana fired a 16-yard scoring pass to Craig, whose third touchdown of the day was a Super Bowl record. And in the fourth quarter, the 49ers mounted a 13-play, 78-yard drive that consumed almost eight minutes and wasn't stopped until Miami's defense held at its 2.

The result of San Francisco's offensive juggernaut was a game-record 537 yards. The key was Montana, the game's most valuable player, who completed 24 of 35 passes for a record 331 yards and also totaled 59 yards rushing, a record for quarterbacks.

"All week, all we heard was, 'Miami, Miami, Miami,'" Montana said. "That motivated us. We felt we had more tools than Miami – passing, running, a great defense – and we wanted to prove it."

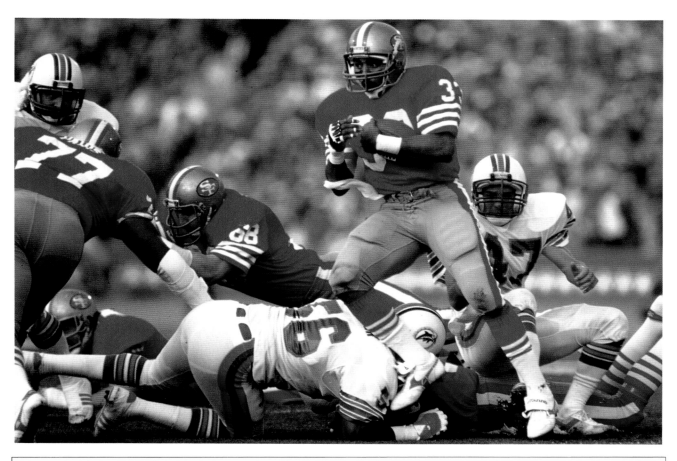

49ers running back Roger Craig (33) set a Super Bowl record by scoring 3 touchdowns on pass receptions of 8 and 16 yards and a run of 2 yards.

Participants

MIAMI DOLPHINS, champions of American Football Conference, and SAN FRANCISCO 49ers, champions of the National Football Conference

Date – January 20, 1985
Site – Stanford Stadium, Palo Alto, California
Time – 3:00 P.M. PST
Conditions – 53 degrees. clearing fog
Playing Surface – Grass
Television – American Broadcasting Corporation (ABC)
Radio – Columbia Broadcasting System (CBS)
Regular Season Records
MIAMI, 14-2
SAN FRANCISCO, 15-1
Conference Championships
Miami defeated the Pittsburgh Steelers 45-28 for the AFC title
San Francisco defeated the Chicago Bears 23-0 for the NFC title
Players Shares
$36,000 to each member of the winning team
$18,000 to each member of the losing team
Attendance – 84,059
Gross Receipts – $20,995,324.00
Officials
Referee, Pat Haggerty
umpire, Torn Hensley
line judge, Ray Dodez
head linesman, Leo Miles
back judge, Tom Kelleher
side judge, Bill Quinby
field judge, Bob Lewis
Coaches
Don Shula, Miami
Bill Walsh, San Francisco

MIAMI	Starters, Offense	SAN FRANCISCO
Mark Duper	WR	Dwight Clark
Jon Giesler	LT	Bubba Paris
Roy Foster	LG	John Ayers
Dwight Stephenson	C	Fred Quillan
Ed Newman	RG	Randy Cross
Cleveland Green	RT	Keith Fahnhorst
Bruce Hardy	TE	Russ Francis
Mark Clayton	WR	Freddie Solomon
Dan Marino	QB	Joe Montana
Woody Bennett	RB	Roger Craig
Tony Nathan	RB	Wendell Tyler
	Starters, Defense	
Doug Betters	LE	Lawrence Pillers
Bob Baumhower	NT	Manu Tuiasosopo
Kim Bokamper	RE	Dwaine Board
Bob Brudzinski	LOLB	Dan Bunz
Jay Brophy	LILB	Riki Ellison
Mark Brown	RILB	Jack Reynolds
Charles Bowser	ROLB	Keena Turner
Don McNeal	LCB	Ronnie Lott
William Judson	RCB	Eric Wright
Glenn Blackwood	SS	Carlton Williamson
Lyle Blackwood	FS	Dwight Hicks

MIAMI	10	6	0	0 – 16
SAN FRANCISCO	7	21	10	0 – 38

Mia – FG von Schamann 37
SF – Monroe 33 pass from Montana (Wersching kick)
Mia – D. Johnson 2 pass from Marino (von Schamann kick)
SF – Craig 8 pass from Montana (Wersching kick)
SF – Montana 6 run (Wersching kick)
SF – Craig 2 run (Wersching kick)
Mia – FG von Schamann 31
Mia – FG von Schamann 30
SF – FG Wersching 27
SF – Craig 16 pass from Montana

TEAM STATISTICS

	Miami	SF
First downs	19	31
Rushing	2	16
Passing	17	15
By penalty	0	0
Total yardage	314	537
Net rushing yardage	25	211
Net passing yardage	289	326
Passes att.-comp.-had int.	50-29-2	35-24-0

RUSHING

MIAMI		SAN FRANCISCO	
Nathan	5 for 18	Craig	15 for 58, 1 TD
Bennett	3 for 7	Tyler	13 for 65
Marino	1 for 0	Montana	5 for 59, 1 TD
		Harmon	5 for 20
		Solomon	1 for 5
		Cooper	1 for 4

PASSING

MIAMI		SAN FRANCISCO	
Marino	29 of 50 for 318, 1 TD, 2 int.	Montana	24 of 35 for 331, 3 TDs

RECEIVING

MIAMI		SAN FRANCISCO	
Nathan	10 for 83	Craig	7 for 77, 2 TDs
Clayton	6 for 92	D. Clark	6 for 77
Rose	6 for 73	Francis	5 for 60
D. Johnson	3 for 26, 1 TD	Tyler	4 for 70
Moore	2 for 1	Monroe	1 for 33, 1 TD
Cefalo	1 for 14	Solomon	1 for 14
Duper	1 for 11		

PUNTING

MIAMI		SAN FRANCISCO	
Roby	6 for 236, 39.3 average	Runager	3 for 98, 32.7 average

PUNT RETURNS

MIAMI		SAN FRANCISCO	
Walker	2 for 15	McLemore	5 for 51

KICKOFF RETURNS

MIAMI		SAN FRANCISCO	
Walker	4 for 93	Harmon	2 for 24
Hardy	2 for 31	Monroe	1 for 16
Hill	1 for 16	McIntyre	1 for 0

INTERCEPTIONS

MIAMI	SAN FRANCISCO	
None	Williamson	1 for 0
	Wright	1 for 0

Far left: Dan Marino runs onto the playing field to the delight of the Miami cheerleaders. Despite setting league records in 1984 for completions (362), yards passing (5,084), and touchdown passes (48), Marino (29 of 50, 318 yards, 1 touchdown, 2 interceptions) was almost totally shut down by the San Francisco defense in Super Bowl XIX.

★ ★ ★ ★

CHICAGO BEARS 46

NEW ENGLAND PATRIOTS 10

Left: Chicago defensive end Richard Dent pressured the New England quarterbacks throughout Super Bowl XX. He finished with 2 tackles, an assist, 1½ sacks, 1 pass defensed, and 1 forced fumble.

The Chicago defense forced six turnovers, returned one interception for a touchdown, scored a safety, and held the New England Patriots to 123 total yards and a record-low seven yards rushing, as the Bears recorded a 46-10 victory, the most lopsided score in Super Bowl history at the Superdome in New Orleans.

In a game that matched two outstanding defenses, the Bears proved superior; the Patriots couldn't stop Chicago's offense, which accounted for 408 yards and four long scoring drives.

The Patriots scored first, following Don Blackmon's recovery of Walter Payton's fumble on the second play of the game. The turnover gave New England the ball on the Chicago 19, but three incomplete passes led to a fourth and 10 and a 36-yard field goal by Tony Franklin.

The Bears came right back. On second and 10 at the 31, Jim McMahon completed a 43-yard pass to Willie Gault. Two runs by Matt Suhey picked up another first down, and, three plays later, Kevin Butler tied the score with a 28-yard field goal.

Two turnovers late in the first quarter helped put the Bears in charge of the game. First, Chicago defensive end Richard Dent, later named the game's most valuable player, sacked New England quarterback Tony Eason, who fumbled the ball away at his own 13. Butler kicked a 24-yard field goal for a 6-3 lead. On New England's first play after the kickoff, Craig James fumbled and Mike Singletary recovered

at the Patriots' 13. On second down, Suhey blasted 11 yards for a touchdown.

In the second quarter, the Bears continued their domination on both sides of the line of scrimmage. McMahon scored from the 2 to cap a 10-play, 59-yard drive that built a 20-3 lead. Two series later, New England head coach Raymond Berry replaced an ineffective Eason with Steve Grogan. Eason had been zero-for-six passing, while being sacked three times. The Bears ended the half with an 11-play, 72-yard drive culminated by Butler's 24-yard field goal.

The halftime statistics provided ample proof of the Bears' effectiveness. They led in first downs 13 to 1, in

Above: Former New England head coach Raymond Berry retired as the NFL's leading receiver. In his 13 years, Berry (82) led the league in receiving three times and played in five Pro Bowls. He took the Patriots to their first-ever Super Bowl in only his second season as head coach.

Opposite bottom: All-pro linebacker Mike Singletary (50) and defensive tackle Steve McMichael (76) team up to trap San Francisco quarterback Joe Montana. Statistically, the Bears had the NFL's best defense in 1985.

Participants
NEW ENGLAND PATRIOTS, champions of the American Football Conference, and CHICAGO BEARS, champions of the National Football Conference

Date – January 26, 1986
Site – Louisiana Superdome, New Orleans
Time – 4:20 P.M. CST
Conditions – 70 degrees, indoors
Playing Surface – AstroTurf
Television and Radio – National Broadcasting Company (NBC)
Regular Season Records
NEW ENGLAND, 11-5
CHICAGO, 15-1
Conference Championships
New England defeated the Miami Dolphins 31-14 for the AFC title
Chicago defeated the Los Angeles Rams 24-0 for the NFC title
Players' Shares
$36,000 to each member of the winning team
$18,000 to each member of the losing team
Attendance – 73,818
Gross Receipts – $23,850,000.00
Officials
Referee, Red Cashion
umpire, Ron Botchan
line judge, Bama Glass
head linesman, Dale Williams
back judge, Al Jury
side judge, Bob Rice
field judge, Jack Vaughan

Coaches
Raymond Berry, New England
Mike Ditka, Chicago

CHICAGO	Starters, Offense	NEW ENGLAND
Willie Gault	WR	Stanley Morgan
Jim Covert	LT	Brian Holloway
Mark Bortz	LG	John Hannah
Jay Hilgenberg	C	Pete Brock
Tom Thayer	RG	Ron Wooten
Keith Van Horne	RT	Steve Moore
Emery Moorehead	TE	Lin Dawson
Dennis McKinnon	WR	Stephen Starring
Jim McMahon	QB	Tony Eason
Matt Suhey	RB	Craig James
Walter Payton	RB	Tony Collins
	Starters, Defense	
Dan Hampton	LE	Garin Veris
Steve McMichael	LT-NT	Lester Williams
William Perry	RT-RE	Julius Adams
Richard Dent	RE-LOLB	Andre Tippett
Otis Wilson	LLB-LILB	Steve Nelson
Mike Singletary	MLB-RILB	Larry McGrew
Wilber Marshall	RLB-ROLB	Don Blackmon
Mike Richardson	LCB	Ronnie Lippett
Leslie Frazier	RCB	Raymond Clayborn
Dave Duerson	SS	Roland James
Gary Fencik	FS	Fred Marion

In Super Bowl XX, the Bears' defense forced 6 turnovers, returned an interception for a touchdown, scored a safety, and held the Patriots to 123 total yards, including a record-low 7 yards rushing.

rushing yards 92 to minus-5, in passing yards 144 to minus-14, and in total yards 236 to minus-19.

The Bears ended any lingering hopes the Patriots might have had the first time they touched the ball in the second half. With a first-and-10 from his own 4-yard line following a punt, McMahon passed 60 yards to Gault. Eight plays later, McMahon sneaked over from the 1 for a 30-3 lead.

Three plays later, the Bears' defense got into the act again. Reserve cornerback Reggie Phillips intercepted Grogan's pass for tight end Derrick Ramsey and returned it 28 yards for a touchdown.

On New England's second play after the kickoff, Stanley Morgan fumbled after making a reception, and linebacker Wilber Marshall recovered, returning

the ball to New England's 31. Three runs by Payton and a 27-yard pass from McMahon to Dennis Gentry gave the Bears a first-and-goal at the 1. Then came the moment America had been waiting for. Defensive tackle William (The Refrigerator) Perry was inserted at running back and banged into the end zone for a 44-3 lead.

The Patriots opened the fourth quarter with their only sustained drive of the day, 12 plays for 76 yards, capped by an eight-yard touchdown pass from Grogan to Irving Fryar. But the Bears had one final humiliation left for the Patriots. With four minutes left in the game, reserve defensive tackle Henry Waechter sacked Grogan in the end zone for a safety and the final 46-10 margin.

CHICAGO	13	10	21	2 – 46
NEW ENGLAND	3	0	0	7 – 10

NE – FG Franklin 36
Chi – FG Butler 28
Chi – FG Butler 24
Chi – Suhey 11 run (Butler kick)
Chi – McMahon 2 run (Butler kick)
Chi – FG Butler 24
Chi – McMahon 1 run (Butler kick)
Chi – Phillips 28 interception return (Butler kick)
Chi – Perry 1 run (Butler kick)
NE – Fryar 8 pass from Grogan (Franklin kick)
Chi – Safety, Waechter tackled Grogan in end zone

TEAM STATISTICS

	Chicago	NE
First downs	23	12
Rushing	13	1
Passing	9	10
By penalty	1	1
Total yardage	408	123
Net rushing yardage	167	7
Net passing yardage	241	116
Passes att.-comp.-had int.	24-12-0	36-17-2

RUSHING

CHICAGO		NEW ENGLAND	
Payton	22 for 61	C James	5 for 1
Suhey	11 for 52, 1 TD	Collins	3 for 4
McMahon	5 for 14, 2 TDs	Weathers	1 for 3
Sanders	4 for 15	Grogan	1 for 3
Gentry	3 for 15	Hawthorne	1 for -4
Thomas	2 for 8		
Perry	1 for 1, 1 TD		
Fuller	1 for 1		

PASSING

CHICAGO		NEW ENGLAND	
McMahon	12 of 20 for 256	Grogan	17 of 30 for 177, 1 TD, 2 int.
Fuller	0 of 4 for 0	Eason	0 of 6 for 0

RECEIVING

CHICAGO		NEW ENGLAND	
Gault	4 for 129	Morgan	7 for 70
Gentry	2 for 41	Starring	2 for 39
Margerum	2 for 36	Fryar	2 for 24, 1 TD
Moorehead	2 for 22	Collins	2 for 19
Suhey	1 for 24	Ramsey	2 for 16
Thomas	1 for 4	C. James	1 for 6
		Weathers	1 for 3

PUNTING

CHICAGO		NEW ENGLAND	
Buford	4 for 173, 43.3 average	Camarillo	6 for 263, 43.8 average

PUNT RETURNS

CHICAGO		NEW ENGLAND	
Ortego	2 for 20, 1 fair catch	Fryar	2 for 22

KICKOFF RETURNS

CHICAGO		NEW ENGLAND	
Gault	4 for 49	Starring	7 for 153

INTERCEPTIONS

CHICAGO		NEW ENGLAND	
Morrissey	1 for 47	None	
Phillips	1 for 28, 1 TD		

 NEW YORK GIANTS 39

DENVER BRONCOS 20

Quarterback Phil Simms completed all 10 of his second-half passes, and the New York Giants went on a 30-3 scoring binge to defeat the Denver Broncos 39-20 in Super Bowl XXI at the Rose Bowl in Pasadena.

Behind quarterback John Elway's adept scrambling and passing, Denver held a 10-9 lead at halftime. The advantage could have been much more, but the Broncos failed to score after driving to a first and goal at the Giants' 1-yard line late in the second quarter, and Denver kicker Rich Karlis missed a pair of short field goal tries in the first two quarters.

The second half, however, belonged to Simms and the Giants' defense.

The blitzkrieg began with a surprise play. After Lee Rouson brought Karlis's kickoff back to the Giants' 37, Simms could take his offense only nine yards in three plays. On fourth-and-one, with punter Sean Landeta standing 15 yards back, his hands up to accept the long snap, the up man, reserve quarterback Jeff Rutledge, moved in under center. Rutledge took the snap and made two yards for the first down.

"You're trying to win the game," said Giants coach Bill Parcells while explaining the call afterward.

Left: Super Bowl XXI most valuable player Phil Simms set Super Bowl records for most consecutive completions (10) and highest compeletion percentage (22 completions in 25 attempts).

Below: While his offensive line did a superb job in handling the Denver defense, Simms (11) threw for 268 yards and 3 touchdowns in Super Bowl XXI.

"This is for the world championship. It's not for faint-hearted people. So you take your shot."

Five plays later, Simms hit tight end Mark Bavaro with a 13-yard touchdown pass and a 16-10 lead. After that, the assault was on. The Giants eventually built a 39-13 lead before the Broncos scored a touchdown with two minutes left.

Simms finished the game with a Super Bowl accuracy record and the MVP award. He completed 22 of his 25 passes for 268 yards and three TDs.

"Every one I threw I liked," he said. "I didn't want one of them back."

Simms (11) and the Giants' offense played conservatively and used a ball-control offensive scheme in 30 miles per hour winds to defeat the Redskins 17-0 in the 1986 NFC Championship Game.

Participants
DENVER BRONCOS, champions of the American Football Conference, and NEW YORK GIANTS, champions of the National Football Conference

Date – January 25, 1987
Site – Rose Bowl, Pasadena
Time – 6:00 P.M. EST
Conditions – 76 degrees, sunny
Playing Surface – Grass
Television and Radio – Columbia Broadcasting System (CBS)
Regular Season Records
DENVER 11-5
NEW YORK 14-2
Conference Championships
Denver defeated the Cleveland Browns 23-20 in overtime for the AFC championship
New York defeated the Washington Redskins 17-0 for the NFC championship
Players' Shares
$36,000 to each member of the winning team
$18,000 to each member of the losing team
Attendance – 101,063
Gross Receipts – $27,500,000.00
Officials
Referee, Jerry Markbreit
umpire, Bob Boylston
line judge, Bob Beeks
head linesman, Terry Gierke
back judge, Jim Poole
field judge, Pat Mallette
side judge, Gil Mace

Coaches
Dan Reeves, Denver
Bill Parcells, New York

DENVER	Starters, Offense	NEW YORK
Vance Johnson	WR	Lionel Manuel
Dave Studdard	LT	Brad Benson
Keith Bishop	LG	Billy Ard
Bill Bryan	C	Bart Oates
Mark Cooper	RG	Chris Godfrey
Ken Lanier	RT	Karl Nelson
Clarence Kay	TE	Mark Bavaro
Steve Watson	WR	Stacy Robinson
John Elway	QB	Phil Simms
Sammy Winder	RB	Joe Morris
Gerald Willhite	RB	Maurice Carthon
	Starters, Defense	
Andre Townsend	LE	George Martin
Greg Kragen	NT	Jim Burt
Rulon Jones	RE	Leonard Marshall
Jim Ryan	LOLB	Carl Banks
Karl Mecklenburg	LILB	Gary Reasons
Ricky Hunley	RILB	Harry Carson
Tom Jackson	ROLB	Lawrence Taylor
Louis Wright	LCB	Elvis Patterson
Mike Harden	RCB	Perry Williams
Dennis Smith	SS	Kenny Hill
Steve Foley	FS	Herb Welch

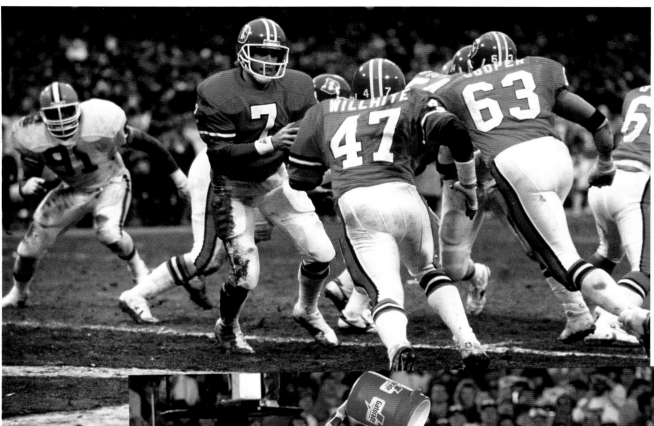

Above: John Elway turns to hand off from his own end zone on the Broncos' 98-yard scoring drive in the fourth quarter of the 1986 AFC Championship Game. This series of downs known as "The Drive," ended with Elway's 5-yard scoring pass to Mark Jackson.

Above: Giants' linebacker Harry Carson gives head coach Bill Parcells a victory shower in the fourth quarter of Super Bowl XXI.

DENVER	10	0	0	10 – 20
N.Y. GIANTS	7	2	17	13 – 39

Den – FG Karlis 48
NYG – Mowatt 6 pass from Simms (Allegre kick)
Den – Elway 4 run (Karlis kick)
NYG – Safety, Martin tackled Elway in end zone
NYG – Bavaro 13 pass from Simms (Allegre kick)
NYG – FG Allegre 21
NYG – Morris 1 run (Allegre kick)
NYG – McConkey 6 pass from Simms (Allegre kick)
Den – FG Karlis 28
NYG – Anderson 2 run (kick failed)
Den – V. Johnson 47 pass from Elway (Karlis kick)

TEAM STATISTICS	Den	NYG
First Downs	23	24
Rushing	5	10
Passing	16	13
By penalty	2	1
Total yardage	372	399
Net rushing yardage	52	136
Net passing yardage	320	263
Passes att.-comp.-had int.	41-26-1	25-22-0

RUSHING

DENVER		NEW YORK GIANTS	
Elway	6 for 27, 1 TD	Morris	20 for 67, 1 TD
Willhite	4 for 19	Galbreath	4 for 17
Winder	4 for 0	Simms	3 for 25
Sewell	3 for 4	Rouson	3 for 22
Lang	2 for 2	Carthon	3 for 4
		Rutledge	3 for 0
		Anderson	2 for 1, 1 TD

PASSING

DENVER		NEW YORK GIANTS	
Elway	22of37for304,1TD,1int.	Simms	22 of 25 for 268, 3 TDs
Kubiak	4 of 4 for 48		

RECEIVING

DENVER		NEW YORK GIANTS	
V. Johnson	5 for 121, 1 TD	Bavaro	4 for 51, 1 TD
Willhite	5 for 39	Morris	4 for 20
Winder	4 for 34	Carthon	4 for 13
M. Jackson	3 for 51	Robinson	3 for 62
Watson	2 for 54	Manuel	3 for 43
Sampson	2 for 20	McConkey	2 for 50, 1 TD
Mobley	2 for 17	Rouson	1 for 23
Sewell	2 for 12	Mowatt	1 for 6, 1 TD
Lang	1 for 4		

PUNTING

DENVER		NEW YORK GIANTS	
Horan	2 for 82, 41.0 average.	Landeta	3 for 138, 46.0 average.

PUNT RETURNS

DENVER		NEW YORK GIANTS	
Willhite	1 for 9	McConkey	1 for 25

KICKOFF RETURNS

DENVER		NEW YORK GIANTS	
Bell	3 for 48	Rouson	3 for 56
Lang	2 for 36	Flynn	1 for -3

INTERCEPTIONS

DENVER		NEW YORK GIANTS	
None		Patterson	1 for -7

WASHINGTON REDSKINS 42
DENVER BRONCOS 10

Right: Super Bowl XXII most valuable player Doug Williams completed 18 of 29 passes for a record 340 yards and 4 touchdowns.

Below: Gary Clark (84) sets up his game-winning touchdown catch in the 1987 NFC title game with a 43-yard reception behind Minnesota cornerback Reggie Rutland (48). The Redskins won 17-10.

The Washington Redskins blitzed the Denver Broncos for 35 points in a record-setting second-quarter barrage and cruised to a 42-10 victory in Super Bowl XXII at Jack Murphy Stadium in San Diego.

The Broncos scored a touchdown on their first play from scrimmage, a 56-yard pass from quarterback John Elway to wide receiver Ricky Nattiel. Later, a 24-yard field goal by Rich Karlis gave Denver a 10-0 lead after one quarter.

If, at this point, someone had told the Broncos that they were about to be outscored 42-0, the laughter would have been so loud that one might not have heard the sound of momentum shifting.

In the next 14 minutes and 17 seconds of playing time, the Redskins beat the Broncos every way imaginable. It looked as if Washington could do anything it wanted. The Redskins scored on five consecutive possessions, on drives of 80, 64, 74, 60, and 79 yards. It took the Redskins a total of 18 plays and 5 minutes and 47 seconds of elapsed time to travel those 357 yards.

Washington's first play of the quarter resulted in quarterback Doug Williams's 80-yard touchdown pass to wide receiver Ricky Sanders. Then Williams

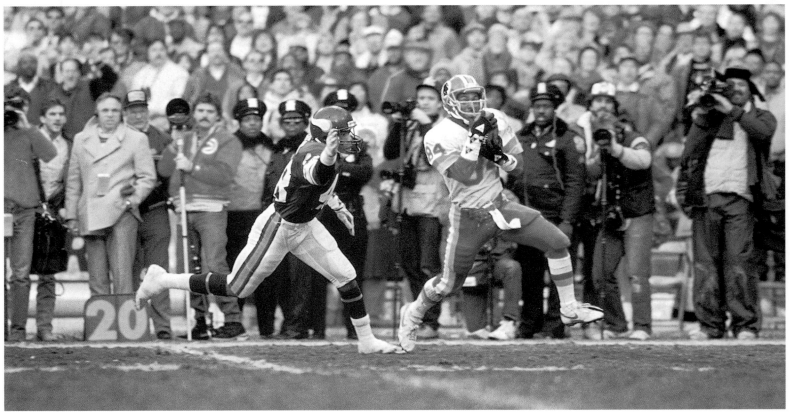

hit wide receiver Gary Clark with a 27-yard scoring pass...14-10. Running back Timmy Smith galloped 58 yards down the right side of the field...21-10. Williams collaborated with Sanders again, this time for 50 yards...28-10. Finally, a soft eight-yard touchdown lob from Williams to tight end Clint Didier ... 35-10. Smith added a four-yard run in the fourth quarter to finish the scoring.

Williams, the game's MVP, completed 9 of 11 passes for 228 yards and four touchdowns in the second quarter alone. Smith ran for 122 yards in the quarter and finished with a Super Bowl record 204 yards rushing.

Ironically, Smith, a rookie who had gained only 126 yards in the regular season and who was not retained after the following season, did not know he would be starting until the game was about to begin.

"We didn't tell Timmy anything," said offensive coordinator Joe Bugel, "because we didn't want him getting sick in our locker room."

Participants
DENVER BRONCOS, champions of the American Football Conference, and
WASHINGTON REDSKINS, champions of the National Football Conference

Date – January 31, 1988
Site – Jack Murphy Stadium, San Diego
Time – 6:00 P.M. EST
Conditions – 61 degrees, mostly cloudy
Playing Surface – Grass
Television – American Broadcasting Company (ABC)
Radio – Columbia Broadcasting System (CBS)
Regular Season Records
DENVER, 10-4-1
WASHINGTON, 11-4
Conference Championships
Denver defeated the Cleveland Browns 38-33 for the AFC title
Washington defeated the Minnesota Vikings 17-10 for the NFC title
Players' Shares
$36,000 to each member of the winning team
$18,000 to each member of the losing team
Attendance – 73,302
Gross Receipts – $28,000,000.00
Officials
Referee, Bob McElwee
umpire, Al Conway
line judge, Jack Fette
head linesman, Dale Hamer
back judge, Al Jury
field judge, Johnny Grier
side judge, Don Wedge

Coaches
Dan Reeves, Denver
Joe Gibbs, Washington

WASHINGTON	Starters, Offense	DENVER
Gary Clark	WR	Mark Jackson
Joe Jacoby	LT	Dave Studdard
Raleigh McKenzie	LG	Keith Bishop
Jeff Bostic	C	Mike Freeman
R.C. Thielemann	RG	Stefan Humphries
Mark May	RT	Ken Lanier
Clint Didier	TE	Clarence Kay
Don Warren	TE-WR	Ricky Nattiel
Doug Williams	QB	John Elway
Timmy Smith	RB	Sammy Winder
Ricky Sanders	WR-RB	Gene Lang
	Starters, Defense	
Charles Mann	LE	Andre Townsend
Dave Butz	LT-NT	Greg Kragen
Darryl Grant	RT-RE	Rulon Jones
Dexter Manley	RE-LOLB	Simon Fletcher
Mel Kaufman	LLB-LILB	Karl Mecklenburg
Neal Olkewicz	MLB-RILB	Ricky Hunley
Monte Coleman	RLB-ROLB	Jim Ryan
Darrell Green	LCB	Mark Haynes
Todd Bowles	RCB	Steve Wilson
Barry Wilburn	SS	Dennis Smith
Alvin Walton	FS	Tony Lilly

Cleveland running back Earnest Byner (44) fumbles at the Denver 3-yard line with 65 seconds remaining in the 1987 AFC Championship Game. The Browns trailed 38-31 at the time and were driving for the tying score. Denver took an intentional safety and won the game 38-33.

| WASHINGTON | 0 | 35 | 0 | 7 – 42 |
| DENVER | 10 | 0 | 0 | 0 – 10 |

Den – Nattiel 56 pass from Elway (Karlis kick)
Den – FG Karlis 24
Wash – Sanders 80 pass from Williams (Haji-Sheikh kick)
Wash – Clark 27 pass from Williams (Haji-Sheikh kick)
Wash – Smith 58 run (Haji-Sheikh kick)
Wash – Sanders 50 pass from Williams (Haji-Sheikh kick)
Wash – Didier 8 pass from Williams (Haji-Sheikh kick)
Wash – Smith 4 run (Haji-Sheikh kick)

TEAM STATISTICS

	Wash	Den
First Downs	25	18
Rushing	13	6
Passing	11	10
By penalty	1	2
Total yardage	602	327
Net rushing yardage	280	97
Net passing yardage	322	230
Passes att.-comp.-had int.	30-18-1	39-15-3

RUSHING

WASHINGTON		DENVER	
Smith	22 for 204, 2 TDs	Lang	5 for 38
Bryant	8 for 38	Winder	8 for 30
Rogers	5 for 17	Elway	3 for 32
Williams	2 for 2	Sewell	1 for -3
Clark	1 for 25		
Griffin	1 for -2		
Sanders	1 for -4.		

PASSING

WASHINGTON		DENVER	
Williams	18 of 29 for 340, 4 TDs, 1 int	Elway	14 of 38 for 257, 1 TD, 3 int.
Schroeder	0 of 1 for 0	Sewell	1 of 1 for 23

RECEIVING

WASHINGTON		DENVER	
Sanders	9 for 193, 2 TDs	Jackson	4 for 76
Clark	3 for 55, 1 TD	Sewell	4 for 41
Warren	2 for 15	Nattiel	2 for 69, 1 TD
Monk	1 for 40	Kay	2 for 38
Bryant	1 for 20	Winder	1 for 26
Smith	1 for 9	Elway	1 for 23
Didier	1 for 8, 1 TD	Lang	1 for 7

PUNTING

WASHINGTON		DENVER	
Cox	4 for 150, 37.5 average	Horan	7 for 253, 36.1 average

PUNT RETURNS

WASHINGTON		DENVER	
Green	1 for 0	Clark	2 for 18

KICKOFF RETURNS

WASHINGTON		DENVER	
Sanders	3 for 46	Bell	5 for 88

INTERCEPTIONS

WASHINGTON		DENVER	
Wilburn	2 for 11	Castille	1 for 0
Davis	1 for 0		

Williams (17) led the Redskins' 35-point second quarter explosion in Super Bowl XXII by passing for a record-tying 4 touchdown passes.

SUPER BOWL ★ XXIII ★

SAN FRANCISCO 49ers 20,
CINCINNATI BENGALS 16

Quarterback Joe Montana threw a 10-yard touchdown pass to wide receiver John Taylor with just 34 seconds remaining to lift the San Francisco 49ers to a 20-16 victory over the Cincinnati Bengals in the most exciting Super Bowl finish to date.

The touchdown capped a 92-yard drive in the closing minutes for the 49ers, who won their third Super Bowl crown of the 1980s and lay claim to the title "Team of the Decade."

Super Bowl XXIII matched the same participants as Super Bowl XVI. The game could not fairly be billed as a rematch, however. Only six players from each side were on the field when the 49ers won their first NFL title with a 26-21 victory over the Bengals in Super Bowl XVI. Elbert (Ickey) Woods, Cincinnati's irrepressible rookie fullback, didn't even have his driver's license in January, 1982.

Super Bowl XXIII still had plenty of intrigue, though. Cincinnati head coach Sam Wyche had been San Francisco's passing game coach under 49ers head coach Bill Walsh (who would retire three days after the game) from 1979 to 1982. Now the student was attempting to upstage his former mentor.

And for a while, it looked as if he would. Sparked by Stanford Jennings's 93-yard kickoff return for a touchdown and Jim Breech's three field goals, the Bengals had a 16-13 lead when the 49ers took over

San Francisco wide receiver Jerry Rice was named Super Bowl XXIII after catching 11 passes for a Super Bowl record 215 yards and 1 touchdown.

Participants
CINCINNATI BENGALS, champions of the American Football Conference, and SAN FRANCISCO 49ers, champions of the National Football Conference

Date – January 22, 1989
Site – Joe Robbie Stadium, Miami
Time – 5:00 P.M. EST
Conditions – 76 degrees, partly cloudy
Playing Surface – Grass
Television – National Broadcasting Company (NBC)
Radio – Columbia Broadcasting System (CBS)
Regular Season Records
CINCINNATI 12-4
SAN FRANCISCO 10-6
Conference Championships
Cincinnati defeated the Buffalo Bills 21-10 for the AFC title
San Francisco defeated the Chicago Bears 28-3 for the NFC title
Players' Shares
$36,000 to each member of the winning team
$18,000 to each member of the losing team
Attendance – 75,129
Gross Receipts – $29,000,000.00
Officials
Referee, Jerry Seeman
umpire, Gordon Wells
line judge, Bob Beeks
head linesman, Jerry Bergman
back judge, Paul Baetz
field judge, Bobby Skelton
side judge, Gary Lane

Coaches
Sam Wyche, Cincinnati
Bill Walsh, San Francisco

CINCINNATI	Starters, Offense	San Francisco
Tim McGee	WR	John Taylor
Anthony Munoz	LT	Steve Wallace
Bruce Reimers	LG	Jesse Sapolu
Bruce Kozerski	C	Randy Cross
Max Montoya	RG	Guy McIntyre
Brian Blados	RT	Harris Barton
Rodney Holman	TE	John Frank
Eddie Brown	WR	Jerry Rice
Boomer Esiason	QB	Joe Montana
James Brooks	RB	Roger Craig
Ickey Woods	RB	Tom Rathman
	Starters, Defense	
Jim Skow	LE	Larry Roberts
Tim Krumrie	NT	Michael Carter
Jason Buck	RE	Kevin Fagan
Leon White	LOLB	Charles Haley
Carl Zander	LILB	Jim Fahnhorst
Joe Kelly	RILB	Michael Walter
Reggie Williams	ROLB	Keena Turner
Lewis Billups	LCB	Tim McKyer
Eric Thomas	RCB	Don Griffin
David Fulcher	SS	Jeff Fuller
Solomon Wilcots	FS	Ronnie Lott

possession at their own 8-yard line with 3:10 left.

Montana, who already had established his reputation with several dramatic rallies throughout his college and professional career, was deliberate and controlled. There was an air of inevitability as he completed short passes to Roger Craig (eight yards), John Frank (seven), and Jerry Rice (seven). After handing off twice to Craig, Montana went to Rice again, this time for 17 yards along the left sideline into Cincinnati territory to the 48. He then found Craig for 13 at the 35, then threw incomplete for Rice.

After an ineligible receiver downfield penalty cost the 49ers 10 yards, Montana found Rice for a 27-yard gain to the 18. Another pass to Craig set up the winning score.

In the final tally, Rice caught 11 passes for a Super Bowl record 215 yards and was named the MVP. Montana, who completed 7 of 8 passes for 97 yards on the final drive, finished with a record 357 yards passing.

Above: Joe Montana (16) passes 27 yards to Jerry Rice on the tenth play of the 49ers' game-winning drive in Super Bowl XXIII. Montana completed 23 of 36 passes for 357 yards and 2 touchdowns.

Right: John Taylor catches the game-winning 10-yard touchdown pass from Joe Montana with 34 seconds remaining in Super Bowl XXIII. It was Taylor's only catch in the game.

49ers' guard Bruce Collie (69), quarterback Joe Montana (16) and center Randy Cross (51)

CINCINNATI	0	3	10	3 – 16
SAN FRANCISCO	3	0	3	14 – 20

SF – FG Cofer 41
Cin – FG Breech 34
Cin – FG Breech 43
SF – FG Cofer 32
Cin – Jennings 93 kickoff return (Breech kick)
SF – Rice 14 pass from Montana (Cofer kick)
Cin – FG Breech 40
SF – Taylor 10 pass from Montana (Cofer kick)

TEAM STATISTICS

	Cin	SF
First Downs	13	23
Rushing	7	6
Passing	6	16
By penalty	0	1
Total yardage	229	451
Net rushing yardage	106	112
Net passing yardage	123	339
Passes att.-comp.-had int.	25-11-1	36-23-0

RUSHING

CINCINNATI
Woods 20 for 79
Brooks 6 for 24
Jennings 1 for 3
Esiason 1 for 0

SAN FRANCISCO
Craig 17 for 71
Rathman 5 for 23
Montana 4 for 13
Rice 1 for 5

PASSING

CINCINNATI
Esiason, 11 of 25 for 144, 1 int.

SAN FRANCISCO
Montana 23 of 36 for 357, 2 TDs

RECEIVING

CINCINNATI
Brown 4 for 44
Collinsworth 3 for 40
McGee 2 for 23
Brooks 1 for 20
Hillary 1 for 17

SAN FRANCISCO
Rice 11 for 215, 1 TD
Craig 8 for 101
Frank 2 for 15
Rathman 1 for 16
Taylor 1 for 10, 1 TD

PUNTING

CINCINNATI
Johnson 5 for 221, 44.2 average

SAN FRANCISCO
Helton 4 for 148, 37.0 average

PUNT RETURNS

CINCINNATI
Horton 1 for 5
Hillary 1 for 0

SAN FRANCISCO
Taylor 3 for 56

KICKOFF RETURNS

CINCINNATI
Jennings 2 for 117, 1 TD
Brooks 1 for 15

SAN FRANCISCO
Rodgers 3 for 53
Taylor 1 for 13
Sydney 1 for 11

INTERCEPTIONS

CINCINNATI
None

SAN FRANCISCO
Romanowski 1 for 0

SAN FRANCISCO 49ers 55

DENVER BRONCOS 10

Right: Joe Montana won his third Super Bowl most valuable player award after completing 22 of 29 passes for 297 yards and a record 5 touchdown passes in game XXIV.

Super Bowl victories by trouncing the Denver Broncos 55-10 in Super Bowl XXIV at the Louisiana Superdome in New Orleans.

The game's outcome was never in doubt as the 49ers scored a touchdown on their first possession and on eight of their 11 possessions before running out the clock in the fourth quarter.

The first time the 49ers had the ball, Montana threw a 20-yard touchdown pass to wide receiver Jerry Rice, one of a record three scoring catches for Rice. Later in the first quarter, Montana connected with tight end Brent Jones on a seven-yard touchdown pass, and San Francisco led 13-3 (the extra point was missed, the 49ers' only error). Before the half was over, fullback Tom Rathman ran one yard for a touchdown, and Montana and Rice combined on a 38-yard touchdown pass to make it 27-3.

The 49ers didn't let up, scoring four more times in the second half and establishing Super Bowl records for points scored and margin of victory. Rathman and Roger Craig ran for scores, and Montana threw touchdown passes to Rice (28 yards) and John Taylor (35 yards).

Montana's last three touchdown passes came on deep post patterns.

"We felt with their two-deep safeties we could use some motion and sneak something down the middle," he said. Montana, who previously had been named the most valuable player in the 49ers' victories in Super Bowl XVI and XIX, earned Super Bowl MVP

Quarterback Joe Montana's record-setting performance led the way as the San Francisco 49ers became the first team in 10 years to repeat as Super Bowl champions and equalled the Pittsburgh Steelers' record four

Opposite: San Francisco fullback Tom Rathman (44), tight end Jamie Williams, and wide receiver Jerry Rice (80) mob running back Roger Craig (33) after his 4-yard touchdown run in the 1989 NFC Divisional Playoffs. Craig rushed for 125 yards on 18 carries in the 49ers's 41-13 win over Minnesota.

Participants
DENVER BRONCOS, champions of the American Football Conference, and SAN FRANCISCO 49ers, champions of the National Football Conference

Date – January 28, 1990
Site – Louisiana Superdome, New Orleans
Time – 5:00 P.M. EST
Conditions – 72 degrees, indoors
Playing Surface – AstroTurf
Television and Radio – Columbia Broadcasting System (CBS)
Regular Season Records
DENVER, 11-5
SAN FRANCISCO, 14-2
Conference Championships
Denver defeated the Cleveland Browns 37-21 for the AFC title
San Francisco defeated the Los Angeles Rams 30-3 for the NFC title
Players' Shares
$36,000 to each member of the winning team
$18,000 to each member of the losing team
Attendance – 72,919
Gross Receipts – $28,500,000.00
Officials
Referee, Dick Jorgensen
umpire, Hendi Ancich
line judge, Ron Blum
side judge, Gerry Austin
head linesman, Earnie Frantz
back judge, Al Jury
field judge, Don Orr
replay official, Al Sabato

Coaches
Dan Reeves, Denver
George Seifert, San Francisco

SAN FRANCISCO	Starters, Offense	DENVER
John Taylor	WR	Vance Johnson
Bubba Paris	LT	Gerald Perry
Guy McIntyre	LG	Jim Juriga
Jesse Sapolu	C	Keith Kartz
Bruce Collie	RG	Doug Widell
Harris Barton	RT	Ken Lanier
Brent Jones	TE	Orson Mobley
Jerry Rice	WR	Mark Jackson
Joe Montana	QB	John Elway
Roger Craig	RB	Steve Sewell
Tom Rathman	RB	Bobby Humphrey
	Starters, Defense	
Pierce Holt	LE	Alphonso Carreker
Michael Carter	NT	Greg Kragen
Kevin Fagan	RE	Ron Holmes
Charles Haley	LOLB	Michael Brooks
Matt Millen	LILB	Rick Dennison
Michael Walter	RILB	Karl Mecklenburg
Keena Turner	ROLB	Simon Fletcher
Darryl Pollard	LCB	Tyrone Braxton
Don Griffin	RCB	Wymon Henderson
Chet Brooks	SS	Dennis Smith
Ronnie Lott	FS	Steve Atwater

honors for an unprecedented third time. He completed 22 of 29 passes for 297 yards posting a record five touchdown passes. He also established Super Bowl career records in every meaningful passing category.

The defeat was especially difficult for Denver and its fans because the Broncos equalled the Minnesota Vikings' record for futility with their fourth Super Bowl loss in as many tries.

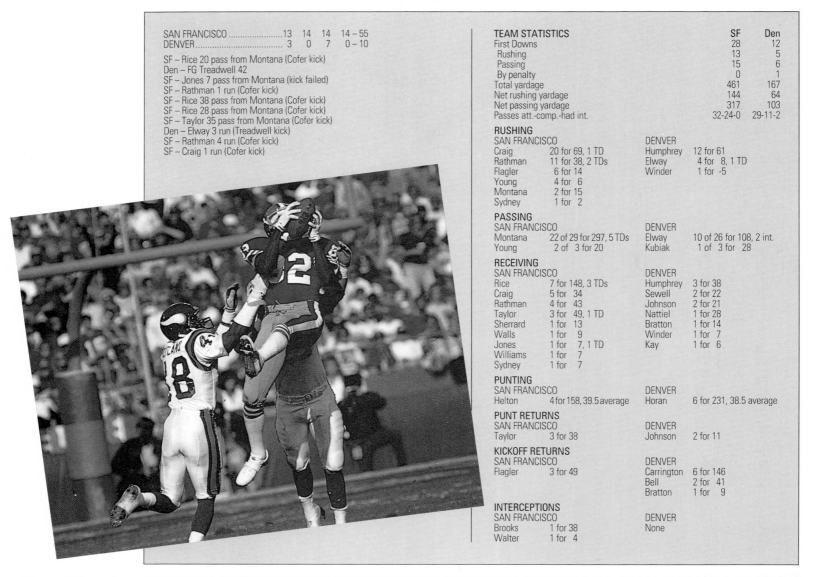

```
SAN FRANCISCO .......................13   14   14   14 – 55
DENVER ...................................  3    0    7    0 – 10
```

SF – Rice 20 pass from Montana (Cofer kick)
Den – FG Treadwell 42
SF – Jones 7 pass from Montana (kick failed)
SF – Rathman 1 run (Cofer kick)
SF – Rice 38 pass from Montana (Cofer kick)
SF – Rice 28 pass from Montana (Cofer kick)
SF – Taylor 35 pass from Montana (Cofer kick)
Den – Elway 3 run (Treadwell kick)
SF – Rathman 4 run (Cofer kick)
SF – Craig 1 run (Cofer kick)

TEAM STATISTICS	SF	Den
First Downs	28	12
Rushing	13	5
Passing	15	6
By penalty	0	1
Total yardage	461	167
Net rushing yardage	144	64
Net passing yardage	317	103
Passes att.-comp.-had int.	32-24-0	29-11-2

RUSHING

SAN FRANCISCO		DENVER	
Craig	20 for 69, 1 TD	Humphrey	12 for 61
Rathman	11 for 38, 2 TDs	Elway	4 for 8, 1 TD
Flagler	6 for 14	Winder	1 for -5
Young	4 for 6		
Montana	2 for 15		
Sydney	1 for 2		

PASSING

SAN FRANCISCO		DENVER	
Montana	22 of 29 for 297, 5 TDs	Elway	10 of 26 for 108, 2 int.
Young	2 of 3 for 20	Kubiak	1 of 3 for 28

RECEIVING

SAN FRANCISCO		DENVER	
Rice	7 for 148, 3 TDs	Humphrey	3 for 38
Craig	5 for 34	Sewell	2 for 22
Rathman	4 for 43	Johnson	2 for 21
Taylor	3 for 49, 1 TD	Nattiel	1 for 28
Sherrard	1 for 13	Bratton	1 for 14
Walls	1 for 9	Winder	1 for 7
Jones	1 for 7, 1 TD	Kay	1 for 6
Williams	1 for 7		
Sydney	1 for 7		

PUNTING

SAN FRANCISCO		DENVER	
Helton	4 for 158, 39.5 average	Horan	6 for 231, 38.5 average

PUNT RETURNS

SAN FRANCISCO		DENVER	
Taylor	3 for 38	Johnson	2 for 11

KICKOFF RETURNS

SAN FRANCISCO		DENVER	
Flagler	3 for 49	Carrington	6 for 146
		Bell	2 for 41
		Bratton	1 for 9

INTERCEPTIONS

SAN FRANCISCO		DENVER	
Brooks	1 for 38	None	
Walter	1 for 4		

Above: *Wide receiver John Taylor leaps to make a catch in the 1989 Divisional Playoff Game against the Vikings. Taylor caught 3 passes for 50 yards and 1 touchdown.*

Right: *San Francisco's Tom Rathman scores his second touchdown in Super Bowl XXIV on a 4-yard run.*

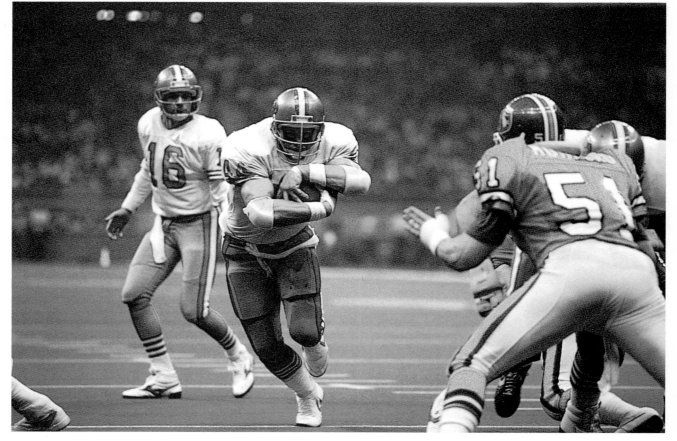

Left: 49ers defensive end Larry Roberts (91) sacks John Elway for a 12-yard loss in Super Bowl XXIV. Elway was sacked four times by the 49ers defense, while his backup, Gary Kubiak was sacked twice.

Below: Jerry Rice (80) catches his third touchdown of the game on a 38-yard pass from Joe Montana. Rice led all receivers with 7 receptions for 148 yards.

INDEX

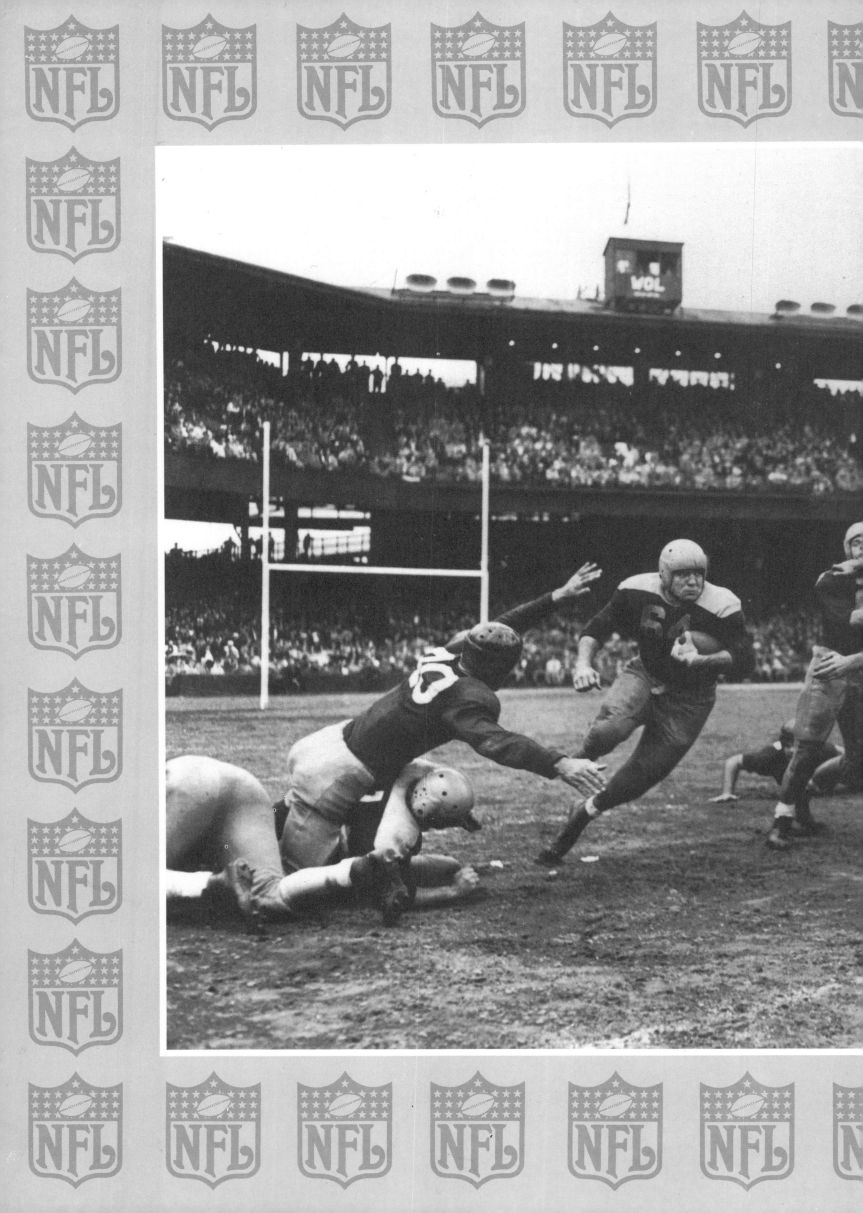